TECHNICAL
AND BUSINESS WRITING

TECHNICAL AND BUSINESS WRITING

A Reader-Friendly Approach

STEPHEN M. FLAHERTY

PRENTICE HALL
Englewood Cliffs, New Jersey 07632

Library of Congress Cataloging-in-Publication Data

Flaherty, Stephen M.
    Technical and business writing : a reader—friendly approach /
Stephen M. Flaherty.
        p.   cm.
    ISBN 0-13-901943-X
    1. Technical writing.   2. Business writing.   I. Title.
T11.F56   1990
808'.0666—dc20   89-16324

Editorial/production supervision: *Mary Carnis*
Cover design: *Wanda Lubelska*
Manufacturing buyer: *David Dickey*

 © 1990 by Prentice-Hall, Inc.
A Division of Simon & Schuster
Englewood Cliffs, New Jersey 07632

Printed in the United States of America
10 9 8 7 6 5 4 3 2 1

ISBN 0-13-901943-X

Prentice-Hall International (UK) Limited, *London*
Prentice-Hall of Australia Pty. Limited, *Sydney*
Prentice-Hall Canada Inc., *Toronto*
Prentice-Hall Hispanoamericana, S.A., *Mexico*
Prentice-Hall of India Private Limited, *New Delhi*
Prentice-Hall of Japan, Inc., *Tokyo*
Simon & Schuster Asia Pte. Ltd., *Singapore*
Editora Prentice-Hall do Brasil, Ltda., *Rio de Janeiro*

Contents

Preface

Engineers and business people are often surprised to discover how much time they spend writing on the job. One recent survey reports that people write about 25 percent of the average workday. Add to this 41 percent performing related activities of reading (23 percent), editing (11 percent), and giving oral reports (7 percent), and only 34 percent of their work time is devoted to activities that do not involve communication skills.

These statistics indicate that effective verbal skills are very important to a technical or business career. As students, you need to prepare yourselves thoroughly for career challenges after graduation. One of the greatest challenges that you will face is to communicate clearly with people on the job. The best preparation you can make in meeting this challenge is to learn and practice the principles of professional writing and public speaking. This book contains the basic information you will need to understand and begin to master these principles. Learning them, however, is not enough. Continuous practice and improvement are necessary to develop mature skill in writing and speaking.

You can use *Technical and Business Writing: A Reader-Friendly Approach* to develop mature communication skills. Chapters One, Two, and Three provide a foundation of the writing process and the written product. They tell you that readers on the job expect particular types of documents that are well organized with a clear purpose and in an appropriate style. To write effectively you have to fulfill these reader needs. You must revise and edit your initial attempts to produce good writing (writing that is free of errors and unnecessary words). You must place yourself in the role of reader and be satisfied with your writing before you send it out. You must write in a style (concise, active voice, coherent) and format (headings, subheadings, and visuals) that make reading comprehension more probable.

Chapters Four through Ten build on this reader-friendly foundation. They are organized around the assumption that when writers communicate on the job, they identify a communication situation, choose a document type and style to deal with it, and shape the content of the message to the situation, document, and style they have chosen.

Each chapter includes an introductory summary and extensive chapter exercises that will help you to organize your writing assignments. Several chapters include discussions of the costs of written communication.

In Chapter One you will discover that specific types of documents require a certain type of style. You will also learn that developing a text consists of several stages and that different audiences require special information written in a special style.

Chapter Two tells you to be friendly to your readers by making sure that they understand your message. You must be aware of readers' information needs. Are they fully or partially informed about your subject? Are they uninformed? In any case, you can be reader-friendly by following the Seven Commandments of Reader-Friendly Writing: be concise, use active voice, write coherently, correct your mistakes, use headings and subheadings, use visuals, and learn word processing.

Chapter Three is about organizing your writing with a purpose. You will learn to compare and contrast, classify, explain causes and effects, break processes down into steps, give examples, describe, and set up an argument. You will see organizational structures for each purpose as well as examples of each.

Chapter Four shows you how to describe mechanisms. This chapter emphasizes using physical qualities of size, shape, color, texture, and methods of attachment to provide readers with word pictures of physical devices. You will also learn to format and use visuals to support a mechanism description.

Chapter Five shows you how to write processes. You will organize procedures into sequences of steps in objective style for a managerial audience. You will learn to explain how each task in a process is performed and to distinguish operator descriptions from nonoperator descriptions.

In Chapter Six you will be writing instructions and manuals. The chapter covers different types of manuals: owner's, user's, technical, instructions. It includes an explanation of writing instructions in the imperative style and the friendly style. You will learn that instructions are written for workers who perform the tasks described—not for managers who oversee them.

Chapter Seven is about letters and memos. It covers the basic structure and conventions of both forms of communication. Specific situations such as ordering products, filing a complaint, resolving a claim, providing instructions, and requesting information are explained. You will also learn about adopting a style suitable for particular memo readers.

Three types of reports are explained in Chapter Eight: proposals, progress reports, and evaluation reports. This chapter covers how to organize a report with an executive summary in the top position. It explains specific requirements for each report type, and offers guidelines on matching the right report with a particular communication situation.

Chapter Nine will guide you through a research project from hypothesis to final draft. It explains the nature and purpose of research and shows you how to develop a working bibliography, collect notes and form a thesis, sketch an outline, write a rough draft, and polish it into a final draft. This chapter also covers several documentation systems.

In Chapter Ten you will learn how to organize, write, and deliver an oral presentation. This chapter distinguishes oral from written communication, explains three speech types (impromptu, extemporaneous, and manuscript), presents three principal speaking purposes (inform, persuade, demonstrate), and includes suggestions on style and the speaking environment.

Appendices provide helpful information on résumés and cover letters, research paper sources, rules for using numbers, word meanings, and abbreviations and symbols.

ACKNOWLEDGMENTS

I would like to thank the following reviewers for their helpful comments and
good advice:

Adalene Flechtner
Lynna Kalna
Cindy Keller
Robert Preissle
Joseph Rice
Maris Roze
Andrea Rutherfoord
Wendy Stocker

I would also like to thank these companies and individuals for giving me
permission to use certain materials:

Apricorn, Inc.
Battelle Memorial Labs
DeVry, Inc.
Adalene Flechtner
Nissan Motor Corporation
Patrick Menter
OCLC
William Rase
Daniel Rose
Star Micronics, Inc

Stephen M. Flaherty

TECHNICAL
AND BUSINESS WRITING

ONE

Writing on the Job

PREVIEW

To produce good writing, you have to make the information fit the document and style that best communicates to readers. Technical and business writing consists of special documents such as memos, reports, manuals, and instructions. It requires up to several stages of text development: brainstorming, clustering, outlining, rough-drafting, revising, proofreading, and producing the final draft. Using a word processor saves time in developing text.

Good professional writing is produced in response to a realistic situation. Writers determine readers' information needs and select the content, document, and style that fulfill them best. Style is very important. In fact, each writing situation prescribes one of the following styles: objective, imperative, friendly, or intimate. The first two are distant styles because they focus more on information than on the reader. The second two are close styles because they focus on either the reader or the writer more than on content.

THE BASICS

Technical and business writing requires several characteristics shared by all writing. Any written communication requires an audience who will read the message (writers often do not see, hear, or speak to any of the audience members except through words), content material that will be shaped into a message, and the writer's plan for turning ideas into logical written communication.

DOCUMENT TYPES

Technical and business writing, in addition, consists of specialized types of documents, such as memos, articles, professional reports, and manuals. Each has certain unique characteristics. For example, a memo has a special heading; its message consists of a central idea expressed in a statement exchanged between members of the same company or organization. An article is an essay written in journals and magazines for a specialized audience within a particular profession or field; different journals and magazines usually require a particular content and writing style.

The mainstay of professional writing, however, is the report. Professional writers must know about several types of reports: progress reports, feasibility studies, evaluation reports, and others. Each type has its own requirements. For example, progress reports contain a summary of the project, an update of work accomplished, a summary of work remaining, and notification of the next planned written contact. Manuals are very practical how-to documents. They consist of instructions, descriptions of materials and parts, and maintenance and troubleshooting guidelines. Other reports have other special characteristics that readers expect to find. Throughout this book you will learn how to write reports, as well as letters and memos. General writing techniques such as definition, process, and description are included in earlier chapters.

STYLE

Style is the way that something or somebody sounds or looks. For example, the punk rock movement has a special form of music, and its followers have distinctive dress, language, and haircut. Punk rock musicians differ in style from country musicians, who have their own type of music, dress, language, and haircut. Adopting a professional style in writing means getting the message to the reader by using the right style to create a positive impression.

Since writers create style through words, style is evident in writing in more subtle ways than it is in music and clothing. Readers perceive a writer's style by the sound of words. When we read, we hear the writer's voice: "Get me out of here!" sounds very different from "The three parts of a floppy disk are the envelope, the square protective covering, and the disk itself." Professional writing tends to be like the style of the second voice: controlled, objective, and well organized.

Although professional writing usually communicates facts, advertising copy and promotional communication employ emotional style to appeal to customers. Sales literature promotes products using an excited tone: "If you want a personal computer that is 100% IBM compatible, take a look at THIS!" and sometimes by stretching the truth: "This is the finest printer on the market today!"

Five useful styles are the objective, conditional, imperative, friendly, and intimate. The **objective style** is factual and is often used for technical writing and nonpromotional business documents. It contains little, if any, mention of the writer (I) or the audience (YOU): "The first two tasks involved in 'booting up' the computer are inserting the system disk into disk drive A and flipping the toggle switch to the up position." The objective style focuses on the subject rather than on reader or writer. The same is true for the **conditional style.**

Writers try to avoid the conditional style because it creates uncertainty: "If one wishes to 'boot up' the computer, one would insert the system disk into disk drive A and flip the toggle switch to the up position." It can be used effectively in conditional situations such as proposals. In proposals, companies compete for business contracts by explaining plans to solve a problem or complete a project for a specified sum of money: "If Danforth Corporation is selected as the provider for these services, Danforth will guarantee all labor and materials for a period of three years." Since the situation is uncertain, the conditional style is appropriate.

The **imperative** and **friendly styles** address the audience by using the second-person pronoun "you" or by using the pronoun "you" understood to form imperative (command) statements. Instructional manuals consist of imperative statements: "First, loosen the hex bolt; second, carefully remove the bolt from the hole; third, clean rust and dirt from the bolt with gasoline." Each statement is a command using the pronoun "you" understood as the subject.

TABLE 1-1   *Summary of Writing Styles*

Style	*Focus*	*Pronoun*	*Documents*
Objective	Subject	He/she/it/they	All
Conditional	Subject	He/she/it/they	Proposals Feasibility studies Uncertain situations
Imperative	Reader	"You" understood	Instructions Manuals
Friendly	Reader	You	Sales literature Advertising copy Memos Letters
Intimate	Writer	I, We	Letters Memos Testimonials Autobiographies

The friendly style creates sales and promotional literature: here the "you" is present. "You'll be pleased to know that the Hydro M85 has all the features that you would expect to find on the higher-priced models." The imperative and friendly styles focus on the reader.

The **intimate style** employs the pronoun "I" to refer to the writer. Memos and letters utilize the intimate style because they are personalized messages: "Bill, I think your proposal regarding changing our cost/benefit analyses has merit. I would like to see more specifics." In sales literature, the first-person style is used in testimonials to products: "I never thought that I would use brand X until I tried it—boy, was I wrong!" The intimate style focuses on the writer.

The five styles are summarized in Table 1-1. Choosing the right style determines the closeness of the writer to readers. The intimate and friendly styles are used easily with memos and letters, but more distant styles can also be used. A letter or memo specifying instructions, for example, is written in the imperative. The same holds true of other styles and documents. No particular style dominates a document, but do expect to see certain styles used more often with certain documents (a few examples: memos and letters written in the intimate or friendly style, proposals and feasibility studies in the conditional style, instructions in the imperative style, and formal reports in the objective style).

Intimate	Friendly	Imperative	Conditional/Objective

Close ⟵———————————————————————⟶ Distant

Throughout the book you will choose the best styles to use in your assignments, so be sure you know thoroughly the five styles described above. But even if you know the right style and the right document to use, you will have to develop your text. The seven stages of text development are discussed next.

TEXT DEVELOPMENT

Since few people can produce a well-written document on the first try, most writers complete one only after performing a series of text development tasks. Seven stages in text development include brainstorming, clustering, outlining, drafting, revising, proofreading, and producing the final draft. Use of these stages depends on the number of facts gathered, the writer's familiarity with the subject matter and document type, and the nature of the intended message. The following steps can be accomplished using a word processor.

Brainstorming

List everything related to the topic. Read through the lists to exclude irrelevant items. Let's review the sequence by means of an example.

Belinda Mitchell, who majored in business, has been employed by Hargrove Industries for two years since her graduation. She is an assistant manager in the Transportation Division. Beginning this week Belinda is required to write her boss a one-page memo that summarizes the most important developments in her area. Friday afternoon at 3:30 she sits down in front of her PC to start composing. She turns on the computer, waits for the A > prompt. After it appears, she inserts her word-processing disk, types in the startup code, hits the RETURN key, and waits for the menu to appear on the monitor screen. She chooses the menu item to enter a new file. The new file name is "Sum Memo 1" because this is the first summary memo she has written. She will store it on her data disk. Belinda begins composing by brainstorming. She lists everything significant pertaining to work that comes to her mind until her computer screen is full:

```
Tariff increase on metals
5 drivers called in sick
85% on-time deliveries
Delivered to 15 new customers
Late to 3 new customers
Union complaints over docking pay
Air freight estimates too high
Need three new drivers by August
Complaints about broken vending machines
Prices on subcontract truckers
Volume forecast for next year 20% increase
```

Clustering

Begin grouping together items on your list that are similar. Cluster items into groups: each may be part of a topic, a separate topic, or part of a larger topic. Try to form clusters that contain unified, specific information. Do not be afraid to eliminate unsuitable material.

Belinda clusters her brainstorming list into groups of items according to subject areas. She uses the DELETE key to eliminate misplaced items and the RETURN key to create spaces between items so that she can change the position of items to form groups. Her computer screen contains four clusters: prices, worker problems, delivery efficiency, and forecasted information.

```
Tariff increase on metals
Air freight estimates too high
Prices on subcontract truckers

Five drivers called in sick
Worker complaints over docking pay
Complaints about broken vending machines
```

85% on-time deliveries
Delivered on-time to 15 new customers
Delivered late to 3 new customers

Need three new drivers by August
Volume forecast for next year is a 20% increase

Outlining

Organize clusters into a logical format. First, identify the central message. This is your **thesis**—your statement of purpose. Next, ask: How can I best organize my information to achieve this purpose? Keep your audience in mind. What information is required to make your message understood? What depth of detail and breadth of coverage is needed to fully follow the logic of your statements? With the answers to these questions, sequence the subtopics in the order that will best support your purpose. Make sure that each subtopic provides the necessary support for the purpose. Finally, do not forget to sequence the introduction and conclusion. Introductions prepare the reader with a thesis and main points. Conclusions remind the reader by reemphasizing main points.

Belinda's purpose is to provide her boss with a summary of significant data for the week. Belinda decides to sequence her information by emphasizing delivery efficiency first, followed by prices, union problems, and forecasted information. Her boss is most concerned with delivery efficiency and prices. Since prices mentioned are unaccrued, she decides that they are of secondary importance. Worker problems are more immediate than forecasts, so she decides to place the union third and the forecasts last.

Belinda wonders how much information to include. Her boss instructed her not to exceed one single-spaced page. She decides to include the percentage of all deliveries made on time in comparison to last year's average and to highlight the names of new high-volume customers who received late deliveries. She will quote tariff increases and compare them with old tariffs to show their impact on expenses. She decides just to specify the worker problems and let her boss ask for more information. Including suggestions for dealing with forecasts seems like a good idea because her boss is always asking for "solutions instead of problems."

Belinda presses the RETURN key to make spaces between items in clusters to insert details. She places introductory details above the clusters and concluding details below them. Now she has three screens of information:

Introduction: Summary of significant data for the week
Four areas of data covered: delivery efficiency, prices, worker complaints, and forecasts

85% on-time deliveries
Last year's average 83%

Delivered on-time to 15 new customers including: General Auto, Forge, Inc, Phillips Ltd, Greystone, Fiber Optics

Delivered late to 3 new customers: Harcourt Machinery, Petersen Labs, and Firerock Corporation—phone apologies made

Tariff increase on metals expected to increase 7% on July 1

> Air freight estimates too high
> 23% higher than rail with 3-day save time
> 18% higher than container 3-week save time
>
> Prices on subcontract truckers
> 4% higher than staff but 9% savings with overhead considered
>
> Five drivers called in sick
> Union complaints over docking pay
> Complaints about broken vending machines
>
> Need three new drivers by August
> General Auto and Forge contracts will require six additional truckloads per week

> Volume forecast for next year is 20% increase
> Hargrove will open an instruments division in January—delivery volume should increase 20%
> Suggestion: contract out business to independents until stable volume growth achieved.
>
> Conclusion: Deliveries are punctual, metals tariff increase will have minor effect on costs, alternative to air freight should be examined, using contract truckers will save money, union problems minimal, and business looks prosperous over the next year.

Rough-drafting

Put all the preceding steps together in prose form for the first time. Compose sentences and paragraphs out of outline items. Start writing with the introduction or the body. Be flexible when writing a rough draft. Just follow the outline and include more information as needed. If necessary, compose sections out of sequence. However, after completing the rough draft, make sure that your writing follows the order of the outline.

Belinda quickly composes the rough draft from the outline:

> To: M. Peters
> From: Belinda Mitchell
> Date: 4/22/88
>
> Subject: Weekly Report
>
> Significant activity occurred in four areas during the week 4/18–4/22: delivery efficiency, prices, union complaints, and forecasts.
>
> Delivery efficiency was 85%, a 2% increase over last year's efficiency rating during the same period. Fifteen new customers received on-time service, including General Auto, Forge, Inc, Phillips Ltd, Greystone, and Fiber Optics. Three new customers received late deliveries: Harcourt Machinery,

Petersen Labs, and Firerock Corporation—phone apologies have been made.

Tariff increases on metals amounting to 7% are expected on July 1. Air freight estimates are too high at 23% higher than rail with a 3-day save time and 18% higher than container with a 3-week save time. The price for subcontract truckers is 4% higher than staff wages but saves 9% on fringe benefit overhead.

Union problems include five drivers calling in sick, complaints from the union steward regarding docking pay, and broken vending machines in the loading dock area.

Forecasts indicate that we will need three new drivers by August to handle six additional truckloads per week due to the General Auto and Forge contracts. The volume forecast for Hargrove will increase 20% by January 1989 due to the New instruments division. I suggest contracting independent truckers to handle the work until the volume stabilizes.

Conclusion: Deliveries are punctual, metal tariff increase will have a minor effect on cost, alternative to air freight should be examined, using contract truckers should save money, union problems are minimal, and business looks prosperous over the next year.

Revising

Review the rough draft to decide on necessary changes. Keep your purpose in mind as you revise. Make sure that the sequence of information is logical and prepares the reader for upcoming information. Do not be afraid to move major sections of your document around. Your revision is complete when you feel comfortable with the purpose, the sequence of main points, the supporting details, and the general "feel" of the document.

Belinda makes the following revisions to her document:

- Changes the heading to "Weekly Summary" to remind Peters that her memo is a summary and not comprehensive.
- Moves the date from the first line to the heading so that it reads "Weekly Summary Report 4/18–4/22." This arrangement immediately identifies the time period.
- Reduces the wordiness of the first line to "Four important areas to report on are. . . ."
- Reduces wording on delivery efficiency by listing items. She defines efficiency as on-time deliveries and decides to compare the percentage with that of the preceding week since recent information is the most important.
- Eliminates the judgment that air freight prices are too high and lists pricing information. Belinda decides that Peters can evaluate the prices.
- Condenses the wording of forecasted information by listing items. Removes the first-person suggestion by changing it to a factual statement of options.
- Eliminates the conclusion as opinionated and repetitive.

Proofreading

Read the document carefully to identify and correct spelling, grammar, punctuation, and wording. Belinda corrects "New instruments division" so that it reads "new Instruments Division."

Final Drafting

The final draft involves typing or word-processing the revised and proofed document. Belinda's final draft now fills her computer screen:

To: M. Peters
From: Belinda Mitchell
Date: 4/22/88

Subject: Weekly Summary 4/18–4/22

Four important areas to report are delivery efficiency, prices, union complaints, and forecasts.

DELIVERY EFFICIENCY

On-time efficiency is at 85%—a 3% drop from the preceding week.

Fifteen new customers received perfect on-time delivery (including General Auto, Forge, Phillips, Greystone, and Fiber Optics).

Three new customers received later deliveries: Harcourt, Petersen, Firerock (apologies have been made).

PRICES

Metals tariff is increasing 7% on 7/1/88.

Air freight rates are 23% higher than rail and delivered 3 days sooner and 18% higher than containers and delivered 3 weeks sooner.

Subcontract truckers charge wages 4% higher than staff but do not require the 9% fringe benefits overhead paid to staff— company savings using subcontractors nets out at 5%.

EMPLOYEE ISSUES

Five drivers called in sick.

Complaints were received from the steward over docking pay for tardiness.

Workers have complained about broken vending machines on the loading dock.

FORECASTS

Three new drivers are needed by 8/1/88 to handle six additional weekly truckloads for General Auto and Forge.

An increase of 20% in delivery volume is anticipated by 1/1/89, a result of activity from the new Instruments Division. Initially using contract truckers would eliminate permanent overstaffing problems.

Contact me for additional information.

Belinda makes some last-minute changes in the final draft, such as adding subheadings and using numbers to designate dates. She saves her memo on her data disk.

Be sure to complete your document in a timely manner. In business, your reader will always want information very soon. Make backup copies of your work in case you lose the original. When using a word processor, this means having two data disks that contain all written work. One disk will be the "original," the other will be the "backup." Keep your disks away from anything magnetic. Information on them can be destroyed through contact with a magnet.

ESTABLISHING THE WRITING SITUATION

Use a realistic situation to make your writing assignments meaningful. Few write anything without an audience and a purpose—even in school you write graded papers for teachers. In this course, try being a little different by creating a realistic situation, one with an audience and purpose that will give your writing details. Identify two or three situations that require an engineer or manager to write. Here are a few suggestions to get you started.

- Explaining a part, process, or concept to a customer
- Training a new employee
- Sharing information with a fellow worker
- Addressing a professional organization

Write your own ideas below.

_____

_____

_____

_____

_____

Consider the documents necessary for your situations.

DECIDING ON A DOCUMENT TYPE

The four suggested situations require different types of documents. You would provide information to a customer with a set of product instructions, use a training manual to train a new employee, share information with a fellow employee in a memo, and address a professional society with a journal article. What documents would your suggestions demand? Consider a newspaper or magazine article, formal report, or chapter in a book—would any of these fit your writing situations? Once you have identified a document type, how do you learn to organize and compose it? An easy way is by studying examples for format and typical content.

DEVELOPING AN APPROPRIATE STYLE

To choose the right style for a situation and document, you must know how you want to be perceived by the audience. Style is the way that the writing comes across to the reader. Whenever people read a document, they perceive the writer to be either close or distant. If you want to be close to the reader, use the intimate or friendly style; if you want to be distant, use the objective or imperative style.

MAKING IT FIT: SITUATION, DOCUMENT, AND STYLE

Consider the following aspects of professional writing:

- Situation (audience and purpose)
- Type of document (set of instructions, training manual, memo, article)
- Style [relationship to reader(s)—intimate/distant]

These characteristics are interrelated. Audience and purpose require a certain type of document, and style is stipulated by the audience, purpose, and document type.

Consider the situation of producing a set of instructions. Instructions tell readers about how to perform a technical or mechanical task. The task must be defined. If you have ever purchased a product that required assembly (such as an electronic kit, home computer, or even a piece of furniture), you are familiar with the format and style of instructions. The format usually consists of a list of tasks. The style is imperative. This brief set of instructions on setting up a general ledger account in a computer illustrates instructional writing:

Completing these steps sets up general ledger account numbers:

1. Enter ''genled'' into the keyboard.
2. Wait for the display on the screen.
3. Find the ''Account Number'' heading at the top of the display.
4. Enter the appropriate account number.
5. Enter the department number and employee number under these headings.

Although an informed reader would easily understand these instructions without an accompanying definition, an uninformed reader would discover little meaning in them. A definition makes understanding the instructions much easier.

A general ledger is a computerized record of a company's financial transactions. It consists of a list of numbers followed by dollar amounts. Each number is actually a three-part code. The first three numbers stand for the category of spending (payroll, machinery, accounts payable); the second two numbers stand for the department (Operations, Advertising, Sales); and the final three numbers represent the employee who spent the funds. See the following example.

250-00-111	$ 25.00
250-00-140	300.00
525-07-000	85.00

Think of a writing situation at school, work, or home that requires instructional writing. Use the general ledger model as a guide and compose a brief set of instructions and an accompanying definition for an uninformed reader. Test your writing on your instructor. Can he or she understand your instructions without the definition? Is understanding improved using the definition?

The audience in the general ledger example is not well defined. Would the instructions and definition of it change for a customer audience?

Customer Audience

Customers read company literature, such as sales brochures and product manuals. These are public relations documents as well as information sources. Companies use brochures to sell products and to convince customers that they made smart purchases. One method of making consumers feel good about a purchase is to make products easier to use through manuals written in the friendly style. For example, the style of a printer manual reads as follows:

Allow us to introduce you to your Gemini printer: "Gemini, this is your new user." "User, this is the remarkable new Gemini—a versatile and dependable printer that lets you do tricks with its dot matrix and bit image capabilities."

This paragraph conveys a friendly message about the product. Practice this style by revising the general ledger definition or your own into the friendly style. Afterward, explain the effect of each revision. Is this style best for communicating information? Why? Why not?

Revision

Explanation of Changes

Employee Audience

The relationship between writer and reader who are employer and employee is formal. You can expect the style to be more distant than the friendly style used for a customer. This relationship is reflected in a company document such as a training manual. The writer presents the company as concerned about making employees happy and productive.

> You should be impressed with our new Imagemaker printer. Its important features include letter quality print, sophisticated graphics, and high-speed laser printing. We have gone to some expense to purchase this state-of-the-art machine. But we believe that our investment is justified if it helps you to perform your job more easily and proficiently.

The tone is friendly and firm. The reader's responsibilities are clear. It is more serious and more informative than the customer-friendly style. Revise either the general ledger definition or one of your own as if you were writing to an employee. Be sure to explain the effect of each change.

Revision

Co-worker Audience

Different relationships exist between equals on the job. They can be friends, working associates, and competitors. Memos between friends are intimate and therefore informal. Working associates share less intimate and more formal memos—not unfriendly, but concise and helpful. Competitors are formal, ranging from terse to polite. Remember that since memos document a writer's words within company files, none are likely to be too informal, too friendly, or too unfriendly. Most will focus on pertinent information.

A memo heading identifies the intended reader, the writer, and the topic of the memo. The following is a memo written between two friendly employees on the topic of the new printer:

TO: Fred Smith, Director of Personnel
FROM: Bill Jones, Director of Documentation
SUBJECT: New Printer
DATE: June 3, 1986

Fred, I thought you might be interested in knowing that our department has just received the new printer that I was telling you about last week. It has some great features, such as a laser printhead, font varieties, letter quality of course, and graphics capability that will absolutely knock your socks off.

The laser creates print by spraying ink through a jet onto the page. You won't believe how quickly it operates.

The company is doing a demonstration of the printer on the 17th of this month. Since your department will be using it rather extensively, I would like to invite you and some of your people down here for the demonstration. I think you'll be impressed.

If you can't make it, no problem, Let me know if and when you can, and I'll arrange for someone down here to check you out on this state-of-the-art masterpiece.

Bill's memo is informative and friendly. He uses several informal words and phrases to get his message across. But he is not too informal. Bill keeps his message focused on the printer and the upcoming demonstration.

How would this memo differ if Bill and Fred shared a different kind of relationship? What if they were simply working associates, or competitors? How would the memo differ in each case? Produce a memo for each of these alternatives and explain how you alter the style in each.

Revisions

_____

_____

_____

_____

_____

Explanations of Changes

_____

_____

_____

Professional Audience (Journal Article)

Journal articles reflect a student–teacher relationship between writer and reader. The writer, as an authority on the subject, teaches the readers. The general audience for a professional article is the profession of experts in the field. Since journal articles represent the profession, they are written with precision on significant topics.

Journal articles emphasize facts. Readers want information. They wish to be challenged by the writer's ideas and knowledge. The objective style of this introductory definition appearing in a journal article is distant and formal:

The Microwave Data Communication System (MDCS) is a network designed to improve data transmission between state agencies by replacing current dependency on the telephone system. Once implemented, the MDCS will be more efficient and reliable than the telephone system because it will eliminate telephone lines and line problems. The MDCS will consist primarily of a central transmitting tower and transmitting antennas located throughout the state. The purpose of this article is to describe the most important characteristics of the MDCS and to explain the three phases of its implementation.

The writer provides a brief, informative definition of the subject using objective style. The writing is clear and concise. The writer does not try to impress the audience by using sophisticated or confusing language.

Attempt to write an introductory definition to a journal article by choosing a topic from a course you are taking. Keep your topic simple.

_____

_____

_____

_____

_____

_____

Discuss your results with your instructor. Is your style objective? How do you know? Are "I" or "you" present in your writing? Can style be objective even if these pronouns are present? (The answer is yes—can you explain why?) Have you expressed opinions or just stated facts?

CONSIDERING COST

When you communicate on the job, you must be aware of costs. In business, everything relates to the bottom line—the profit or loss statement at the end of a revenue period. Memos, letters, reports, proposals, brochures, and journal articles written by company employees cost a certain number of dollars or cents to produce.

Three types of cost are actual, opportunity, and the estimated cost of error. **Actual costs** include the value of the paper, ink, machine use, and labor invested in each communication. Document types vary in actual cost depending on length, personnel involved, and types of machines being used. Long reports involving high-salaried employees, FAX communications, laser printers, and long hours will be expensive in comparison to routine memos announcing meetings.

Opportunity costs are an estimate of what the company could have earned using the same resources in a different activity. For example, if $25,000 is invested in researching and writing an unsuccessful proposal for a $1,000,000 contract, the company lost the opportunity to use $25,000 to generate revenue from another source. Opportunity cost is part of the risk of doing business.

The **estimated cost of error** measures the expense of miscommunication. Documents with incorrect information can cause employees and customers to damage machines, policies to be interpreted differently than intended, and personal injuries on the job. Companies are usually responsible for errors in their documents, and these errors can be very expensive.

Companies hope for a favorable cost/benefit ratio. Management plans to spend specified amounts on documentation for routine business communication as well as for gaining and maintaining business contracts. The cost of error, however, is something that businesses cannot always plan on. That is one reason that courses in business and technical writing stress precision and correctness. When the meaning is unclear, costs often increase.

CHAPTER ASSIGNMENT

1. Consider each of the following situations, and explain how you would make the information fit. Produce samples of writing to indicate the style you would use in each.

- You purchased a radio that stops working after two weeks.
- The procedure used at work is inefficient, and you have an idea for improving it.
- Your project at school requires an explanation of operation.
- The student organization you belong to wants to communicate an appeal to raise money for the United Way.
- Your younger brother/sister in high school who is taking a class in your college major asks you to send a written explanation of a basic concept.

2. Identify commands from a word-processing program such as WordStar or WordPerfect that will help you to perform text processing stages. Indicate the procedure used on your word processor (or computer with word-processing software) for completing each stage. Identify commands that work best with each stage.

Stage	*Command(s)*	*Procedure(s)*
Brainstorming		
Clustering		
Outlining		
Rough-drafting		
Revising		
Proofreading		
Final drafting		

In Chapter 1 you have learned about characteristics governing professional writing situations. You have had an opportunity to revise some examples so that they are more consistent with newly introduced situations. In Chapter 2 you will be learning about some important characteristics of the written text itself.

TWO

Being Reader Friendly

PREVIEW

Being **reader friendly** means designing your document so that readers can easily understand it. You should consider how much readers know about your topic. Target your writing for readers in the middle range. Avoid writing exclusively for those at the extremes of ignorance or full understanding. Be concise, so that you do not waste time. Use the active voice, so that readers see clear connections between subjects and verbs. This saves time and avoids confusion. Write coherently by using transitions to show relationships. Readers appreciate knowing how and why statements are connected. Correct errors. They distract and they lessen reader confidence in you. Organize with subheadings so that readers can follow major divisions. This aids in comprehension and scanning. Use visuals to illustrate. They communicate quickly and efficiently. Try using a word processor. It will make revising and storing your work a lot easier.

THE BASICS

Good writing communicates. This seems simple, but sometimes writers forget the information needs of readers. They assume that readers know too much or too little. This leads to either boredom or confusion. Readers differ in intelligence, knowledge, and experience, so their information needs and preferences also differ.

CONSIDERING AUDIENCE AWARENESS

Consider your readers' awareness of your topic. Is it informed or uninformed? Informed readers share your knowledge. They are experts who are trying to learn more. Uninformed readers do not share your knowledge. They read to learn basic information. Both require standard sections of information, such as introductory summary, background, definitions, explanation of ideas, illustrations, and conclusions—although these may be presented differently to each type of audience.

Think of your readers as being on a 10-point scale:

1 2 3 4 5 6 7 8 9 10

Uninformed ————————————————————— Informed

Most in your audience will be in between the extremes of total ignorance at point 1 or total knowledge at point 10. Readers at 1 and 2 or 9 and 10 will learn little because they will be too unprepared for the topic or too informed to be interested in reading about it. You can exclude those at the extremes.

Target your writing for readers in the range 3 to 5. Those who need basic information will get it, while those who do not can scan past it quickly and go on to the "meatier" sections. How do you adjust writing for readers in the range 3 to 5? Obey the seven commandments of reader-friendly writing:

1. Be concise.
2. Use active voice.
3. Write coherently.
4. Correct your errors.
5. Organize with subheadings.
6. Use visuals.
7. Learn word processing.

Commandment 1: Be Concise

• Replace complex words with simple words to convey the same meaning.

Complex	Simple
nomenclature	name
terminate	end
miniscule	tiny
commencement	beginning

Think of simpler words for the following complex ones.

analyzation _____

finalize _____

amorphous _____

antithesis _____

• Avoid vague language by using specific, detailed descriptions.

> Replace "Manufacturing fiber optics is a complex process" with "The two steps involved in manufacturing fiber optics are, first, making the preform containing the core and cladding, and second, drawing the fiber and coating it."

Replace these vague expressions with specific, detailed wording:

This is a tough project.   ⸺⸺⸺⸺⸺⸺

Company A has a big market share.   ⸺⸺⸺⸺⸺

The new model is quite competitive.   ⸺⸺⸺⸺⸺

The future is uncertain.   ⸺⸺⸺⸺⸺⸺

- Use the objective style as much as possible.

  Instead of "First, the mechanic should have adjusted the carburetor," use "First, the mechanic adjusts the carburetor."

Revise these sentences into objective style:

I feel that the estimates will be a tad too high.

⸺⸺⸺⸺⸺⸺⸺⸺

When the turboencabulator is fully assembled, it should be running like a top.

⸺⸺⸺⸺⸺⸺⸺⸺

I hope to present three main points that should consist of conceptual descriptions, assembly advice, and maintenance tips.

⸺⸺⸺⸺⸺⸺⸺⸺

⸺⸺⸺⸺⸺⸺⸺⸺

You can expect some pretty high evaluations on this procedure.

⸺⸺⸺⸺⸺⸺⸺⸺

- Keep the vocabulary understandable for readers in the range 3 to 5.

  Andgates and nandgates, buses and buffers, semiconductors and filters may be understandable to readers in the range 6 to 10, but those in the range 3 to 5 need definitions or plain English terms.

Can you define these terms? If you cannot identify some of them, you are not alone. Many readers in the range 3 to 5 would have difficulty as well.

CPU   _____

LAN   _____

Market share   _____

Marginal cost   _____

LED   _____

EOM   _____

AI   _____

Project displacement   _____

Transducer   _____

Hurdle rate   _____

- Limit the use of words that end in *-ize* (e.g., maximize, minimize, optimize, or formalize).

> "To maximize profits, we must minimize expenses by formalizing our accounts: all this should optimize our market position" really means "We can gain market share by reinvesting higher profits gained from cutting expenses."

- Use parallel wording. Keep coordinate ideas parallel by using the same types of words, phrases, or clauses to denote each idea.

> "The four steps in the process are:
>   sanding rusted areas
>   application of the primer
>   to sand the primer
>   finish up with the top coat of paint"

> can be improved with parallelism to

> "To complete the process:
>   sand rusted areas
>   apply the primer
>   sand the primer
>   apply the finish coat of paint."

- Avoid old-fashioned expressions; use language that is current.

"The findings suffer a precocious quality and thus are totally unacceptable" is understandable to the reader in the 1990s as "The data do not support the findings."

- Avoid clichés.

	Instead, use	
hands-on		practical
quick as a flash		very fast
last but not least		final
state of the art		current

Replace these clichés with meaningful words:

plain as day   _____

overkill   _____

light of day   _____

cost-effective   _____

- Avoid repetitive phrases.

Repetitive	*Improved*
basic essentials	essentials
advance plan	plan
close proximity	proximity
small in size	small

Make these repetitive expressions concise:

first priority   _____

visible to the eye   _____

current status   _____

absolutely perfect   _____

• Edit wordy phrases.

Unedited	Edited
on a daily basis	daily
in most cases	usually
at this point in time	now
the reason being that	because

Edit these wordy phrases down to single words:

most of the time   _____

is generally accepted   _____

on the basis of   _____

significant number   _____

Commandment 2: Use Active Voice

Active voice makes the subject of the sentence the doer of the action. **Passive voice** makes the subject the receiver of the action. Active voice clarifies the relationship between subject and verb, making your writing easier to understand.

A study conducted by John Kirkman indicates the effectiveness of active voice in improving readability. He had scientists read two versions of the same information: Brown's version, written in passive voice, and Smith's version, written in active voice. An excerpt from Brown's version:

It was discovered that total removal of the adrenal glands effects reduction of aggressiveness and that aggressiveness in adrenalectomized mice is restorable to the level of intact mice by treatment with corticosterone.

An excerpt from Smith's version:

The first experiment in our series with mice showed that total removal of the adrenal glands reduces aggressiveness. Moreover, when treated with corticosterone, mice that had their adrenals removed again became as aggressive as intact animals.

Notice that the passive "it was discovered" and "aggressiveness . . . is" from the Brown version are replaced with the active "experiment . . . showed" and "reduces aggressiveness" in the Smith version. Scientists rated the Smith version as more appropriate, interesting, precise, and explanatory. They found the Brown version more difficult to read.

Commandment 3: Write Coherently

Coherent writing contains transitional devices that show the reader how information is related. The following paragraph contains several transitional devices.

Currently, *supercomputers* are used to aid *scientists* in aerospace technology. *For example,* at Lockheed–Georgia Company a Cray X-MP/24 *supercomputer solves* complex fluid *flow* equations by *simulating aerodynamic flow.* The *solutions* tell *scientists* the direction and strength of *airflows simulated* by the *supercomputer. Scientists* can use these data to design better aircraft.

All the italicized words are transitional devices that hold the paragraph together either by indicating the nature of the information (for example) or by referring to a word used earlier. The pattern of repeated words consists of the following:

Supercomputers–supercomputer–supercomputer
Scientists–scientists–scientists
Solves–solutions
Flow–flow–airflows
Simulating–simulated

Locate transitional devices in the following paragraph.

Fiber optics is a branch of physics that focuses on transparent fibers made of glass or plastic. Light may travel through the optical fibers over distances ranging from a few centimeters to over 100 miles. The fibers can work individually or in groups. Some individual fibers have diameters measuring less than 0.001 inch. Each optical fiber has two parts: the inner part, a pure glass core, and the outer cladding, made of nontransparent glass.

Compare these transitional devices with standard transitional expressions such as *furthermore; in addition to; first, second, third, . . . , and finally.* You should discover that devices used in the fiber optics paragraph work better because they are less noticeable.

Commandment 4: Correct Your Errors

• Properly punctuate all sentences and independent clauses.

Sentences and independent clauses must contain a subject and verb, and they often also contain an object or complement.

The mechanic removes the oil plug by turning it counterclockwise with a $\frac{3}{8}$-inch open-end wrench.

"Mechanic" is the subject. "Removes" is the verb. "Plug" is the object. The rest of the sentence consists of two prepositional phrases ["by turning it counterclockwise" and "with a ⅜-inch open-end wrench"]. The latter two elements depend on the independent clause [the mechanic removes the oil plug] for their meaning.

Placing a subordinating word in front of the sentence makes it incomplete:

> When the mechanic removes the oil plug by turning it counterclockwise with a ⅜-inch open-end wrench

The sentence now consists of a subordinate clause [when the mechanic removes the oil plug] and two prepositional phrases. An easy way to revise this long sentence fragment into a complete sentence is to create a new independent clause by inserting a subject and main verb:

> When the mechanic removes the oil plug, he or she uses a ⅜-inch open-end wrench to turn it counterclockwise.

It is once more a complete sentence: a subordinate clause [when the mechanic removes the oil plug], an independent clause [he or she uses a ⅜-inch open-end wrench], and an infinitive phrase [to turn it counterclockwise].

• Be sure that introductory phrases and clauses and all adjectives and modifiers clearly refer to an intended noun or pronoun.

> Rewrite the following humorous statements to clarify the meaning that seems to be intended.
>
> An invisible car came out of nowhere, struck my vehicle, and vanished.

> I told the police that I was not injured but on removing my hat, I found that I had a fractured skull.

> When I saw that I could not avoid a collision, I stepped on the gas and crashed into the other car.

> The pedestrian had no idea which direction to go, so I ran over him.

The indirect cause of the accident was a little guy in a small car with a big mouth.

_____

_____

In my attempt to kill a fly, I drove into a telephone pole.

_____

_____

I pulled away from the side of the road, glanced at my mother-in-law, and headed over the embankment.

_____

_____

I was thrown from my car as it left the road. I was later found in a ditch by some stray cows.

_____

_____

The accident happened when the right door of a car came around the corner without giving a signal.

_____

_____

I had been driving my car for forty years when I fell asleep at the wheel and had an accident.

_____

_____

These statements are excerpts from insurance company claims reports.

- Use a comma to separate each of three or more items in a list, including the last two:

> Completing the process requires the following tools: digital oscilloscope, needle-nose pliers, soldering gun and desolderer.

Because there is no comma between the last two items in the list, they appear to comprise one unit. Place a comma before the "and" to indicate that they are separate units:

> Completing the process requires the following tools: digital oscilloscope, needle-nose pliers, soldering gun, and desolderer.

- Avoid abbreviations: use symbols or write out the proper word.

> See Appendix E for a list of symbols.

- When using symbols, define them, avoid confusing similar ones, and punctuate them as words.

> Megahertz (MHz) equals 1000 cycles per second. Millihertz (mHz) equals 0.001 of a cycle per second. Despite the similarity in the appearance of MHz and mHz, the value of each is quite different.

- Hyphenate words or a word and numeral compounded to form a single adjective.

> This company operates on a 52-week year.

> That code resembles an embedded-print command.

- Capitalize the following.

> Company and product names
>> Hewlett-Packard, Hughes Aircraft, General Electric, Westinghouse
>>
>> IBM-PC, Big Mac, Coke, Soft-White Bulbs

> Government agencies, departments, and divisions
>> Federal Bureau of Investigation, Justice Department, Division of Natural Resources

> Organization names
>> Society for Technical Communication, the United Way, American Management Association

> Proper nouns, except those in common usage
>> Capitalize the names of places (America), regions (Middle East), people (Albert Einstein), days of the week (Monday), and months (January).
>>
>> Do not capitalize directions (east), seasons (spring), or commonly used proper nouns (diesel, ampere, watt).

- Be sure to use words to denote their correct meanings. See the list of commonly confused words below.

Terms	A	AN
Meanings	(used before a word beginning with a consonant sound)	(used before a word beginning with a vowel sound)

Terms	ABILITY	CAPACITY
Meanings	being able to perform	power to contain

Terms	ABOUT	APPROXIMATELY
Meanings	rough estimate	accurate estimate

Terms	ACCEPT	EXCEPT
Meanings	to receive	exclude

Terms	ADVISE	INFORM
Meanings	to counsel	to provide information

Note: "Advice" is a noun meaning "counsel."

Terms	AFFECT	EFFECT
Meanings	to influence	a result, to result in

Terms	ALL TOGETHER	ALTOGETHER
Meanings	every item or person together	entirely

Terms	ALLUDE	REFER
Meanings	to reference indirectly	to name

Terms	ARE	OR
Meanings	to be (verb)	(conjunction used between two possibilities)

Note: "Our" is a first-person possessive pronoun.

See Appendix D for more words.

- Use numerals to denote units of measure, time, dates, page numbers, percentages, money, and proportions.

5 centimeters	15 minutes	December 25	page 32
12%	$25.00	3/5	

- Otherwise, write out all numbers of less than 10 and use numerals for numbers greater than or equal to 10.

one two three four five six seven eight nine

10 11 12 13 14 . . . 100 . . . 1000 . . . 10,000 . . . 100,000 . . . 1,500,000

- Numbers in the millions may be denoted with both numerals and words.

1.5 millions

See Appendix C for more number rules.

Commandment 5: Organize with Subheadings

A logical organization allows you to develop and arrange ideas so that the audience can easily understand them. Reports have three sections: introduction, body, and conclusion. The **introduction** explains the topic, the purpose, and the major subtopics of the report. It provides readers with a summary of main points so that they know what to expect in the body.

The **body** of the report consists of a delivery of the expected information in the sequence specified in the introduction. If the reader's expectations are violated by a poorly written or misleading introduction, the message will not be communicated successfully.

The **conclusion** complements the body and fulfills the purpose stated in the introduction. Conclusions reemphasize and support main points with findings, recommendations, and supporting facts in appendices. Conclusions vary according to the reader's needs.

The following model provides an outline of report elements.

Introduction

    Description of the Topic
    Explanation of the Purpose of the Report
    Statement of the Scope (Area Covered) of the Report
    List of Specific Subtopics (Subheadings) to Be Covered

Body

    Subtopic 1
    Subtopic 2   Note that each subtopic will probably
    Subtopic 3   be identified as a subheading.
    Subtopic 4
    Subtopic 5

Conclusion

    Findings? (list findings to be explained)
    Recommendations? (list recommendations to be argued)
    Appendices? (supporting facts, tables, visuals)

Using headings and subheadings provides readers with several benefits. Each provides a break in the text and relief from the otherwise constant flow of information. Headings show major divisions in a document. Subheadings tell readers the subtopic of each major division. They also act as transitional devices showing a change in subject matter.

Readers find subheaded reports less intimidating. They can scan subheadings and form a plan for reading. All readers will not read the entire report. Some will read only the vital sections. Subheadings enable them to locate those sections quickly. Busy managers appreciate subheaded documents because they save time.

Main headings introduce a major section of a report. Second-order subheadings designate the large divisions within a major section. Third-order subheadings indicate divisions within second-order subheadings. Subheadings help organize a report into an outline prior to writing by arranging main, second-order, and third-order subheadings into an outline.

Wide margins create white space that enables the reader's eye to focus

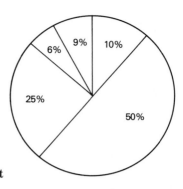

FIGURE 2-1   Pie Chart

easily on each subheaded section. Thin margins create a cluttered page—the clutter of words distracts the eye, making comprehension difficult. Leave 1-inch margins on all four sides of a document. Skip lines between paragraphs. Leave extra space between distinct sections of a document.

Commandment 6: Use Visuals

These are several standard types of visuals, described below.

Pie Chart

The pie chart demonstrates percentages as slices of a pie. Think of total tax dollars as being the 100% entity, and imagine how these dollars have been spent by labeling the slices in Figure 2-1.

Vertical Bar Chart

The vertical bar chart represents a total amount (not necessarily as a percentage) as a vertically rising bar and shows subamounts as different sections on the bar. Think of total research dollars (in the millions) as the total amount of the bar in Figure 2-2; label the subamounts as areas of spending.

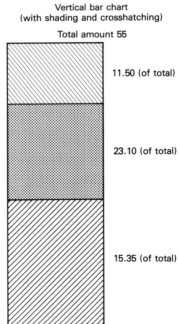

FIGURE 2-2   Vertical Bar Chart

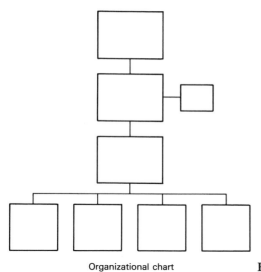

Organizational chart

FIGURE 2–3   Organization Chart

Organizational Chart

Organizational charts (Figure 2–3) show the power or hierarchical relationship among members of a company, government entity, or organization. Think of your workplace or school and imagine how you, your boss, or teacher might fit into such an organizational grid.

Flowchart

Flowcharts illustrate sequential steps in a process. Can you think of a process that would fit into the flowchart shown in Figure 2–4? Make up a flowchart of your typical Wednesday at school.

Horizontal Bar Chart

A horizontal bar chart shows a relationship among several categories. The numbers on the horizontal axis in Figure 2–5 could represent dollars (probably in the thousands or millions), percentage increases, or units such as numbers of new businesses (probably in the thousands). The categories, represented by each horizontal bar, would be different types of the same entity. For example, if Figure 2–5 measures increases of new businesses in thousands, each bar

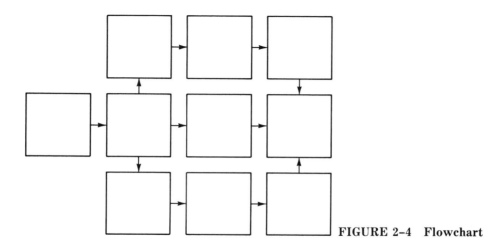

FIGURE 2–4   Flowchart

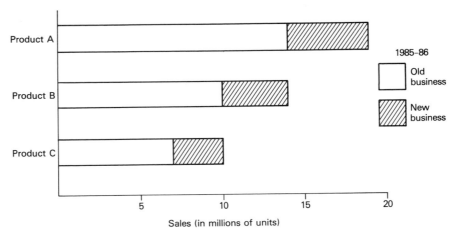

FIGURE 2-5   Horizontal Bar Chart

would represent each type of bar: the clear portion of the bar would be thousands of old businesses and the crosshatched areas would be additional thousands of new businesses. Both areas of each bar would represent total thousands of businesses in each category. Try making a horizontal bar chart showing the grade level achieved in each school subject you are now taking. *Hint:* Divide the horizontal axis into the grades 50, 60, 70, 80, 90, and 100.

Graph

A graph shows the relationship between two variables. In Figure 2-6 the vertical axis measures price and the horizontal axis measures quantity. As the quantity increases—moves left of the origin—the price moves up above the origin. This graph indicates that as price increases, the quantity available for sale also increases. Any two variables can be measured in relation to each other. Try plotting a graph that shows the relationship between the time you spend on your schoolwork (the horizontal axis) and your grade-point average (the vertical axis).

Multiline Graph

A multiline graph functions exactly like a single-line graph, except that two lines are shown to indicate two measured entities. In Figure 2-7 fixed and variable costs are shown in relation to quantity sold and production costs.

Tables

Tables consist of columns of related information. Sometimes, the same numbered item in each column should be compared or contrasted. For example, Table 2-1 could be titled "Sources of Known Chemical Pollutants." Column heading 1 would name all the sources (each item under this head would be a source of chemical pollution). Column heading 2 would be titled "Percent Derived from the United States" (each item under this head would be a percentage). Column heading 3 would be "Percent Derived from Outside the United States." Try setting up Table 2-1 as described above by imagining possible sources and percentages of chemical pollution in and out of the United States.

Some tables are constructed with columns that are independent of each other. The columns in Table 2-2 are independent of each other.

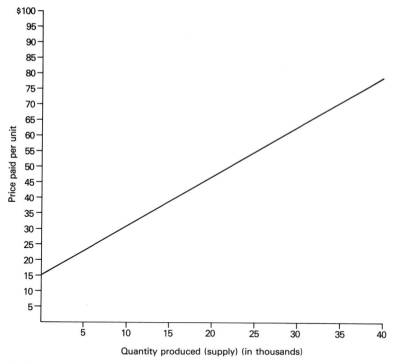

FIGURE 2-6   Line Graph

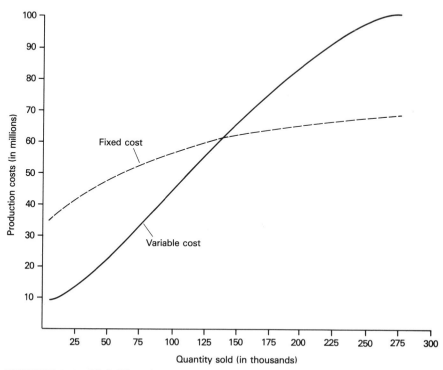

FIGURE 2-7   Multiline Chart

33

TABLE 2-1

TABLE 0-0 *Table Title*

Column Heading 1	Column Heading 2	Column Heading 3
Item 1	Item 1	Item 1
Item 2	Item 2	Item 2
Item 3	Item 3	Item 3
Total 1	Total 2	Total 3

TABLE 2-2

TABLE 0-0 *Preliminary List of Topics To Be Addressed in Final Report*

Reinforcement Fibers	Polymers	Structural Types
Carbon	Thermoplastic [TP]	Polymer/fiber composites (TP & TS)
Boron	Polyolefins	
Silicon carbide	Acrylics	
Alumina	Nylons	Polymer/filler composites (TP & TS)
Aramid	Thermoset [TS]	
Ceramic	Epoxy	
Glass	Acrylic	Polymer/polymer composites (TP & TS)
Metal	Unsaturated polyester	
	Phenolics	Laminates
	Polyimides	Multilayer films
		Blends/alloys
		Graft and block copolymers

Particulates	Composites Characterization
Silica	Reinforcement filler/polymer interactions
Carbon	Mechanical and other physical properties under stress conditions
Cross-linked polymeric microspheres	Analysis of composite structures subjected to severe environmental exposure conditions
Other inorganics	Reaction cure analysis
	Quality control analysis

Source: Battelle, Columbus Division, Columbus, Ohio.

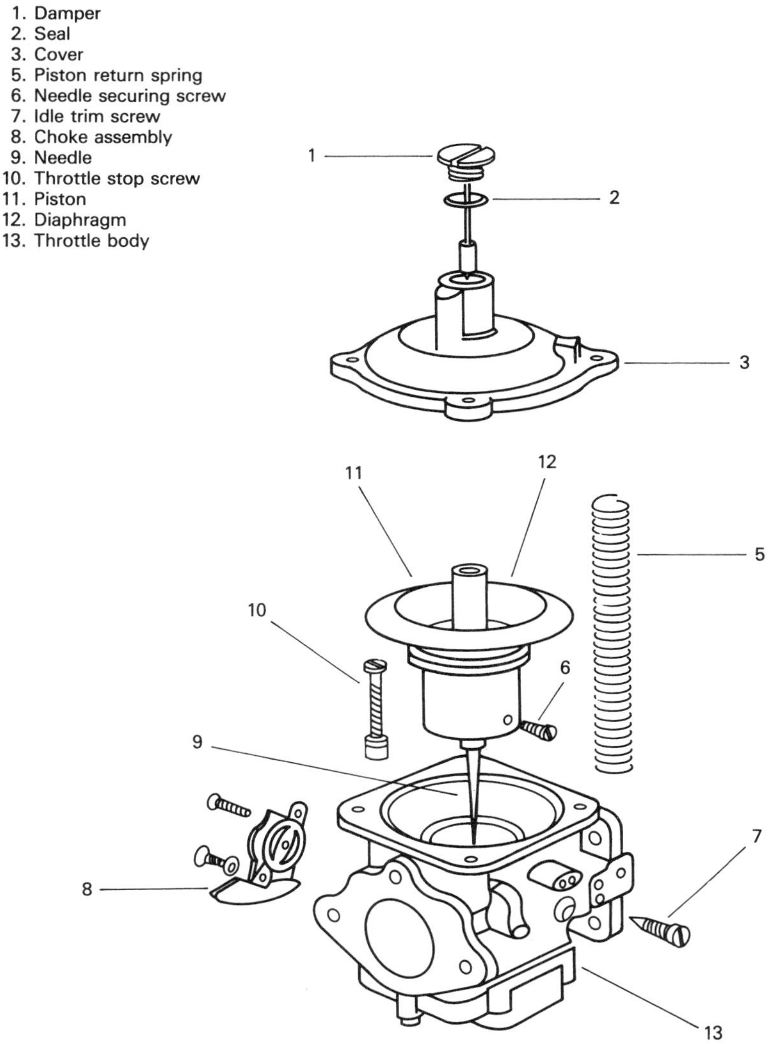

1. Damper
2. Seal
3. Cover
5. Piston return spring
6. Needle securing screw
7. Idle trim screw
8. Choke assembly
9. Needle
10. Throttle stop screw
11. Piston
12. Diaphragm
13. Throttle body

FIGURE 2-8   Line Drawing

Line Drawings

Line drawings can be functional, such as the exploded drawing of a carburetor in Figure 2-8; or they can provide visual reinforcement, such as the visuals in Figure 2-9. Can you think of any textbook descriptions you have read recently that would be easier to understand with a line drawing?

Program Schedules and Organization

Proposals, progress reports, and research reports often contain program schedules such as Figure 2-10 and program organization charts such as Figure 2-11. Could any of the other charts discussed earlier be used to structure program schedules or organization?

Databases are created by database producers, who acquire and analyze documents. Database producers create machine-readable records for these documents and store them on magnetic tapes or disks. These tapes or disks are forwarded to Information Providers as content to online databases, and frequently are used in the production of printed indexes (fig. 1-1).

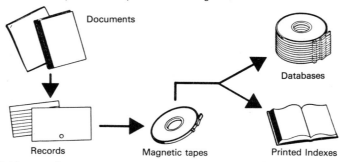

Fig. 1-1 Database producers

Information providers obtain databases from database producers and/or create their own, mount the databases on their own computers, and make them available to users for searching (fig. 1-2).

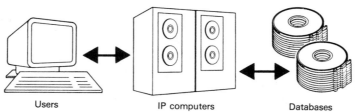

Fig. 1-2 Information providers

The OCLC LINK service links users to information provider systems and databases and provides additional services as well (fig. 1-3).

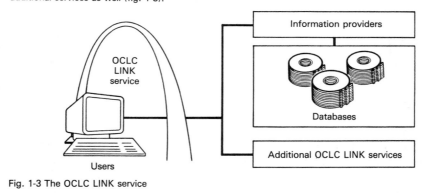

Fig. 1-3 The OCLC LINK service

FIGURE 2–9 Line Drawing (Courtesy of Online Computer Library, Dublin, Ohio; ©1986 OCLC, reprinted with permission)

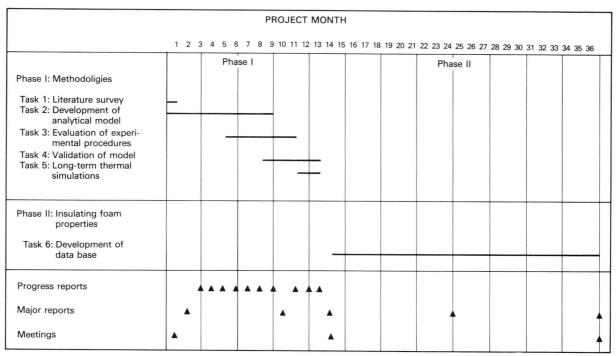

FIGURE 2-10   Program Schedule (Courtesy of Battelle, Columbus Division, Columbus, Ohio)

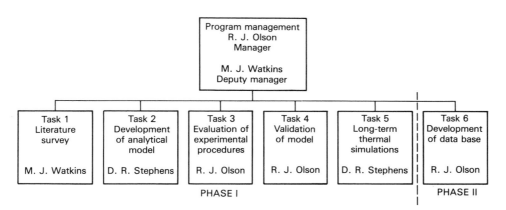

FIGURE 2-11   Program Organization Chart (Courtesy of Battelle, Columbus Division, Columbus, Ohio)

Next are shown several additional innovative approaches to presenting visual information.

Schematic Outline of a Plan

Fibers
Particulates
Polymers & monomers
Composite fabrication
Composite aging
Identification of instrumentation and analytical methods for characterizing composites systems
Final report description and evaluation of identified analytical methods

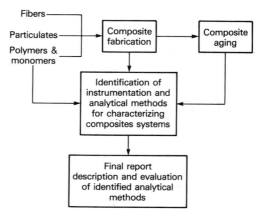

FIGURE 2–12 Schematic Outline of a Research Plan (Courtesy of Battelle, Columbus Division, Columbus, Ohio)

Circle Diagrams to Show Domain

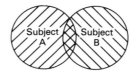

Subject A
Subject B
Indicates that the domain includes both areas represented by each circle
Subject A
Subject B
Indicates that the domain includes only area common to both subjects
Subject A
Subject B
Indicates that domain includes area exclusive to subject A

FIGURE 2–13 Circle Diagram

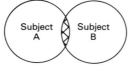

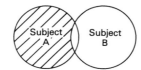

Reproduction of a Computer Screen

NOTE: The system supplies the product name, price, and product number (in fig. 5–31). The quantity default is 1, which you may change.

OCLC LINK/OCLC PRODUCTS ORDER FORM

Page 1 of 2

Product Name   : CATALOGING: USER MANUAL _____
Price   : $20.00 _____
OCLC #/Prod. Code : #10848550/800 _____
Quantity   : 1 _____
        *   *   *   *   *

METHOD OF PURCHASE
  No-charge : __
  Bill   : __
  Prepay   : __

Need by (Allow 4 weeks for delivery)
                 : _____

METHOD OF SHIPMENT
  UPS   : __
  Mail 4th class   : __
  Next-day service : __

Purchase Order Number (opt.): _____
  ^D[CR] − move to command line ^A − insert character ^B − delete character
  ^D[cmd][CR] − execute [cmd]   Enter Help on command line for assistance.

Edit Form: _____

Page 2 of 2

SHIPPING INFORMATION
Name   : _____
Title   : _____
Messaging ID   : _____
Telephone No.   : _____
OCLC Symbol/Network : _____

  Institution : _____
  Street   : _____
            : _____
  City   : _____
  State   : _____
  Country   : _____
  Zip Code : _____

  ^D[CR] − move to command line ^A − insert character ^B − delete character
  ^D[cmd][CR] − execute [cmd]   Enter Help on command line for assistance.

Edit Form: _____

Fig. 5–31 OCLC LINK ON-ORDER Screen

FIGURE 2-14 Reproduction of Computer Screen (Courtesy of Online Computer Library, Dublin, Ohio; ©1986 OCLC, reprinted with permission)

Hierarchy of Options

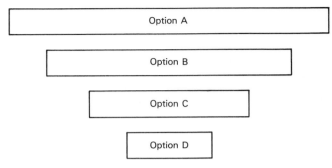

NOTE: Option A is the broadest option
Option D is the most limited (focused) option

FIGURE 2–15   Hierarchy of Options

When composing a document that will contain a number of visuals, you should think out the tables, drawings, and charts that you will need. Following is a sequence of drawings and tables taken from a research proposal.

Tables

The technical approach to developing the basic thermal property data base will follow the procedures discussed in Task 4b. Table 1 details the foam types and range of foam densities that will be considered. A total of 25 foam type and density combinations will be evaluated, with multiple tests run on several of the specimens. The data from these tests will be reported in the format of graphs and charts of measured data, and in a reduced format suitable for direct input to the Task 2 moisture permeation model.

TABLE 1.   *Basic Thermal Property Test*

Conditions	Foam Types:	Polyurethane, Polyvinyl Chloride
	Foam Density:	2, 5, 10, 12, 16, 20, 24 lb/ft^3
	Total Specimens:	25
Output:	Permeability Versus Vapor Pressure Differential	
	Thermal Conductivity Versus Moisture Content	

FIGURE 2–16   Table (Courtesy of Battelle, Columbus Division, Columbus, Ohio)

The test matrix for Task 6c is shown in Table 2. Basically, the test matrix provides for a number of different foams to be tested at four temperature differentials, with a sufficient number of specimens tested at a given condition to provide a measure of the repeatability of the results. Although the long-term thermal conductivity data collection subtask is planned to last 18 months, the experimental setup should allow continued exposure if it proves desirable to extend the testing.

TABLE 2. *Long-Term Exposure Tests*

Foam Type:	Polyurethane, Polyvinyl Chloride
Foam Density:	5, 10, 15, 20 lb/ft^3
Inner Wall Temperature:	60, 100, 150, 200 F
Bath Temperature:	40 F
Total Specimens:	16

FIGURE 2-17   Table (Courtesy of Battelle, Columbus Division, Columbus, Ohio)

The total costs for the Phase I research program are \$356,000. The distribution of effort currently envisioned is shown in Table 3. As discussed above, only the work for Phase I is formally being offered at this time. For reference, Phase II costs are anticipated to be of the same order of magnitude as Phase I, given the scope outlined in the technical discussion.

Initially, the participation of 10 companies at \$350,600 per company is being sought. When 7 companies have joined, Tasks 1, 2, and 3 will be started. Tasks 4 and 5 will be added when full funding has been attained.

TABLE 3. *Estimated Distribution of Effort*

		Estimated Effort
Phase I:	Task 1—Literature Survey	3%
	Task 2—Development of Analytical Model	32%
	Task 3—Evaluation of Experimental Procedures	25%
	Task 4—Validation of Model	29%
	Task 5—Long-Term Thermal Simulations	11%
	Total	100%

FIGURE 2-18   Table (Courtesy of Battelle, Columbus Division, Columbus Ohio)

Drawings

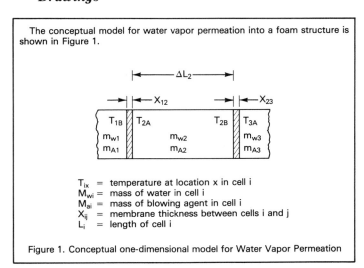

The conceptual model for water vapor permeation into a foam structure is shown in Figure 1.

T_{ix} = temperature at location x in cell i
M_{wi} = mass of water in cell i
M_{ai} = mass of blowing agent in cell i
X_{ij} = membrane thickness between cells i and j
L_i = length of cell i

Figure 1. Conceptual one-dimensional model for Water Vapor Permeation

FIGURE 2-19   Drawing (Courtesy of Battelle, Columbus Division, Columbus, Ohio)

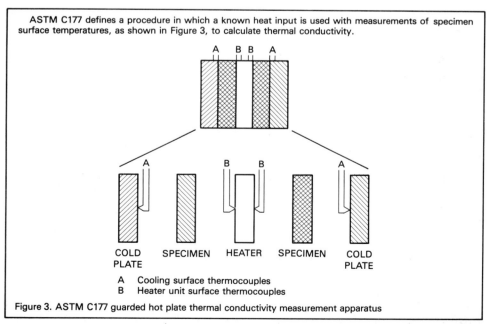

In this setup, a specimen is sandwiched between a hot plate and a heat flow meter/cold plate as shown in Figure 2. By measuring the temperatures of the hot and cold plates and the temperatures at the face of the heat meter (a device of known thermal conductivity), the thermal conductivity of the specimen under test can be determined.

A   B,C D

A

B C   C   D

PLATE 1   SPECIMEN   HEAT FLOW   PLATE 2
                          METER

A, D Plate surface thermocouples
B   Heat meter surface thermocouple
C   Heat Meter Thermopile

Figure 2. ASTM C518 heat flow meter thermal conductivity measurement apparatus

FIGURE 2-20 Drawing (Courtesy of Battelle, Columbus Division, Columbus, Ohio)

ASTM C177 defines a procedure in which a known heat input is used with measurements of specimen surface temperatures, as shown in Figure 3, to calculate thermal conductivity.

A   B B   A

B   B

A   A

COLD   SPECIMEN   HEATER   SPECIMEN   COLD
PLATE   PLATE

A   Cooling surface thermocouples
B   Heater unit surface thermocouples

Figure 3. ASTM C177 guarded hot plate thermal conductivity measurement apparatus

FIGURE 2-21   Drawing (Courtesy of Battelle, Columbus Division, Columbus, Ohio)

The third concept to be evaluated addresses the issue of identifying an inexpensive method to determine the amount of moisture intrusion into a foam specimen. In the concept shown in Figure 4, one load cell is required for every specimen. Because of range and accuracy demands, such load cells are likely to be expensive, and would thus drive experimental testing costs up for large-scale (many specimens), long-term insulation moisture exposures. In addition, long-term (i.e., 3 years) reliability of such load cells may be questionable. To address these issures, Battelle proposes to determine if an accurate, repeatable correlation exists between the moisture gain and the ac impedance of a specimen.

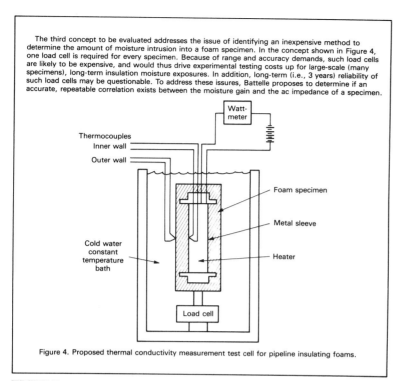

Figure 4. Proposed thermal conductivity measurement test cell for pipeline insulating foams.

FIGURE 2–22   Drawing (Courtesy of Battelle, Columbus Division, Columbus, Ohio)

In the ac impedance tests, a specimen is immersed in an aqueous electrolyte as shown in Figure 5. Periodic measurement of the impedance of the specimen, along with measurement of specimen weight, will yield a direct correlation which will allow substitution of the ac impedance measurements for the more expensive load cell measurements.

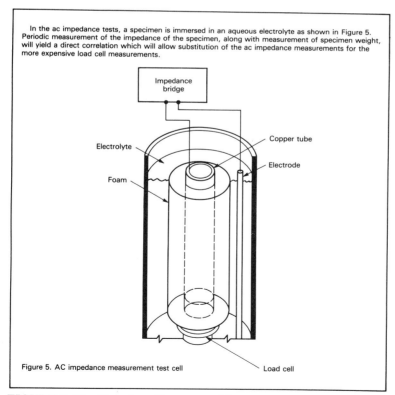

Figure 5. AC impedance measurement test cell

FIGURE 2–23   Drawing (Courtesy of Battelle, Columbus Division, Columbus, Ohio)

With reference to Figure 6, a parallel-plate/moist-foam capacitor can be placed in a bridge circuit to measure the capacitance of the unknown plate-foam capacitor. The capacitance of a number of specimens with various geometries and known moisture contents can be measured to establish the correlation between capacitance and moisture content.

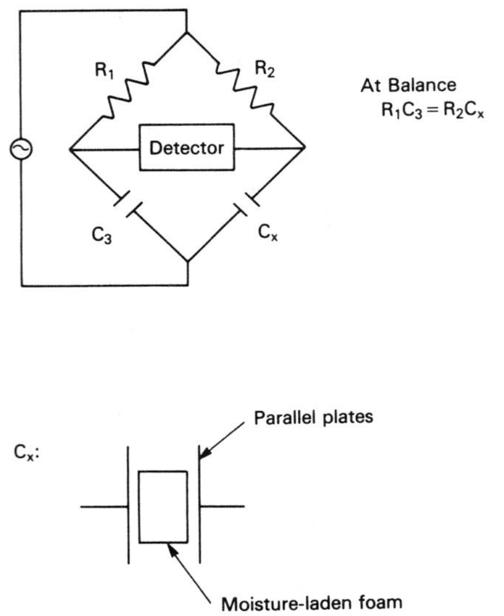

At Balance
$R_1 C_3 = R_2 C_x$

Figure 6. Electrical capacitance method for determining the moisture distribution in a pipeline insulating foam

FIGURE 2-24 Drawing (Courtesy of Battelle, Columbus Division, Columbus, Ohio)

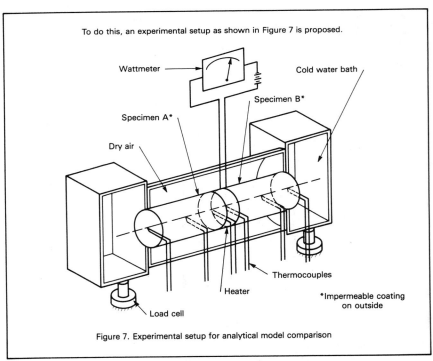

To do this, an experimental setup as shown in Figure 7 is proposed.

*Impermeable coating on outside

Figure 7. Experimental setup for analytical model comparison

FIGURE 2-25 Drawing (Courtesy of Battelle, Columbus Division, Columbus, Ohio)

Charts
See Figures 2–10 and 2–11.

Commandment 7: Learn Word Processing

If you have not already taken advantage of word processing, you should give it a try. With some time and effort devoted to learning one of the popular word-processing software packages, you will save considerable time and effort in completing your writing assignments in all the courses you take later. Two currently popular software packages are WordStar and WordPerfect; but there are many more from which to choose. The most exciting development has been the advent of desktop publishing systems on the Apple Macintosh and more recently on the IBM. You should consider the following points about any word-processing software that you consider:

1. Be sure that the software is compatible with the type of computer you will be using. Some programs are designed for certain computers. Some can be used on several types. WordStar can be used on both the IBM and Apple personal computers, but to use it on the Apple, a special CPM operating card must be added at considerable cost.

2. Be sure that the software that you choose can perform all the functions that you will need for your particular kind of work. If you wish to use your computer exclusively to write, one of the standard word processing packages will probably be suitable. If, however, you need to integrate your reports with original graphs, charts, and tables, you may wish to consider an integrated software package such as AppleWorks or Lotus. In addition to word processing, these packages can create spreadsheets for calculating and graphing information and databases for storing and organizing information.

3. Consider additional equipment that you will need to make your computer operational for word-processing software. Some printers are sold with IBM-compatible setups: not very useful if you have a different kind of computer. Be sure to inquire about a printer interface card. There are many different types. The less expensive ones usually have limited graphics capabilities. If you are planning on doing graphics, you may wish to buy a more expensive interface that has graphics capabilities.

Is word processing worth all the hassle and expense? It depends on how willing you are to learn it and how important you believe becoming proficient on a computer is to your future. The following list will give you an idea of the benefits of word processing.

1. You can see your text in printed form on the monitor screen before you print out a hard copy—seeing the text gives you a sense of its length, quality, and physical appearance.

2. You can edit the text before printing out a hard copy. The editing capabilities of word-processing software packages differ; however, if you use a comprehensive package such as WordStar, you can perform a great number of editing functions, such as the following:
   a. Delete words, sentences, paragraphs, or sections.
   b. Move the positions of text sections.
   c. Insert words, sentences, or paragraphs.

    d. Move freely to various points in the text.

    e. Combine textual material from different files.

    f. Use a spelling checker to detect and correct errors.

There are many other more sophisticated editing functions that a word processing program such as WordStar can produce as well.

3. You can save your document on disk, so if your hard (printed) copy is lost or misplaced, you will be able to print a new one quite easily. You can also save reports and assignments for later use and referral. These can be updated or revised at any time.

4. You can use print commands to produce highlighted, double-stroked, or fancy-font titles, headings, and subheadings throughout your document. These should improve the readability and appearance of your document.

5. Some word-processing programs have commands for footnoting and endnoting that are quite useful to research paper writing. Using these commands will enable you to produce a very sharply documented research report.

Word-processing software will not, of course, write your papers for you; but after you invest some time in learning how to use it, it will become a very useful tool that should eliminate some of the drudgery from writing, such as "whiting out" typed sentences and continuously balling up written pages that do not quite hit the mark.

CONSIDERING COST

The Seven Commandments of Reader-Friendly Writing weigh heavily in determining the cost of documents. Writing that communicates an intended message saves money. You know about actual, opportunity, and error costs. But what about the cost per communicated message? Every document has such a cost. You find it by taking actual cost (materials and labor) and dividing it by the number of readers who actually comprehend the intended message. For example, if you spend $5000 producing sales brochures and 5000 people read and understand the sales brochure, your cost per message communicated is $1.

Every person who reads a message does not understand it. Some readers are so busy they just look at documents or scan them. Some think they understand the message when they really do not. The cost per impression or contact is much less than the cost per communicated message. If for $5000 you produced and distributed 10,000 sales brochures, your cost per impression or contact would be $0.50. But since only half the people who received brochures took time to read and comprehend the message, the cost per communicated message is $1.

Determining cost per contact is easy, but determining cost per communicated message is very difficult, especially for documents with a large circulation. It may be too expensive to conduct a survey to determine this cost. The cost per communicated message of reports written for a limited audience is easier to determine because readers can provide feedback to indicate how well they received an intended message.

How can you minimize the cost per communicated message? Employing the Seven Commandments of Reader-Friendly Writing helps because you make writing easy for readers to understand. Proposals, memos, reports, and essays that are reader friendly have a much better chance of being read and understood.

CHAPTER ASSIGNMENT

1. You are in a new management position. For your first assignment you must outline a report explaining why sales have decreased in your new division over the past two years. You are not responsible for the decline, but your superior wants you to investigate this problem and explain any causes you can determine. "Put it in pictures," he tells you. "I want as many visuals as possible. I want to be able to look at it and understand it in a split second." After researching, you determine the following causes:

- New competitors have taken market share from your company
- Warranty claims on your product have increased in the last three years
- Your factories have more old machinery than do those of your competitors
- Actual demand for your product has decreased in the past three years
- Labor costs for your company are higher than those of foreign competitors
- Your manufacturing plant is operating at only 65% capacity.

Decide on a sequence of visuals to illustrate these facts.

2. You have a new employee who keeps submitting written reports that are difficult to understand. You arrange an appointment to discuss this problem. Develop a strategy for explaining to the employee how the reader-friendly writing saves the company money.

In Chapter Two you learned how to make your document reader friendly. You should write for readers in the lower-middle range of subject knowledge, and you should employ the writing style and format that makes your writing easy to understand.

THREE

Defining Purpose and Organization

PREVIEW

A simple definition explains the fundamental characteristics of a term by identifying the term (DOS), the classification of the term (type of computer operating system), and its unique characteristics (disk operating system). An extended definition explains more completely the physical characteristics, functions, and applications of a term. An extended definition of DOS could consist of contrast/comparison of DOS with another type of operating system (such as a tape system or a keypunch card system), classification of major types of disk operating systems, a process analysis or a set of instructions on the operation of DOS, a cause-and-effect explanation of the operation of DOS, and examples of disk operating systems. You could also define DOS by describing the physical characteristics of its components.

The introduction of an extended definition contains a simple three-part definition of the term, an explanation of the significance of the term, and a list of major aspects of the term to be explained in the body. Explain major aspects of the term in the body. Conclude by listing findings, making recommendations, offering support material, and reemphasizing main points.

THE BASICS

You will use definitions to explain business and technical words. Simple definitions are formed in three parts: term, classification, and unique characteristics, as illustrated in the table below:

Term	Classification	Unique Characteristics
DOS	type of computer operating system	disk operating system
CPU	part of the computer	central processing unit—links hardware to software
IRA	investment plan	tax-deductible retirement account

Extended definitions explain a term thoroughly by describing physical characteristics, functions, and/or applications. Organization for an extended definition is provided below.

Introduction

- Three-part definition of the term
- Significant uses of the term
- List of major points to be discussed in the body

Body

- Discussion of each major aspect cited in the introduction

Conclusion

- Findings, recommendations, and/or supporting data

METHODS OF DEFINING

Definitions can be written in several ways. Five methods are: contrast/comparison, classification, process, cause and effect, and exemplification. Consider the expression "market share." It is defined as the percentage of consumers who purchase a competitive brand. An extended definition of market share could consist of three examples of brands in the same product market, classification of three popular types of products and market shares of competitive brands in each market, a process analysis of how market share is determined, a contrast/comparison of brands within the same market, or a cause-and-effect explanation of why some brands have high market shares. These methods provide logical structures that show relationships possible among the facts and ideas of your topic. They also provide standard outlines that help organize your writing. You can use these methods of defining to develop ideas and organize writing.

Contrast/Comparison

Contrast/comparison defines by showing differences (contrast) or similarities (comparison) between a defined term and another term the reader already knows. Examples of this method include contrasting or comparing two models of a machine (a digital oscilloscope and a conventional oscilloscope), two processes (programming a job in BASIC and programming it in COBOL), two uses of technical knowledge (calculating after-tax profit using LIFO and FIFO accounting systems), and two methods of performing a technical task (soldering, desoldering, troubleshooting).

Contrast/comparison employs either block or alternating structure. Block puts term 1 in the first half of the writing and term 2 in the second. Alternation divides the text by criteria. See the outline of a contrast of LIFO and FIFO accounting methods below.

Block Outline

Introduction

The profits reported for tax purposes are affected by the accounting system used. Last in, first out (LIFO) calculates the cost of goods sold by adding up the cost of most recent additions to inventory. First in, first out (FIFO) calculates cost of goods sold by adding up the cost of the oldest additions to inventory. The system that produces a higher cost of goods sold will also produce a lower taxable income, and therefore, a lower tax bill.

- Definition of the two topics to be contrasted or compared

The LIFO system totals the cost of all inventory items sold by assuming that the most recent additions to inventory are sold first. The FIFO system totals cost of inventory by assuming that the oldest items in inventory are sold first. Neither system actually accounts for when actual inventory items were sold. LIFO and FIFO simply make their respective assumptions for accounting purposes.

- Purpose of the contrast or comparison

Contrasting LIFO and FIFO systems shows the usefulness of each system in inflationary (prices are increasing) and deflationary (prices are declining) economies. During inflation, LIFO will produce a lower tax bill because the cost of goods sold will be higher. During deflation, FIFO will produce a lower tax bill because the oldest inventory items are the most expensive.

- Listing of major points of contrast or comparison in the correct order of mention

1. Both systems total inventory costs—LIFO starts totaling costs of the most recent additions until the number of units sold has been reached; FIFO starts with the oldest additions.
2. Both systems are based on assumptions. The actual goods sold may be old or new additions to inventory. Companies use the system that yields the desired results.
3. FIFO is usually used during inflationary periods because the cost of recent inventory items will be higher. Cost of goods sold will be higher. Taxable income will be lower. Fewer tax dollars will be paid. LIFO is used during deflationary periods when the cost of old inventory items is higher. Tax dollars will be saved because of lower taxable income.
4. When companies wish to show a higher profit to distribute a larger dividend and increase the value of stock, they may use an inventory method that produces a higher taxable income.
5. The Internal Revenue Service audits the use of FIFO and LIFO.

Body

Part 1: Detailed description of topic 1
Point 1
Point 2
Point 3
Point 4

Part 2: Detailed description of topic 2
Point 1 (Comparison or contrast to point 1 in part 1)
Point 2 (Comparison or contrast to point 2 in part 1)
Point 3 (Comparison or contrast to point 3 in part 1)
Point 4 (Comparison or contrast to point 4 in part 1)

Conclusion

Findings, recommendations, and supporting material

Alternation Outline

Introduction

(Same as for the block outline style)

Body

Point 1: Application to topic 1
Comparison or contrast to topic 2
Point 2: Application to topic 1
Comparison or contrast to topic 2
Point 3: Application to topic 1
Comparison or contrast to topic 2
Point 4: Application to topic 1
Comparison or contrast to topic 2

Conclusion

Findings, recommendations, and supporting data

Helpful Hints

1. Confine yourself to either contrasting or comparing. Attempting to define by doing both at the same time will be confusing.
2. Define a term by comparing or contrasting it to only one other term. Attempting to use more will require too much jumping back and forth between too many areas. You will have to contrast or compare topic 1 to topic 2; then topic 2 to topic 3; then topic 1 to topic 3; and all points made about one topic must be explained in terms of the other two.

Suggestion: Discuss with your instructor how to complete the body and conclusion of the sample outline contrasting FIFO and LIFO.

Classification

Classification defines by organizing information into categories. Any body of facts can more easily be understood when defined into categories. Classification can be useful in situations such as defining types of electronic components (diode, transistor, and resistor), major types of a particular software package (the several types of spreadsheets), and the three types of business involved in the distribution of products (manufacturing, wholesale distribution, and retail outlets).

Be certain that each category created is unique. No item in one category can be placed correctly in another category. To ensure this, use unique criteria to define each category. For example, the three electronic components mentioned above are unique because each component performs a different function in an electronic circuit. If two of the components performed the same function, only two categories would exist. One would be invalid.

A classification definition of businesses is structured as follows.

Introduction

Three types of business are involved in producing and channeling products to customers: manufacturers, wholesale distributors, and retail outlets.

- *Definition of the terms and categories*

Manufacturers produce finished products or parts from raw materials. Wholesale distributors channel products to companies that resell them. Retail outlets sell products directly to customers.

- *Criteria of each category*

Manufacturers are involved exclusively in the production of goods. Wholesale distributors purchase goods from the manufacturer and resell them. They do not make products. Retail outlets purchase goods from wholesalers to sell to customers. Retailers do not usually buy directly from manufacturers.

- *List of categories*

Category 1: manufacturers: any company that produces goods from raw materials

Category 2: wholesale distributor: any company that buys goods in large quantity from manufacturers to resell at a profit to retailers

Category 3: retail outlet: any company that buys goods from a wholesaler to sell directly to consumers

---

Body

> Description of category 1
> Description of category 2
> Description of category 3

Conclusion

> Reemphasis of major points

Helpful Hints

1. Use the same criteria to create all the categories.
2. Be sure to have at least two items in any category (one item is really not enough to constitute a category).
3. Try to invent new and refreshing categories to explain information.
4. Avoid including too much information in one category.

Suggestion: Develop an outline for each of the three categories specified in the body of the model outline on business types. What points would you emphasize in the conclusion?

Cause and Effect

Cause and effect defines either by showing the reasons (causes) something (effect) happened or by tracing the result(s) [effect(s)] of a chain of events. Situations needing a cause-and-effect definition include explaining what causes an LED or LCD to light up, describing the chain of events that lead to the issuing of a bond, showing the market changes created by the miniaturization of computer hardware, or explaining the events that occur when a machine is operating properly.

Be certain that the "causes" are in fact responsible for the effect being described. Events that occur prior to an effect are not always responsible for it. Also, do not make the mistake of attributing one cause as being responsible for one effect. Most effects are produced by more than one cause.

A sample outline for a cause-and-effect definition on miniaturization of computer hardware follows.

Introduction

Since the creation of the first electronic computer after World War II, computer components have been made smaller. Today there is a revolution in miniaturization of computer hardware.

- *Definition of the cause*

Miniaturization means making something that was once large tiny by comparison. Computer components that were once over a foot in length are now a fraction of an inch in size.

- *Description of the effects to be explained*

Miniaturization has contributed to several important changes in computer products. It has helped to decrease cost because of techniques developed to mass produce tiny components. It has aided in increasing memory capacity in computers. Today's computers have thousands of times more capacity than those made just 10 years ago. It has contributed to multiplying the number of computer products available. Once we had mainframes. Today we have a variety of microcomputers and portables.

- *Importance of understanding the effects*

As research and development of computer technology continues, we can expect to see a variety of innovations that will have big impacts on business.

- *Listing of the effects to be discussed in the body*

1. Cost decreases
2. Memory increases
3. More product variety

Body

> Effect 1
> Effect 2
> Effect 3

Conclusion

> Findings, recommendations, supporting data

Helpful Hints

1. When showing causes and effect(s), simplify by classifying causes into three types: *contributory* (a cause that contributes to a given effect), *necessary* (a cause that must be present for the effect to occur but cannot alone create the effect), and *sufficient* (a cause that by itself produces the effect).
2. Focus on either causes or effects, but not both. Usually, discuss an effect in the introduction and then explain how the effect was produced by several causes. You can also focus on a particular cause

in the introduction and, in the body, explain important effects the cause has produced.

Suggestion: Work in groups and develop outlines for each section of the body of the model outline on computer miniaturization. How would you avoid attributing all three effects solely to miniaturization? Do you think other causes were involved in these effects? What findings, recommendations, and supporting data would your group provide for the conclusion?

Process

Process defines by describing the steps of a technical or business procedure. Situations calling for a process definition include describing the steps of soldering electronic components to a breadboard, installing a car radio, handling a customer complaint, and making copies of data disks on a disk drive.

When defining by process, be sure to describe *how* steps are performed. If a reason why steps are performed is needed, it should be confined to the introduction or the section heading of the document. Arrange steps in the order in which they are performed.

An outline for process definition of handling a customer complaint follows.

Introduction

A customer with complaints must be treated with respect and concern. Get as much information as possible about the exact nature of the complaint by following the procedure outlined below.

- *Definition of the process*

The customer complaint procedure ensures the customer that we are actively solving the problem, gathers information to determine what happened, decides a course of action on the complaint, and suggests whether the complaint indicates a widespread problem. If it does, a strategy for solving the problem is determined.

- *Statement of the importance of the process*

Successful handling of customer complaints communicates our goodwill and concern for our customers. It enables us to keep customers who might be lost because of dissatisfaction. It provides our company with a positive reputation and marketing appeal.

- *List of equipment, materials, and tools necessary to perform the process*

You will need a complaint form and pencil, and you must be on-line so that you can call up a current customer purchase file.

- *List of major steps in the process*

1. Introduce yourself and ask "May I help you?"
2. Listen carefully. As soon as you determine that the call is a complaint, begin to fill in the complaint form at once.
3. Don't stop the customer. Wait until he or she stops speaking.
4. Apologize for any inconvenience experienced by the customer.
5. At the same time, quickly scan the form and ask questions to fill in any blanks on the form. Be sure that the form is completed.

6. Get the customer's name, account number, phone numbers at home and at work, and times during the day when he or she can be reached.

Body

All steps structured similarly:

Purpose of the step

Tools, equipment, and material needed

Number of and identification of acts or substeps

Description of each act or substep, including an explanation of how tools, equipment, and materials are used

Expected result(s) of performing the step correctly

Suggested corrective measures if the step is not successfully completed;

Transition to the next step in the process

Conclusion

Cautions and dangers

Helpful hints on correctly performing the process

Statement of overall expected results

Suggestions for maintenance if necessary

Helpful Hints

1. Process definitions are organized chronologically, so be sure to include all steps; gaps in the description will confuse the reader.
2. Describe steps in detail: a clear explanation of how steps are performed is essential to communicating the process to the reader.
3. Finally, cautions, dangers, warnings, helpful hints, statements of expected results, and maintenance suggestions should all be included to help the reader to grasp the complexity and purpose of the process.

Suggestion: Explain how you would keep the body of the customer complaint model from becoming too long. Is paragraph organization the best type to use here? Can you suggest a better organization? How would you fill in the four sections of the conclusion?

Exemplification

Exemplification defines by illustrating information with pertinent examples. A good example simplifies and clarifies complex information. You can define by using actual examples or by using analogies.

Examples show how information is actually put to use. Good situations for using examples are showing three ways that a data base system saves time and money, describing three humorous television advertisements, and providing examples of products that are price elastic and price inelastic.

Analogy

Analogies make complicated operations, devices, or tasks easier to understand by illustrating their similarity to very simple and familiar operations, devices, or tasks. For example, to simplify understanding the flow of current through electronic components, use the analogy of flowing water. Compare a resistor, which allows no current through, to a closed hose nozzle, which allows no water through; a diode, which allows all the current through, to an opened hose nozzle; and a semiconductor, which allows half the current through, to a half-opened (half-closed) hose nozzle. Another analogy is illustrating a computer operating as a series of stop-and-go traffic lights; when programmed, the computer reads the programmer's inputs as a series of stop's and go's in a particular pattern that has a specific meaning.

Analogies should be simple (flowing water, stop-and-go light, games of dominoes or checkers) so that the reader will understand quickly and easily. Similarly, keep examples simple and straightforward. Include just enough information in examples to help the reader to define the intended message.

Following is an outline for exemplification of price elastic and inelastic products.

Introduction

Price elasticity measures consumer response to price increases and decreases. Goods are price elastic when consumers buy them less as prices increase and more when prices decrease. Goods are inelastic when consumers buy them in the same quantity despite price fluctuations.

- *Definition of the topic*

Price elasticity measures consumer behavior in response to price changes.

- *Importance of the message*

Companies must be aware of the price elasticity of their products to avoid under- and overpricing them.

- *Summary of main points*

Consumers can respond to price changes three ways: buy more, buy fewer, or buy the same quantity.

Goods are price elastic when consumers buy fewer as the price increases.

Goods are inelastic when consumers buy the same quantity despite price increases.

When consumers buy more as price increases, goods are inversely elastic. Consumers consider them desirable luxury items because of a higher price.

Inelastic goods have few substitutes. Elastic goods have at least several substitutes.

- *List of the actual examples/analogies*

Inelastic goods: gasoline, diamonds, education
Elastic goods: soda pop, butter, new cars

Body

Example/analogy 1
Example/analogy 2

Example/analogy 3

(Each section should include:

an explanation of the example/analogy in relation to the intended message
description of the example/analogy
and a point-by-point explanation of how the example/analogy simplifies and clarifies the message)

Conclusion

Explanation of major points of the information
Reemphasis of how the examples/analogies illustrate the intended message

Helpful Hints

1. Use exemplification freely with any other methods of defining.
2. Actual examples and analogies can be used together.
3. Exemplification is much more flexible than classification because you do not have to categorize as rigidly, and you can provide examples and analogies that overlap in meaning to a certain degree. Exemplification illustrates and supports factual information, while classification divides factual information into unique classes.

Suggestion: Develop a plan to form transitions between each of the examples in the body of the price elasticity model. How will you keep descriptions of examples from being too repetitive? What main points would you choose to emphasize in the conclusion?

Description

Description defines by creating through details a mental image of an item, mechanism, or procedure. All writing contains description, but it can still be used as a dominant defining method. Description provides information about physical characteristics. It is most used to define parts of mechanisms, such as a cathode ray tube, a computer printer, an electronic component or circuit, or a disk drive or diskette. It should be an objective, straightforward detailing of physical characteristics such as size, shape, color, finish, texture, and methods of attachment. In Chapter Four you will learn to write mechanism descriptions.

Introduction
- Purpose of the document
- Importance of the message
- General description of the mechanism or item
- Listing of the major physical characteristics or parts to be described

Body
- Description of each characteristic (size, shape, color, finish, texture, methods of attachment)

Conclusion
- Summary of major points

Helpful Hints

Description follows a general-to-specific pattern. When defining by description, you will describe in the introduction the general physical characteristics of the entire topic, and later, in the body of the report, describe each characteristic in detail.

Suggestion: Think of a good topic for the description outline and try filling in the outline.

Argumentation

Argumentation defines by convincing readers that some ideas are truer or more accurate than others. In professional writing, argumentation is used to write proposals or feasibility studies. A proposal identifies a problem and "proposes" a plan for solving it—the proposal with the best argument for solving the problem usually is accepted.

Feasibility studies analyze problems and argue for or against the probable success of a proposed solution. The company awarding a contract for a proposal might have feasibility studies conducted on the three most promising proposals and award the contract to the one most likely to succeed. In industry, proposals are written for projects such as designing a part for a machine, writing software or documentation, and manufacturing and marketing all kinds of products.

Argumentative documents differ, but they do share an essential structure, as outlined below.

Introduction

- Presentation of the problem or issue
- Summary of the proposed solutions or viewpoints
- Summary of the favored solution or viewpoint
- List of major points to be made to support the solution or viewpoint favored and reject others under consideration

Body

- Detailed discussion of:

    Reasons for rejecting other solutions or viewpoints
    Reasons for accepting favored solution or viewpoint

Conclusion

- Summary of major points

Helpful Hints

1. Be sure to avoid logical fallacies. Proposed solutions to problems must be the product of correct reasoning. Typical reasoning fallacies to beware of include presenting an unproven statement as true, using an analogy to prove a point, taking a position in reaction to a person rather than to facts or reason, confusing chronological events with cause and effect, mistaking fact for opinion, and providing incomplete evidence as complete because it supports a popular viewpoint.

2. Argumentation follows either an inductive (specific to general) or deductive (general to specific) order. The validity of inductive rea-

soning depends on the reasons for arriving at a general conclusion. For example, if you observe one minor instance of cost overage in a project, you would probably not conclude that the project was going to be tremendously over budget; if you discover several major cost overages, you may be justified in arriving at that conclusion.

3. Deductive statements are valid if your assumptions are logical. If you assume that computerization is expensive and the solution to a problem requires computerization, you will probably assume that the solution will be expensive. The reader may agree or, realizing that the cost of computerization is steadily decreasing, disagree and request more detailed information.

Suggestion: Take an issue that is currently of great concern to you and form an argumentative presentation using the outline provided.

CONSIDERING COST

How important is choosing the best organization for your topic? Documents that communicate are cost-effective. They pay for themselves in improved worker productivity and increased sales revenue. Documents that do not communicate are costs without benefits. They can even decrease productivity and revenue by creating confusion in workers or a negative impression of the company with customers. Defining your topic, establishing a simple and logical organization, and sequencing main points to match reader expectations will help to get your message across.

In Chapter Three you have learned about simple definitions, extended definitions, organizational outlines, the importance of sequencing, and many helpful hints on each type of definition. In Chapter Four, you will learn how to write mechanism descriptions.

CHAPTER ASSIGNMENT

Write an extended definition to a specific audience (such as a customer, boss, fellow employee, friend, or the profession in general) for a specific purpose (to instruct, to train, to share information, to inform the profession in a detailed and formal manner), as a whole document or as part of a larger document (memo, product instructions, training manual). Choose any of the audience relationships, purposes, and types of documents discussed in Chapter Two, or invent your own.

Describe in detail below the audience, purpose, and type of document that you intend to write.

Audience

Purpose

Type of Document

Once you have established these communication criteria, you must outline your extended definition according to the model provided in Chapter One.

Introduction

Three-part definition of the term (term, classification, unique characteristics)

Significant uses of the term

List of major aspects to be discussed in the body

Body

Discussion of each major aspect to be included in the body

Aspect 1

Aspect 2

Aspect 3

Aspect 4

Aspect 5

(Include additional aspects if necessary)

Conclusion

Will you conclude a *summary* of major facts? If so, list them below.

Will you also or instead conclude with an explanation of *findings*? If so, list them below.

Will you also or instead conclude with recommendations? If so, list them below.

Now that you have chosen your topic, established your audience, purpose, and document type, and outlined your extended definition, you should write your rough draft. The rough draft is the first prose writing that you will do. There is really no set procedure for writing a rough draft.

Probably, the easiest way for you to accomplish this initial writing is to refer to your outline and revise into paragraphs all the information that you have jotted down. Remember that each paragraph ordinarily begins with a topic sentence and is developed by the sentences that support the factual information stated in the topic sentence.

Your introductory paragraph should consist of at least three sentences: the three-part definition, the significant uses of the term, and the list of major aspects to be explained in the body of the extended definition. But it may be longer than three sentences. If you devoted a separate sentence to each of the major uses of the term, the introductory paragraph might be five, six, or seven sentences in length rather than three.

The number of sentences in each paragraph is not as important as the quality of each sentence. Each should communicate information clearly and concisely. Each sentence and each paragraph should be written with close attention to quality and the influence each has on the entire document. As you write, you should be asking yourself if what you are writing is consistent with and beneficial to the entire document. Are the words that you choose appropriate for the purpose and audience and consistent with the rest of the language in your document?

Be sure to read through everything after you get the rough draft completed to check for complete coverage of content; appropriateness and consistency of words, sentences, and paragraphs; and organization. The structure must be logical. In an extended definition the best organization to follow is to discuss first the most important aspects of the term defined. Save less important aspects for later discussion. Always discuss the least important aspect last. Exclude any unimportant aspects in your definition. You will just waste the reader's time.

Before beginning your rough draft, read the following introductory paragraphs and critique them according to the criteria mentioned above.

Computed tomography is a medical, diagnostic technique used to investigate the health of internal organs and tissues. Computers are used to reconstruct the internal structure from x-ray transmissions taken at many angles.

The advantage of a computed tomographic scan over conventional x-ray study is that the scanner displays a thin cross section of tissue, while the conventional x-ray displays a profile view with all the internal structures superimposed.

When all the structures are superimposed, the diagnostician cannot tell which structure is causing a light or dark spot on the film. But if a cross section is displayed, only one structure is being observed at one time. The purpose of this definition is to explore advancements and current technology in the field of computed tomography.

Answer the following questions about this introductory paragraph:

1. Who is the writer's intended audience?

2. What is the writer's purpose?

3. In what type of larger document would the definition be included? Or what type of document is the definition supposed to be?

4. What specific improvements would you suggest in the writing of this paragraph to clarify audience, purpose, and documentation?

5. Evaluate the paragraph structure for topic sentences, developing sentences, and clear pattern of organization.

6. Evaluate each sentence in the paragraph for clarity, punctuation, and variety.

7. Evaluate the wording in the paragraph for clarity, consistency, and appropriateness.

8. Summarize your critique of the paragraph by listing its strong and weak points.

Strong Points	*Weak Points*

Now begin writing your own rough draft. Once you have completed it, put it aside for as long as possible and then evaluate it as you have the paragraph on tomography. Have someone else evaluate it, too. After these two evaluations, revise the rough draft according to your own advice and that of a friendly editor. Cross out words, change sentences around, squeeze new information in between lines of old information. After your revision, you can rewrite your rough draft into a preliminary final draft. Have this edited as well, especially for little errors in spelling and punctuation.

Now rewrite your preliminary final draft into your real final draft and submit it for a grade. If you have placed effort into your work, you should be pleased with the grade; but do not be surprised if you have to make some more improvements on your next paper. Writing is a process of planning, outlining, drafting, revising, and rewriting.

FOUR

Describing Mechanisms

PREVIEW

The sample reports in this chapter use description as a method of defining, although they also contain process, exemplification, and simple definition. Since your assignment in this chapter will be to write a mechanism description, review "description" as a defining method in Chapter Three. Remember, description provides readers with a mental picture of the topic. When written in objective style, description is a factual detailing of physical characteristics. When written in friendly style, it is a persuasive or sales type of detailing of physical characteristics. Friendly style speaks to the reader. Objective style speaks about the topic. When mixed, these styles are used to speak to the reader about benefits of product features.

THE BASICS

In this chapter you will describe mechanisms. A mechanism description is a part-by-part explanation of the physical characteristics of a machine, item, or object. It includes information such as size, shape, color, texture, weight, and methods of attachment. It should follow the general outline provided below.

Introduction

Identification of the mechanism
Explanation of its purpose
Description of the overall mechanism
Visual of the entire mechanism
List of major parts to be described

Body

Description of each part following a logical order of mention (top to bottom, right to left, first to last in operation) using criteria such as size, shape, color, texture, weight, and methods of attachment.

Conclusion

Summary statement of how the parts should smoothly operate to achieve the mechanism's purpose

ESTABLISHING THE WRITING SITUATION

First you must establish your audience and purpose. Two situations that require mechanism descriptions in business are selling to retail customers and selling to industrial customers. Most products require a mechanism description. Retail products often come with assembly instructions or a user's manual; either of these will contain a brief, illustrated mechanism description. An industrial customer purchasing a product or contracting to have one produced requires a detailed mechanism description. It will be illustrated with a clear explanation of all the parts of the product.

Mechanism descriptions are widely used. Businesses require them to document the products they produce as well as the products they purchase. These descriptions inform buyers and sellers as to exactly what is being bought and sold. Knowing how to write mechanism descriptions is important to your career. You will be writing them, reading them, or supervising others who write and read them. As a practice exercise, consider how a mechanism description could be used in a memo, a training manual, and a journal article in the spaces provided below. Can you think of additional situations in which a mechanism description would be appropriate? List and explain them below in the space provided.

Memo:

Training Manual:

Journal Article:

Other Suggestions:

A memo topic could be one of a wide variety of items, anything from information about a new copier to product specifications. A training manual description could be a machine or product that a person will be trained to use. A good topic for a trade journal article would be increased efficiency of internal combustion engines using turbochargers, so the article would have a mechanism description of a turbocharger.

DECIDING ON A DOCUMENT TYPE

The type of mechanism description that you produce depends on the reader's information needs and the document you are using. A description of a jet engine will be much more detailed and sophisticated than an exploded drawing of the parts of a bicycle for a retail customer. Consider whether your mechanism description will comprise an entire document or a section of a document. Descriptions in assembly instructions and user's manuals are a section of a larger document. Complicated, expensive products require the description to be a separate document. Industrial firms contracting companies to develop or produce products require detailed mechanism descriptions to verify that products have been produced according to specifications.

DETERMINING VISUALS

Line drawings and photographs work best to illustrate mechanism descriptions. Parts should be labeled, either directly on the visual or by numbers that correspond to a parts list placed beneath the drawing. Exploded drawings show how individual parts fit into the mechanism. Individual drawings of parts can be included if they are available. Colored drawings are more eye-catching, but they are also much more expensive than line drawings. Unless color of parts is important to understanding the mechanism, color graphics should be used in promotional literature, where it is more cost-effective.

DEVELOPING AN APPROPRIATE STYLE

Retail mechanism descriptions are written with a mix of objective and friendly styles. Documents that accompany retail products have two functions: to inform about the product and to sell the customer on the product and company. The description below illustrates this dual role.

A Primer of Your Printer's Basic Components

This section is provided for those of you who are new to computer printer technology, and for now only want to know the most basic information about how the Gemini works. Figure 1 shows what is called an ''exploded'' view of Gemini 10X's major components, and Figure 2 is an elementary logic block diagram for both models. But because the Gemini printers are so well designed, it isn't necessary to know detailed information about how it works—just that it does.

When you turn the **power switch** ''on,'' the alternating current is converted into direct current for the **power unit**. The direct current powers the motors and the printhead, as well as providing power to the **control board**. The control board does just that: controls the printer by means of a maze of transistors, resistors, diodes, capacitors, and **integrated circuits** (ICs for short).

The control board contains the ROMs and RAMs, as explained in the glossary at the back of the manual. For now, it is enough to know that the control board is the ''brains'' of the machine. In fact, your new printer is smart enough to realize when it has finished printing a short line, and instead of the printhead making an unnecessary trip along the rest of the blank line, Gemini moves the paper up automatically, so that no time is wasted before the next characters are printed. That is why Gemini is said to be logic-seeking.

The control board also contains the buffer that allows your computer to send a batch of information to be printed, which Gemini then stores until it can get to it. Although Gemini is a fast printer, computers communicate data even faster. The buffer can accommodate 816 characters of memory, with an optional buffer that can expand to 4K or 8K. Computer memory is measured in terms of K, meaning kilobytes. A kilobyte is 1,024 bytes, and a byte equals one letter of the alphabet (or a symbol, or a number).

The printout is accomplished by the **printer mechanism,** also shown in Figure 1 and represented in Figure 2. The printer mechanism can produce a variety of typographical styles and sizes (including superscripts and subscripts), variable line spacing, adjustable tabs, and block graphics. In addition, the Gemini is outstanding for the full range of papers upon which it can print.

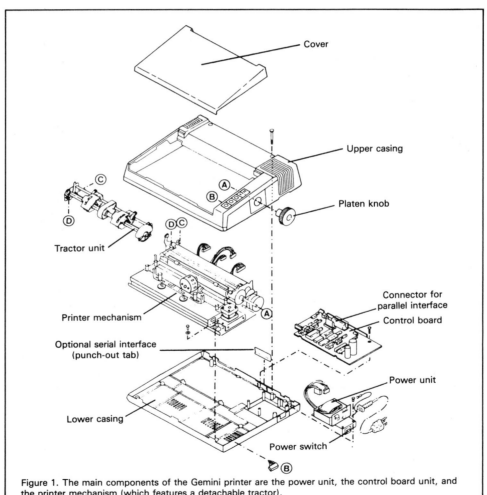

Figure 1. The main components of the Gemini printer are the power unit, the control board unit, and the printer mechanism (which features a detachable tractor).

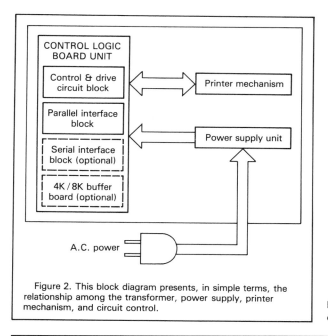

CONTROL LOGIC
BOARD UNIT

Control & drive
circuit block

Parallel interface
block

Serial interface
block (optional)

4K / 8K buffer
board (optional)

Printer mechanism

Power supply unit

A.C. power

Figure 2. This block diagram presents, in simple terms, the relationship among the transformer, power supply, printer mechanism, and circuit control.

Figures 1 and 2 are reprinted courtesy of Star Micronics, Inc.

The writer avoids most technical terms and provides clear definitions of ones that are used. Because of careful word choice and an organization based on the functioning of the printer components, the description is readable and understandable. It is useful to the beginner who wants a general understanding of how the printer operates.

The description is also a persuasive sales document. By including several sales plugs, avoiding difficult technical information, and communicating physical aspects of size, shape, color, finish, and texture with a drawing instead of with words, the writer makes the description easy to read.

At what audience range is this document targeted? Do you think it is 3 to 5? Higher or lower? Technical experts and industrial readers would probably want to know more. The description below illustrates a style more appropriate for the expert or industrial reader.

The 16-Block Digital Memory Device

The purpose of this device is to store 16 digital pressure curves, in sequence, repeatedly. Each block has in it 3600 separate storage locations, or words as they are sometimes called, and each location is 14 bits in length. Each complete curve has 3600 fourteen-bit words.

The device was designed principally for use in analyzing pressure curves in internal combustion engines, although it could be incorporated to store any digital value. This digital memory device has a major advantage over analog devices. A small loss in pressure that could be missed by an analog gauge can be stored in the digital memory device indefinitely and played back later at a rate of speed that allows an operator to locate it. This playback feature is a tremendous aid in pinpointing problem areas in pressure output.

The device looks like a standard rectangular computer circuit board that is covered with integrated circuit chips, ICs. It is 15 inches long, 8 inches wide, and $\frac{1}{2}$ inch thick. It is composed of five basic parts:

Input
Memory
Input/output memory addressing
Memory refresh addressing
Control circuitry

Input

The input is comprised of two 8-bit latches—these are temporary storage devices. The 8 means that there are 8 different input bits that can be latched at the same time. This latch allows, upon receipt of a 0.1-degree pulse, temporary holding of the 14 input bits. Each latch is a 20-pin IC chip, a 74C374. Each chip is rectangular: 1.01 inches long, 0.3 inch wide, and 0.29 inch thick. These latch chips feed directly into the memory chips and are active only during a write sequence.

Memory

The memory is comprised of fourteen 65,536 × 1-bit dynamic random access memory (RAM) chips. The figure 65,536 indicates the number of bit locations on each chip, and the × 1 means that each word character is one bit in length. Thus one bit from each of the 14 memory chips combines with the others to comprise one word of input. Each memory chip is a 16-pin IC, a MCM6665. Each chip is rectangular: 0.75 inch long, 0.24 inch wide, and 0.4 inch thick. The RAM chips control the entire device: input goes to them first and output originates from them.

Input/Output Memory Addressing

The input/output memory addressing controls the incoming data by storing the data in specific places in memory; it controls outgoing data by reading memory and correctly selecting appropriate data for output. It accomplishes these tasks with the use of four binary-coded (BC) IC counters. The counters operate in sequences of 0 to 15 (16 values) up to a total of 3600 (which equals 225 0-to-15 sequences). The lower three counters count from 0 to 3600 to indicate when one complete pressure curve has been stored.

The upper counter, the fourth one, tabulates the number of pressure curves that have been stored. After each storage of a pressure curve, the lower three counters are reset to 0 and the upper counter is increased by one. The upper counter keeps an account of which block of memory (which stored pressure curve) is being used. Each counter is a model 4516 sixteen-pin chip. Each chip is rectangular: 0.75 inch long, 0.24 inch wide, and 0.4 inch thick. These addressing chips enable an operator to locate and analyze specific areas of stored data.

Refresh Addressing

The refresh addressing device is used to maintain data when the input is coming in at a slow rate of speed. Dynamic RAM has the potential to be lost if it is not accessed often enough. The refresh addressing device accesses RAM every 2 milliseconds by sending a "refresh" pulse into every location in memory. There are 128 refresh row addresses in memory. Two BC counters control which address row is being refreshed during each refresh cycle. These two counters are model 4516 sixteen-bit IC chips; they are the same size as described above.

Control Circuitry

The control circuitry ensures proper sequencing of circuit operation. It is composed of two decade decoded counters. The counters have 10 decoded outputs that are normally low and go high (true) only at their respective decoded time slots. This means that the count of zero has its own output line; the count of one has its own output line; each value has its own output line up to the value of nine. Through these two counters the general timing of the circuitry is controlled. For example, on a count of 02 the refresh addresses are incremented, and on a count of 23 the input/output memory addresses are incremented. Each counter consists of a model 4017 sixteen-pin IC chip. These chips are rectangular: 0.75 inch long, 0.24 inch wide, and 0.4 inch thick.

Circuit Operation

The overall circuit operation of the 16-block digital memory device consists of the following steps:

1. Upon receipt of a 0.1-degree pulse, the two 8-bit latches input the incoming data and hold them.
2. This 0.1-degree pulse allows the control circuitry to initiate a write or read sequence, depending upon operator selection, after the next complete refresh cycle.
3. After the refresh cycle has taken place, the input/output addresses are incremented, and when the control circuitry has reached the write/read point (count of 44), a write into memory or a read from memory will be executed.

This sequence is repeated indefinitely as long as power is maintained.

This style is objective. It is not written for readers in the range 3 to 5. It is targeted to readers in the range 6 to 10. What does the writer do differently? Since the readers are knowledgeable, technical terms are not defined and ICs are not described because readers already know what they are. The writer does, however, provide model numbers of the parts because informed readers will probably want to know them. Since the style is objective, the writer concentrates on facts and offers no biased statements. There are no sales plugs in this description.

Suggestion: Recommend to your instructor visuals to illustrate the 16-block digital memory device.

What about the style for uninformed readers who want in-depth information? Writing for this audience is a challenge because it consists of range

3 to 5 readers who want technical information. The following description of a loudspeaker is in a style for this type of audience:

The Loudspeaker

Loudspeakers are important in business and industry because they are used in important devices such as telephones, stereo systems, public address systems, television sets, and computers. The loudspeaker is an electrical device that accepts an input signal from an amplifier and reproduces the signal as sound waves. As shown in Figure 1, it consists of a metal frame that houses a cone that is attached to a coil of wire. The coil of wire moves or vibrates in the vicinity of a magnet to produce sound from electrical signals.

Frame

The frame is the main housing of the loudspeaker. The purpose of the frame is to hold the parts in correct alignment. It is a bowl-shaped piece of metal that is often gold or silver in color with a 5-inch-diameter opening at the top and a 1-inch-diameter opening at the bottom. The sides of the frame are open in four equal sections of approximately 1 square inch. The cone is positioned to fit into the 5-inch opening at the top of the frame. The magnet assembly fits into the 1-inch hole at the bottom. Two male terminals that measure $\frac{1}{4}$ inch each are attached to the outside of the frame to provide the electric current by accepting the input signal from the amplifier.

Cone

The cone is the most important part of the loudspeaker. It moves back and forth to produce sound waves. The cone is shaped like a bowl. It fits inside the frame and is glued to the top rim of the frame. Both are approximately 5 inches in diameter. The diameter of the cone diminishes to about $\frac{3}{4}$ inch at the bottom of the frame, where it is connected to the voice coil (a moving coil of wire that accepts the electrical charge from the male terminals to vibrate the cone to produce sound waves). The cone must be strong, yet light; it is usually made with a special high-quality material that is ordinarily black in color.

Magnet Assembly

The magnet assembly is the part that makes the speaker operate. The magnet assembly is made of iron and magnetic pieces that work together to form a magnetic field around the voice coil. It is $2\frac{1}{2}$ inches in diameter and hollow inside to allow for placement of the voice coil. It is approximately $\frac{3}{4}$ inch in depth. It is glued to the bottom of the frame.

Voice Coil

The voice coil, which is placed inside the hollow portion of the magnet assembly, consists of many turns of fine copper wire wrapped and glued to a short plastic tube called a bobbin. It is glued to the bottom of the cone so that it rests inside the magnet. Opposite ends of the fine copper wire of the voice coil are connected to each of the male terminals located on the frame.

As current is passed intermittently through the terminals and copper wires, an electric field produced around the voice coil causes the coil to move back and forth. The connected cone also moves back and forth and produces vibrations in the air. The human ear perceives these vibrations as sound.

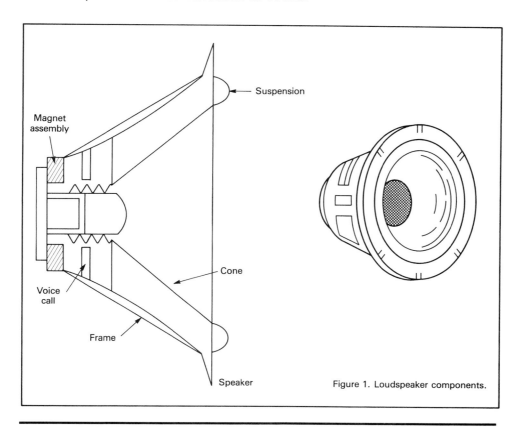

Figure 1. Loudspeaker components.

Notice the careful explanation of each part of the mechanism using the same criteria: purpose of the part in the mechanism, shape, method of attachment to other parts, size, and material. The writer patiently avoids technical terms, uses simple sentences, and explains the uses of the mechanism, to help readers understand how the parts fit and work together.

MAKING IT FIT: SITUATION, DOCUMENT, AND STYLE

Depending on your firm's resources and your product's marketability, mechanism descriptions may be necessary in several documents: operations manuals, proposals, trade journal articles, public relations documents, and ad copy. Each document will be aimed at a target audience and each audience will be approached with a predetermined style. Consider the following company news release about a new product.

The Circuitmate DM-73 Digital Multimeter

The Circuitmate DM-73 digital multimeter (see Figure 1) is the newest addition to the Beckman line of digital multimeters. It is the first multimeter ever designed to be actually hand-held during operation. This meter was produced with the computer technician, television repairman, and electronics student in mind. The DM-73 is capable of measuring ac and dc voltage, resistance, and continuity. It cannot measure ac or dc current.

   The DM-73 is intended primarily for use in computer circuit board and television repair. It can also be used by electronics students as a learning tool in the analysis and design of small circuitry. The DM-73 is best used when a measurement must be taken in some hard-to-reach spot, such as between multilevel computer boards or inside a television set; however, it also makes measuring all circuits easier because the technician can actually hold the meter during circuit analysis. With the use of a DM-73, a technician or repairperson can more easily troubleshoot all areas of a circuit to locate faulty components quickly and easily.

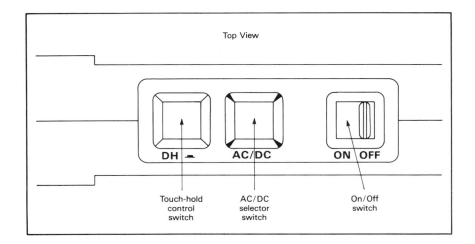

Front View

Grounding Probe

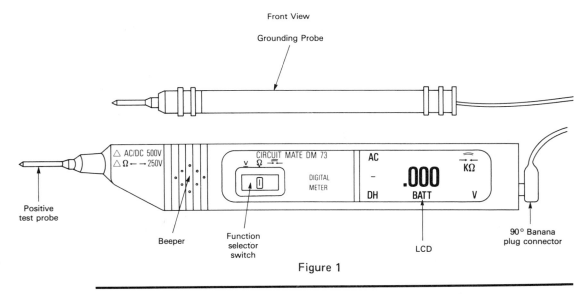

Figure 1

Assuming that you will use this introductory description for all the documents you produce, try to formulate a plan for developing content and style appropriate for different audiences:

1. *Retail audience:* technician, repairperson, or student who wants to know how easy the product is to operate

   a. *Content:* what facts should you include?

   b. *Document type:* sales pamphlet, owner's manual, journal article, etc.

   c. *Style:* objective, conditional, friendly, imperative, intimate

2. *Industrial audience:* technical expert, business manager, interested layman who wants to know specific technical and physical characteristics of the product—perhaps the reader's company is considering distributing the DM-73 or the reader is a journalist who has been assigned to write an article about the DM-73 for a trade publication

   a. *Content:* What facts should you include?

   b. *Document type:* Owner's manual, trade journal article, etc.

   c. *Style:* objective, conditional, friendly, imperative, intimate.

Now compare your plans to the documents a writer actually produced on this subject for retail and industrial audiences. Analyze each one, and consider the decisions the writer made about content, document type, and style.

Retail Audience: technician, repairman who wants to know how easy the product is to operate
Document Type: sales brochure

The body of the DM-73 is made of durable plastic, so you will not have to worry about damaging it during use. It can really take the punishment. The entire length of the meter is a mere 6.5 inches from tip to rear (see Figure 1). You can hold and operate the meter easily in one hand without any difficulty. It has some innovative features, such as an *easy-to-read LCD, helpful function symbols, autoranging capability,* and *touch-hold control.* Despite its portable size, the DM-73 is fully equipped with the following features:

- Continuity testing beeper
- Three-position function selector (voltage/resistance/continuity)

- Easy-to-read and scratch-proof LCD display
- Digital-hold switch
- Ac/dc selection switch
- Gripping-traction on/off switch
- Easy-to-access battery compartment
- Recessed banana jack
- Grounding probe (including the probe, connecting wire, and banana plug)

The DM-73 has some operational features that will really make using it a "breeze." The LCD display has a 3.5 digital readout with a maximum reading of 1999—so when you use the DM-73, your readings will be easy to see and you won't have to worry about any readings going off the scale. The LCD will display some very useful symbols to accompany numerical readouts:

(—)	Shows you are reading a negative voltage value
(AC)	Shows you are measuring ac voltage
(V)	Shows you are in the meter voltage position
(K)	Shows the meter is ready to measure resistance
(DH)	Shows touch-hold control is operating
(Ω)	Shows continuity is present
(Batt)	Shows batteries need to be replaced

But the DM-73 has even more. You've probably already noticed that there's no scale selector switch on the DM-73. That's because you won't need one. The DM-73 is **autoranging**: it *automatically selects the proper range* for your measurements. If you're measuring resistance, the (K) symbol tells you to multiply the value displayed, with the decimal properly positioned, by 1000.

The **touch-hold control** feature of the DM-73 will really make taking measurements a "snap." Touch-hold control allows you to take a measurement on a component and to *hold the measurement on the LCD even after you have disconnected the lead from the component.* All you have to do is press the DH button to "memorize" the reading. You can take the meter out, disconnect the leads, record your reading, and then press the DH button again to clear the LCD for the next reading. You don't have to keep glancing at a display as you do with conventional multimeters, and you don't have to position yourself in awkward places to get a reading.

The DM-73 has all the features to make your job easier and to make your readings more accurate. It is *portable* (only 6.5 inches in length); it has a *complete array of functions*; its LCD is *easy to read* and it displays *helpful symbols*; it is *autoranging*; and it features *touch-hold control.*

The DM-73 is available at your local Beckman dealer.

Notice that information is limited to facts of interest to a retail customer such as the quality of the DM-73, its capabilities, and how it makes work easier. The only exact measurement included is the size of the entire multimeter. Users do not care about the size of each part, but they do care about the size of the entire tool because size affects its usefulness. Parts are listed for easy reading and to show that the DM-73 has a full range of capabilities.

Unique characteristics (portability, LCD characteristics, autoranging, and touch-hold control) are major attractions to customers, so they are emphasized, first, in the introduction, then in the body, and finally, they are reemphasized in the conclusion. Boldface letters are used to bring the reader's eyes to these unique characteristics throughout the document. The writer keeps reminding readers how the DM-73 will make work easier because the retail buyer, the technician, is most concerned with usefulness.

The writer uses a mix of friendly and objective styles to create the impression of speaking directly to readers, as in a sales presentation. The purpose of this document is to inform and persuade about product benefits. Pure objective style is inappropriate here because it is used simply to describe physical characteristics. It would lack persuasion. Objective style is appropriate for informing industrial readers of a product's technical characteristics.

Industrial Audience: technical expert, businessman, or layman who wants to know specific technical and physical characteristics of the product—perhaps the reader's company is considering distributing the DM-73 or the reader is a journalist who has been assigned to write an article about the DM-73 for a trade journal

Document Type: technical product report from the Product Development Division to the Marketing Division

This report provides the Marketing Division with information on the physical characteristics and innovative features of the Circuitmate DM-73 requested during the March 17, 1989 prereport teleconference. After reading it, Marketing should understand enough about the physical size, composition, and major innovations of the DM-73 to develop promotional literature and media plans to support wholesale and retail customers.

The major innovations of the DM-73 are the following:

1. It is a stylish hand-held multimeter. This is evident from Figure 1.
2. It is very durable—however, it is not shatterproof, so the product should be sold with maintenance instructions.
3. The autoranging and touch-hold control features enable users to take faster and more accurate readings by selecting scales automatically and by recording and preserving measurements after the lead has been disconnected.
4. The ac, dc, and resistance scales include a wide range of values, and though they are not as precise as some meters, they are precise enough for scales given.

This report consists of the following sections:

1. Description of Physical Characteristics
2. Listing and Explanation of Numeric Values and Symbols That Appear on the DM-73's Liquid Crystal Diode
3. Explanation of the Autoranging Feature
4. Explanation of the Touch-Hold Control Feature
5. Explanation of Limits, Scales, and Accuracies of All Measurable Operations

Refer to Figure 1 for visual reinforcement of the following descriptions.

Description of Physical Characteristics

The DM-73 is made of durable plastic; it is gray and orange. The overall length of the meter with the grounding probe removed is 6.5 inches from the tip to the rear. The TIP of the meter is 0.75 inch long and it is conical in shape at the probing end. At the front end, the tip threads into the main body of the meter. The tip is made of polished metal alloy, and it is 0.1875 inch thick. Because the tip is very sharp, it may be inscrewed. Before placing it in the breast pocket for carrying, a user should unscrew the tip, remove it, and place it in a protected storage area.

The **built-in continuity beeper** is located 2.25 inches below the tip. The beeper is discernible as a 0.5-inch-diameter area that consists of a circumference of tiny holes in the ribbed plastic side of the DM-73. A small speaker, located beneath the holes, sounds a beep when the meter is being used to test a component for electrical continuity.

The **function selector** is a three-position slide switch that is used to select one of three types of measurements: voltage, resistance, or continuity. The symbols for these three characteristics are located to the side of the switch to indicate where the raised portion of the switch should be placed. The switch is made of white plastic. Except for the raised portion, it is recessed 0.125 inch so that the user can select the proper setting with the thumb of the hand holding the meter. This eliminates the need to use two hands during operation. The DM-73 is the only hand-held multimeter with this feature.

The **liquid-crystal diode** (LCD) is located 1.0 inch from the rear of the meter. The LCD is 1.0 inch wide by 0.5 inch wide. The window housing the LCD is recessed 0.0625 inch to prevent scratching and maintain the visual integrity of the LCD.

On the top of the meter, there are three pushbutton switches (see Figure 1): the **digital hold** (DH) **switch**, the **ac/dc selector switch**, and the **on/off switch**. The digital hold switch is made of yellow plastic. It is 0.1875 inch square. In the nonoperating position, the switch stands 0.1875 inch above the top of the meter. In the operating position, the switch is flush with the top of the meter. The ac/dc selector switch is made of white plastic. It is the same size as the digital hold switch. It is constantly flush with the top of the meter in both operating and nonoperating positions. The on/off switch is a two-position slide switch located beside the ac/dc selector switch. It is 2.25 inches from the rear of the meter. Its top is ribbed to give the user gripping traction to accommodate one-hand operation of the meter. The on/off switch is 0.25 inch long and 0.125 inch wide.

The **battery compartment** is located in the rear of the meter. It is 1.0 inch deep. The cover is made of gray plastic; it is 0.75 inch long and 0.5 inch wide. Three plastic extensions attached to the top edge of the cover slide into three holes located at the top edge of the compartment to hold the cover in place.

The **grounding probe** consists of three parts: the **probe,** the **wire,** and the **banana plug.** The probe is 5.0 inches in length; it consists of a polished, metal-alloy tip and a gray plastic handle. The tip is 0.75 inch long and conical in shape at the test point. The handle is 4.25 inches long and 0.1875 inch in diameter; it has a 0.125-inch hole through it from end to end to allow the wire to feed through to the tip. The wire that connects the tip to the banana plug is an 18-gauge, single-conductor, stranded wire insulated with a 0.25-inch plastic jacket for protection and flexibility. It is soldered at one end to the tip and at the other end to the banana plug. It is 34.0 inches long. The banana plug is a rectangular piece of metal alloy 0.185 inch long and 0.125 inch wide. It is attached to a plastic plug connector that insulates the connection between the wire and the plug. The connector is 0.5 inch long and 0.32 inch wide.

Listing and Explanation of Numeric Values and Symbols That Appear on the DM-73's Liquid Crystal Diode

The DM-73 LCD has a 3.5 digital readout with a maximum value reading of 1999. When a circuit is overloaded the LCD will flash a 1 continuously. Readings for voltage, resistance, and continuity appear on the LCD. Seven symbols also appear with numerical readouts. These are listed below along with a brief explanation:

(−)	Reading a negative voltage value
(AC)	Measuring ac voltage
(V)	The function selector is in the voltage position
(K)	The function selector is in the resistance position
(DH)	Touch-hold control is operating
(Ω)	Continuity is present in the circuit being tested
(BATT)	Batteries need to be replaced

Explanation of the Autoranging Feature

The DM-73 is an **autoranging** multimeter. This means that it automatically selects the proper range for its measurements. That is why it does not have a scale selector switch. This feature eliminates all the guesswork that goes along with proper scale selection. During autoranging, the numeric digits hone in on the actual value that is being measured, while the decimal point, if one is required, floats through the ranges to select the proper one. For example, if resistance is being measured, the (K) symbol will instruct the user to multiply the value displayed, with the decimal properly placed, by 1000.

Explanation of the Touch-Hold Control Feature

The **touch-hold control** feature of the DM-73 means that a user can record a voltage or resistance value on the LCD and hold it on the LCD even after the leads are removed from the component. The user simply must press the digital hold button after taking the reading for a few seconds. To conduct a subsequent measurement, the user must clear the LCD by again pressing the digital hold button.

Explanation of Limits, Scales, and Accuracies of All Measurable Operations

DC voltage can be measured on the DM-73 from 1 millivolt (mV) up to 500 volts (V). The dc position has four ranges: 2 V, 20 V, 200 V, and 500 V. The ranges given indicate the most dc voltage that can be measured on that particular scale—the least dc voltage that can be measured on a scale is the highest value from the previous scale. For example, the 20-V scale can measure up to 20 V and down to 2 V. The accuracy of each scale is within 0.5% for the 2-V and 20-V scales, 0.7% for the 200-V scale, and 1.0% for the 500-V scale. These accuracy figures measure the percentage of error that can be associated with the measured values. This percentage is taken from the nameplate value of the electronic components being measured.

AC voltage has the same scales, limits, and ranges as dc voltage. The accuracy of all ac measured values for all scales is 1.0% above or below the nameplate value of the component being measured.

The **resistance** scale can measure from 1.0 ohm up to 20,000,000 ohms. The resistance scale has four ranges: 2 kilohms (kohms), 20 kohms, 200 kohms, and 2000 kohms. The stated scale value is the largest value that can be read within any scale; the stated value of the preceding scale is the lowest value that can be read in any scale. For example, 20 kohms is the largest value that can be read in the 20-kohm scale; 2 kohms is the smallest value that can be read in the 20-kohm scale because it is the stated value of the scale that precedes the 20-kohm scale. The accuracy of the first three scales (2 kohms, 20 kohms, and 200 kohms) is plus or minus 0.7%. The accuracy of the 2000-kohm scale is plus or minus 1.2%. These given percentages are of the nameplate value of the component being tested.

Conclusion

The Product Development Division hopes that Marketing will be able to use this report to begin planning a program for advertising and distributing the DM-73.

Objective style is used because the writer's main purpose is to inform, not to persuade; the Marketing Division's task is to use the report as an information source to develop promotional literature for the DM-73. Through a pre-report teleconference Product Development knows Marketing's information needs: a thorough mechanism description of the product, including size, shape, color, material, and texture of all parts. Marketing also wants to know about the functioning of the product, so the writer includes innovative characteristics of the DM-73's operation. To emphasize these, the writer summarizes the most important features of the product in the introduction.

The writer uses forms of the verb "to be" throughout most of this document. When describing an object, "be" verbs are inevitable. Phrases such as "The handle is 4.25 inches long" and "The wire is 18 gauge" are the core of the mechanism description, and avoiding these and some passive constructions is impossible. However, notice that despite the extensive use of "to be," the writer has written a clearly understandable report by avoiding complex and compound/complex sentences. And the writer has used active voice: "A user can record a resistance or voltage value . . . ." whenever possible.

Now that you have seen two different documents for the two different writing situations, compare them to what you had planned above prior to reading these documents:

1. How did your suggested content, document type, and style differ from the ones that the writer produced?

2. Was your intended audience different from the writer's? If so, how would your style and type of document differ for your intended audience?

3. Do you think that the writer did a good job in producing the documents? What improvements would you suggest?

4. Did the writer make any wrong decisions in planning strategy for producing the documents? If so, what were they, and what alternatives would you suggest?

5. Do you think the styles of the documents are consistent with the introductory paragraph to be used with both documents? What revisions should be made in the introductory paragraph?

6. Revise the introductory paragraph for each audience in the spaces provided below.

Retail Document

Industrial Document

CONSIDERING COST

The cost of a mechanism description depends on its degree of accuracy, the depth of information, and the nature of visuals to be included. Descriptions that must be extremely accurate require painstaking measurement and explanation of importance of specific dimensions: for example, showing why this product's dimensions help it to outperform a competitor's. High-performance equipment and technical products often must be described very precisely. Their usefulness depends on their precision. Costs rise because highly technical staff (who are well paid) spend time contributing to the content of the description.

Information has a cost derived from time spent either compiling research or conducting tests and experiments. Professional researchers and consultants review reference works and periodicals. Research and development scientists conduct experiments and tests. Mechanism descriptions that require in-depth details require more research time and will be more expensive.

Color visuals are generally more expensive than black-and-white sketches. The process of creating color visuals involves more labor to perform technical artistic work. Visuals that must be very accurate will cost more than those that can be "eyeballed" for precision. Precise graphics may require computer simulation or professional drafting. Both processes are performed by skilled technical professionals, whose time is expensive.

The actual writing of the description by a technical writer or a journalist adds more expense. Technical and nontechnical staff must meet to discuss the document several times during its composition. Finally, the quality of material used to produce a document affects final costs. Glossy finish paper is more expensive than 20-pound bond.

How do companies decide how much to spend? Most determine the benefits they will derive from a mechanism description document. If it can generate revenue, companies will be willing to spend more on the right features of the document. If it is a low-level requirement, not a high consideration in selling, they will probably spend less. One final comment: Documents reflect the image of a company, so no company with a good reputation to maintain will turn out substandard documents.

In Chapter Four you have learned how to write mechanism descriptions for several different audience types, employing objective and friendly styles. In Chapter Five you will write process descriptions.

CHAPTER ASSIGNMENT

Your assignment is to write a mechanism description report either for a retail audience (a user of the mechanism such as the technician who will purchase the DM-73) or an industrial audience (an employee in the Marketing Department who needs to understand the DM-73). Your readers are in the range 3 to 5. They have a general understanding of the topic but are uninformed about its physical makeup.

Provide a visual to reinforce your description. It should be a hand drawing, a tracing of another visual, or a photocopy of a published visual—be sure to give credit to your sources of tracings and photocopies. Label all the parts of the visual so that the reader can identify them while reading your description.

Identify and explain below the item, audience, purpose, and type of document you intend to use to complete your assignment.

Item to Be Described (product and use)

Audience (retail consumer, industrial expert, or other)

Purpose (Why is the document being produced?)

Type of Document and Style (retail manual, industrial product description, other; second-person friendly style, third-person indicative style, other)

Discuss the results of your preplanning with your instructor before you begin to outline your report. Be sure to check the consistency of your choices in each category mentioned above.

Now that you have established your communication criteria, outline the report according to the organization for description provided below. (You may wish to review the section on description provided in Chapter 2.)

Introduction

Purpose of the Report

Importance of the Item to the Reader

General Description of the Item

List of Major Physical Parts

Body (Describe the size, shape, color, finish, texture, and methods of attachment of each part as is appropriate for the style and document type)

Part 1

Part 2

Part 3

Part 4

Part 5

etc.

Conclusion (How do the main parts and their most important characteristics contribute to the functioning of the mechanism?)

Point 1

Point 2

Point 3

etc.

Now that you have established your writing situation and outlined your document, you should begin writing your rough draft. As you do this, keep the following tips in mind:

1. Write the introduction as a single paragraph with a sentence devoted to each part of your introduction outline. List the major parts of the mechanism vertically.
2. Be sure that the list of parts in the introduction is arranged in the same sequence that will be used to describe the parts in the body. Consider organizing the list into a sequence such as order of operation, left to right (or some other spatial arrangement), or by method of attachment.

3. When writing the body, develop a separate paragraph from each item in the vertical list of parts in the introduction. Form a topic sentence that states the importance of the part to the mechanism. Develop each paragraph by describing the characteristics of each part (size, shape, color, etc.) in the same sequence. Conclude each paragraph with a transitional device that will lead into the next part to be described. (*Hint:* Consider describing the method of attachment last.)

4. In the conclusion, consider briefly describing how the parts function during operation and/or emphasizing the most important characteristics of the parts.

Before you begin writing the rough draft, consider the following document. It is the body of a report that was sent back for revision. It is supposed to be a mechanism description of a flashlight that was written to enable the Product Development Division to consider ways to design a new product.

Case

The case is the main body of the flashlight. It holds the contents of the light and protects them from damage. The case is usually made of metal or plastic.

Top

The top screws onto the case and holds the contents in the case. The top is made of plastic.

Switch

The switch is used to turn on and off the light. The switch connects the circuit together inside the light, which makes the light operate.

Spring

The spring is used to keep the batteries in contact with each other and also in contact with the bulb.

Batteries

The batteries are the power supply for the flashlight.

Bulb

The bulb may be the most important part because it emits the light and without it the bulb would be worthless.

Bulb Keeper

The bulb keeper hold the bulb inside the reflector and it also keeps it in the right position for the best reflection.

Reflector

The reflector focuses the light from a bulb into a directional beam.

Lens

The lens protects the bulb from being broken. The lens is made of glass or plastic.

The writer included the following conclusion:

Conclusion

A flashlight is a handy tool that enables one to see in the dark. I have discussed in this report the physical appearance and parts of a flashlight.

How would you suggest that the writer revise the body of this document in the following areas:

Style

Physical Description

Paragraphing

Sentence Structure

Wording

Why would you as manager of the New Products Division accept or reject this document? (The introduction was consistent with the rest of the document.)

Discuss with your instructor your suggestions and conclusions about the flashlight description. What does your evaluation of this report indicate to you about the characteristics you should achieve in your own report?

Now it is time for you to begin to write your rough draft. After you have completed it, consider the following points of advice:

1. Put it aside for as long as possible before trying to write the final draft.

2. Have at least two other people read, edit, and evaluate it. Consider the advice of these editors when revising the paper and writing the final draft.

3. When you rewrite the rough draft, do it section by section (introduction, body, conclusion) first, and then read over the entire document for consistency between sections. Provide transitions wherever they are needed at that point in your writing.

4. After revising, read over the introduction to make sure that it is still consistent with the rest of your paper. Add any information to the introduction that you believe would make the reading of the document easier for the reader.

5. Devote a period of concentrated effort to revising your report and to preparing the final copy. Careless errors in content and writing, such as leaving out important information, inaccurate or poorly worded descriptions, misspelled words, and punctuation errors are often just the result of not spending enough time reading over and thinking about your writing.

6. Keep the reader in mind. Keep asking yourself: "Will the reader to whom I am writing understand this description?" "Will the reader be pleased with this style of writing?" "Have I left out any information that the reader will need to understand this document?" Remember, the reader, not you, is the final judge of your writing.

FIVE

Describing Processes

PREVIEW

The examples in this chapter are organized as step-by-step descriptions. All process descriptions are written in the objective style. The imperative style is used for instructions. The CRT report is a nonoperator description because it explains how parts automatically operate within the CRT. The report to Mr. Anderson is an operator process description because it is written about a user operating the Mapple Network Computer.

A process description explains and describes how steps in a procedure are performed. To do this well, you have to:

1. Define the process.
2. List parts and materials necessary.
3. Break steps into individual tasks.
4. Organize into a logical sequence.

The conclusion should emphasize most important characteristics of the process and explain expected end results of a completed process.

THE BASICS

A process defines by explaining how steps in a procedure are performed. Process descriptions are written for managers and not for readers who will actually perform the process, so the objective style is used.

ESTABLISHING THE WRITING SITUATION

Process descriptions are frequently used to handle situations similar to these:

1. A business manager wants to understand the processes performed by employees to manage them more skillfully.
2. A systems engineer discovers a process that will make doing a better job easier.
3. Students need to understand the process of semiconducting or computer memory storage to do well on a test.

4. A research scientist needs to understand the process of laser operation to keep informed about the discipline and to apply it to research.

These are all examples of writing situations that call for a process description. Indicate below a document type and style that will fulfill **reader needs** in each situation:

Situation 1

Situation 2

Situation 3

Situation 4

Process descriptions usually are written in objective style. They should be thorough, clear, and logically organized. Review the process method of defining in Chapter Three, and you will see the step-by-step format you should use.

The content of the description will depend on your readers' needs. Business managers will want enough details about employees' job tasks to be able to understand how busy they are and how hard they work. A scientist doing research with lasers will want to know how they operate as well as the scientific principles underlying their operation.

Two basic types of process descriptions are operator and nonoperator. An operator description explains how a person performs a process. It is outlined as follows:

Introduction

Definition and purpose of process
Purpose of the report
Tools/materials required
List of major steps

Body

Explanation of each step including:
Purpose of the step
Tools/materials needed
Description of each substep
Transition to next step

Conclusion

Summary of process
Critical information:
Dangers (Can cause physical harm)

Warnings (Can cause machine damage)
Cautions (Can disrupt process/cause danger)

For example, soldering a joint is a good topic for an operator description. You would describe each task that a technician performs when soldering.

Nonoperator descriptions explain how a machine functions during operation. It is outlined similarly, except for the following difference: Tools and materials information is replaced by principle of operation information. Instead of explaining how tools and materials are used, the nonoperator description explains how parts function according to the principle of operation.

For example, electronic circuits operate by the principle of electron flow. A nonoperator description of a semiconductor would explain how electrons behave as they move through various parts of a semiconductor device.

One important distinction: A process description is *not* an operation manual or a set of instructions. It is *not* intended for readers who will perform the process being described. For example, business managers receiving process descriptions of job tasks will not perform those tasks; they will read the descriptions to understand how employees perform the tasks.

DECIDING ON A DOCUMENT TYPE

The document should fit the needs of the writing situation. For example, a scientist who needs a thorough explanation of a fiber optic system would want to receive a detailed scientific report rather than a memo. A business manager needing a quick list of employee job tasks would be satisfied with a memo. If the scientist needs only a list of major operational steps in a fiber optic system, a memo would be sufficient. If the business manager needs a detailed description of job tasks, a report will be necessary. When deciding on a document type, always consider your reader's needs and select a document type to fulfill those needs.

DETERMINING VISUALS

Line drawings that emphasize parts used in a process work well with process descriptions. They give readers a sharp mental image of an operating part. Exploded drawings are especially helpful. Flowcharts illustrate the sequence of steps in a process. They allow readers easily to keep track of steps.

DEVELOPING AN APPROPRIATE STYLE

Process descriptions should be written in the objective style. The imperative style is not appropriate because it is used for operation manuals and sets of instructions that are intended for end users. Process descriptions are intended for managers or researchers who want to understand a process without performing it. Examples of these two styles are provided below.

Objective Style

Process Description of Assembling
a Rotating Sales Display Tree

The technician arrives on the job site and examines the parts in the sales-display-tree kit to make sure that all parts are present and undamaged. The following parts are in the kit (see Figure 1):

Part	Description
A	Base
B	Main shaft
C	Rotor support
D	Rotor
E	Display limbs

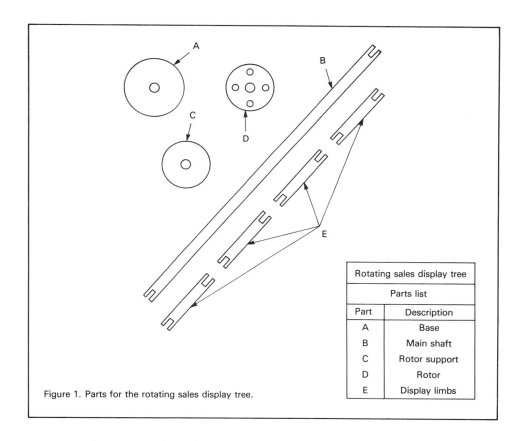

Figure 1. Parts for the rotating sales display tree.

Rotating sales display tree	
Parts list	
Part	Description
A	Base
B	Main shaft
C	Rotor support
D	Rotor
E	Display limbs

Once parts have been located, identified, and examined, the technician performs the following five steps:

1. The *base* (part A) is placed on a flat and level surface and the *main shaft* (part B) is inserted into the center hole of the base by sliding it in far enough that the end of the main shaft is just flush with the bottom of the base.

2. Next, the technician slides the *main shaft* (part B) through the center hole of the *rotor support* (part C). The rotor

support slides 2 to 3 inches down from the top of the main shaft.

3. Now the *rotor display* is assembled by inserting each of the *display limbs* (part E) into the side holes of the ROTOR (part D).

4. The technician now slides the assembled *rotor display* through the center hole down the top end of the *main shaft* until it rests on the *rotor support*.

5. Finally, the technician places the assembled display tree on a countertop and attaches the display items to the limbs.

Note: The technician should be very careful to keep the bottom of the MAIN SHAFT flush with the bottom of the BASE—otherwise, the tree may topple over.

Imperative Style

After arriving on the job site, perform the following tasks:

1. Examine the sales-display-tree kit to make sure that all parts are present and undamaged.

2. Find the following parts in the kit:

Part	Description
A	Base
B	Main shaft
C	Rotor support
D	Rotor
E	Display limbs

After locating, identifying, and examining parts, assemble the display tree by performing the following five steps:

1. Place the *base* (part A) on a flat and level surface and insert the *main shaft* (part B) into the center hole of the base—be sure to slide the main shaft into the base far enough so that it is flush with the bottom of the base.

2. Slide the center hole of the *rotor support* (part C) on the *main shaft* (part B) down 2 to 3 inches from the top of the main shaft.

   Caution: Keep the bottom of the main shaft flush with the bottom of the base—otherwise, the tree may topple over and cause injury or be damaged.

3. Assemble the *rotor display* by inserting each of the *display limbs* (part E) into the side holes of the *rotor* (part D).

4. Slide the *rotor display* through its center hole on to the *main shaft* until the rotor display rests on the *rotor support*.

5. Place the assembled display tree on a countertop and attach display items appropriately to the limbs.

The imperative style consists of a sequence of commands—they tell the reader what to do. The objective style consists of an explanation of what is to be done rather than a series of commands that tell the reader what to do. The process description reader is the technician's manager—a person who wants to know what the employee is supposed to do on the job. The instruction reader is the technician—a person who will actually perform the process.

The formats of the two documents are similar and they contain basically the same information. The difference between them is the style of the writing. The objective style is the one to use for process description.

Also, when determining style, consider the two types of process descriptions: operator and nonoperator. The description of the display-tree assembly above is an operator process description. The following description of the operation of a photovoltaic cell is a nonoperator process description.

Introduction

A photovoltaic cell is a device that uses light photons to stimulate electrons and produce electrical energy. This device is coming into common use in products such as solar calculators and watches. The cell operates according to the principle of electron flow. Negatively charged electrons are attracted to positive charges and repulsed by negative charges. The four main steps in the operation are:

1. Release of electrons
2. Creation of static barrier
3. Passage through static barrier
4. Storage of charge

Body

Release of Electrons

As the light photons strike and penetrate the surface of the cell, they add energy to the already negatively charged atoms of silicon (n-silicon; see Figure 1). An electron from the silicon's outer shell is freed and attracted to the positively charged silicon (p-silicon) because an electron is by nature negatively charged.

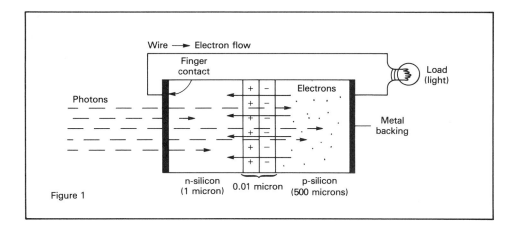

Figure 1

Creation of Static Barrier

A static barrier is created between the *n*-silicon and the *p*-silicon as electrons line up along the edge of the *p*-silicon and protons (positively charged atomic particles) line up along the edge of the *n*-silicon.

Passage through Static Barrier

As photons continue to "excite" and free electrons, the excited electrons pass across the static barrier to the *p*-silicon. The increasing number of electrons in the *p*-silicon are attracted to the positively charged static barrier on the edge of the *n*-silicon; however, the negatively charged static barrier prevents them from passing to the positive barrier.

Storage of Charge

The photovoltaic cell functions by attracting these electrons across the static barrier by use of a low-resistance finger contact (Figure 2), which draws in the electrons and stores them in a metal backing as a future electrical charge.

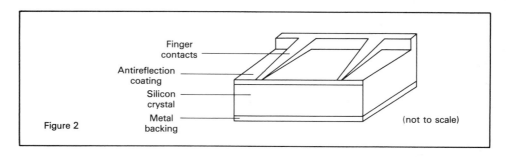

Figure 2   Finger contacts / Antireflection coating / Silicon crystal / Metal backing   (not to scale)

Describing nonoperator action can be confusing. You can avoid confusing the reader by using these guidelines to achieve a clear style:

1. Devote one sentence to each step in the process.
2. Be clear about which parts are involved in each step.
3. Explain carefully the relatedness of each step in sequence.
4. Provide a reinforcing visual.

1. In the example above, the writer attempts to use these guidelines in composing the process. Keeping in mind that the description has been taken out of context, evaluate how successful the writer has been in using the suggested guidelines:

1. Devoting one sentence to each step

2. Being clear about which parts are involved in each step

3. Explaining the relatedness of steps to each other

4. Providing a reinforcing visual

2. Who is the writer's intended audience? Are the readers in the range 3 to 5? Why?

3. How would you conclude the report?

Discuss your answers with your instructor and consider them in completing your own writing assignment in this chapter.

MAKING IT FIT: SITUATION, DOCUMENT, AND STYLE

Imagine a situation in which you may find yourself a few years from now, and develop a document and an appropriate style for the audience defined by the situation. You have graduated and been hired on your first job. You are a professional in a technical company working with a project team that is developing an updated version of an already successful personal computer (PC), the Mapple II. You are in a training situation—learning the ropes of the company by providing services for technical and nontechnical people on the team.

The team is deciding on a monitor to include with the updated version. The team has narrowed its options to a liquid-crystal display (LCD) or a cathode-ray tube (CRT). Members are divided. Some want the LCD because Mapple's primary competitor, Data Specific, has included an LCD in its new portable PC. You notice that the technical members prefer the CRT, whereas the nontechnical members want the LCD. At one of the meetings, Monica Brenner, a technical member, speaks up to defend the CRT:

> Because it has such a wide scope of visual applications, it is difficult to see the CRT as a thing of the past. Even after considering the LCD, the CRT is still outstanding. LCDs are far more limited than CRTs in the types of images they can produce. In fact, companies such as Mitsubishi and Sony are developing small, very high quality CRTs because they produce optimum visual reproduction.

The nontechnical members are unconvinced. She suggests that they be educated about the technology supporting the CRT and LCD: "Once you are educated about the processes of operation of both mechanisms, I think that you'll agree that the CRT is the best type of display to use in the Mapple III." The nontechnical people agree to learn about the operation processes of both monitor types, but they insist that somebody neutral should do the research and write the reports.

All eyes come to rest on you. Monica smiles at you and asks if you would "mind terribly" putting together a couple of brief reports, one on each type of monitor. You agree to produce the reports. After the meeting, you ask Monica for some guidance. She tells you: "Just put together something appropriate. You'll figure it out. We'll need the CRT report in two days—nothing too long or overly complex; just get the basic facts down so that even they [motioning to the nontechnical members] can understand them."

At the Mapple Corporation Learning Resources Center, you ask the director for the quickest available general information on the operation process of the CRT. She directs you to technical encyclopedias. After looking through several of them, you find an applicable process description in the *Illustrated Science and Invention Encyclopedia*. You bring some note cards with you to copy down information on the parts of the CRT, the steps in its operation process, and its future applications. You have decided that this is the information that the team will find most useful.

You organize the information into a rough draft by writing for each step a brief paragraph explaining the parts of the CRT used and tasks involved in the completion of that step. You add an introduction that states the purpose of the report and lists the parts and steps. To compose the final draft, you place these sections in proper order and revise the descriptions for grammar and vocabulary. You place headings in the report to identify the main steps. Since the information is lengthy, you decide to put it into report form with a memo addressed to the Monitor-Project Team. Your final report is produced below.

MAPPLE CORPORATION

INTEROFFICE MEMORANDUM

TO: Monitor-Project Team

FROM: [Your Name]

SUBJECT: CRT Operation Description

The accompanying report is provided to the Monitor-Project Team to provide technical background on the operation of the cathode ray tube (CRT). This information was requested at the last Monitor-Project-Team meeting (date). An accompanying report on the operation of the liquid crystal display (LCD) will be provided at a future date per request by the team. Additional information on the CRT will be provided at this time if requested.

[The Report]

CRT Operation Description

Introduction

This report provides a description of the process of operation of the cathode ray tube (CRT; Figure 1). The CRT is a voltage-controlled device that converts electrical signals into visual images by controlling the scanning by electrons of a fluorescent screen. There are four major parts of the CRT involved in the process:

> Electron gun (Figure 2)
> Focusing system
> Deflection system
> Fluorescent material

These parts interact to create a visual image on the screen. The four major steps in the production of that image are:

> Producing the electron beam
> Focusing
> Aiming
> Producing the image

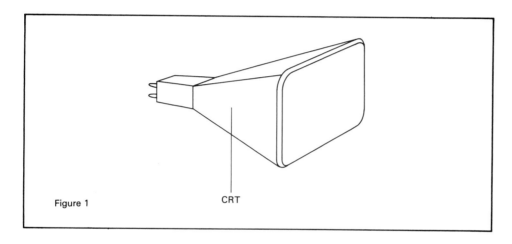

Figure 1

CRT

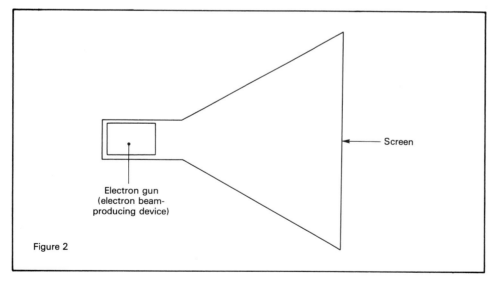

Screen

Electron gun
(electron beam-
producing device)

Figure 2

Producing the Electron Beam

Before an image can be produced on the CRT, the electron beam must be formed. Production of the beam requires the interaction of the following parts of the electron gun: heating element, cesium cover, and positively charged case (see Figure 3). An input voltage is applied to the terminals of the heating element, causing it to heat the cesium cover. The metal cesium will produce electrons when heated. (An electron is a negatively charged atomic particle: it attracts a positive charge and repels a negative charge.) The positively charged case around the cesium cover attracts the freed cesium electrons. As the electrons move toward the positive charge, some escape a $\frac{1}{32}$-inch hole located at the front end of the case to form the electron beam.

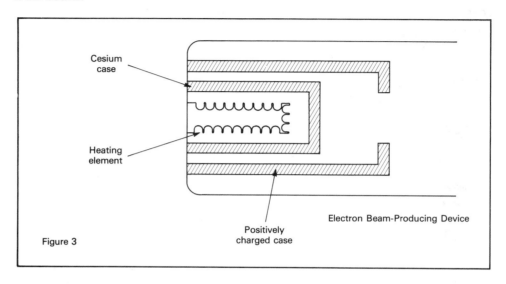

Cesium case

Heating element

Positively charged case

Electron Beam-Producing Device

Figure 3

Focusing the Electron Beam

As the electron beam exits the electron gun, it is too dispersed to be of use in creating an image on the CRT screen. To be of any use in producing an image, it must be focused like sun rays are focused by a magnifying glass. The focusing system, which consists of an accelerator and a focus ring (see Figure 4), first accelerates and then focuses the electron beam as it moves toward the CRT screen. The accelerator is an electromagnetic field that speeds up the beam. The focus ring, whose diameter is about the size of a pencil point, is an additional electromagnetic field that forces the accelerated beam into a convergent path as the beam reaches the screen.

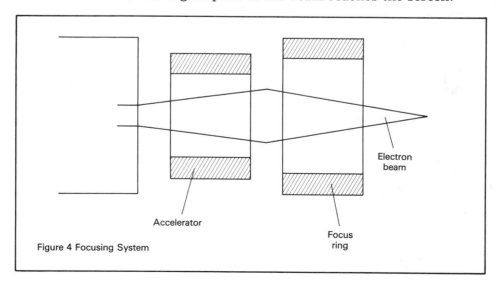

Electron beam

Accelerator

Focus ring

Figure 4 Focusing System

Aiming the Electron Beam

Aiming is necessary to make the beam scan the entire screen, and scanning is what ultimately produces the image on the screen. Scanning is accomplished by the use of deflection plates positioned around the perimeter of the screen.

These plates are alternately charged positive and negative to make the beam move right to left, left to right, top to bottom, and bottom to top in varying frequencies. The pattern of the beam's motion will decide the image created on the screen. For example, the beam moves right when the right deflection plate is positively charged to attract the negatively charged electrons that comprise the beam, and the left deflection plate is negatively charged to repel the electrons. It moves left when the deflection plates are oppositely charged. It moves up when the top deflection plate is positively charged and the bottom is negatively charged, and it moves down when those plates are oppositely charged. The beam is influenced by both sets of plates simultaneously to produce diagonal motion.

Producing the Image

The final step in the operation of the CRT is to produce the image. To accomplish this, a thin layer of fluorescent material that glows on contact with the electron beam is applied to the inside of the screen. Silver-activated zinc sulfide or zinc cadmium are commonly used materials. As the electron beam scans the screen, the fluorescent material lights it up according to the pattern created by the frequency of the changing charges of the deflection plates that control the scanning of the electron beam. The intensity of the beam changes to produce light and dark areas in an image, and spots on the screen will retain their glow until the beam can scan them once more—this property is termed persistence.

Conclusion

The electron beam scans a CRT screen about 25 times per second in black-and-white models and more often in color models. It is simple to keep clean and maintain because all parts are sealed, but they must be kept in a vacuum for proper operation. The CRT operates at about 300 volts. The future prospects for CRT development include faster scanning and smaller dots for higher-quality images. With these modifications in design should come more and diverse areas of application.

[Bibliography]

"Cathode Ray Tube." *The Illustrated Science and Invention Encyclopedia,* 1977 ed., pp. 528–30.

At the next meeting, everyone praises the clarity of your CRT report. One of the nontechnical committee members, however, raises an important point: "How are we supposed to know whether the CRT is really superior to the LCD until we get the report on the LCD and have one of our technical colleagues explain the differences in terms of product quality and dollars and cents?"

Monica looks a bit perturbed, and then speaks up: "Yes, I agree. The sooner we get the LCD report, the sooner we will be able to make a decision based on the technical and economic facts. However, a number of us on this committee will be out of town next week for the National Computer Association convention in Dallas, so I suggest that we delay the LCD report until we return—perhaps we can find some valuable information at the convention on CRT and LCD research and development."

As the meeting breaks up, Fred Anderson, one of the nontechnical committee members speaks to you: "I was very impressed with your report. You know, many of us have been having difficulty understanding our new computer system. We just can't understand the manufacturer's documentation. Knowing how to access that data base is very important to our work. We need that information. I don't want to ask you to write up an entire user's manual, but could you write a simple description explaining how to operate the system? I can pass the information on to some of our people, or I can get one of our staff members to write up a manual." You agree to help out.

Since this is an operator description, you gather a large number of facts by taking notes as you operate the computer system. You also refer to a number of books on computer operation. After a week, you give Anderson the following report:

[Memo]

TO: Fred Anderson, Vice President, Marketing

FROM: [You]

SUBJECT: Description of Operating the Mapple Computer Network

DATE: _____

[Report]

This document will describe how to perform the following tasks on the Mapple Network Computers:

     Turning on the Computer
     Entering the User Identification Code
     Entering the User Password
     Selecting Information

INTRODUCTORY EXPLANATION

The Mapple Network is a data-base system. A data base is a very detailed collection of information files that can be integrated and accessed in various combinations and formats to fulfill user needs. For example, the Personnel Department often uses files of information on employees to decide which benefits represent the best purchase. They might accomplish this by comparing the costs to an employee's gross salary of similar health insurance programs to arrive at a percentage of gross salary figure; the Mapple Network would contain the employee files with the health insurance cost data.

The Marketing Department has its own set of files stored in the computer. These include figures on buying habits and business profiles of customers, including information on primary product or business activity, number of employees, gross and net sales figures, and a number of other statistics on each customer. The data base for the Marketing Department compares changes in a customer's business profile to changes in the customer's buying habits. This information enables Mapple Marketing to identify crucial market factors that influence customer buying habits.

To access this vital information, however, the user must learn a few simple steps to operate the computer.

TURNING ON THE COMPUTER (See Figure 1)

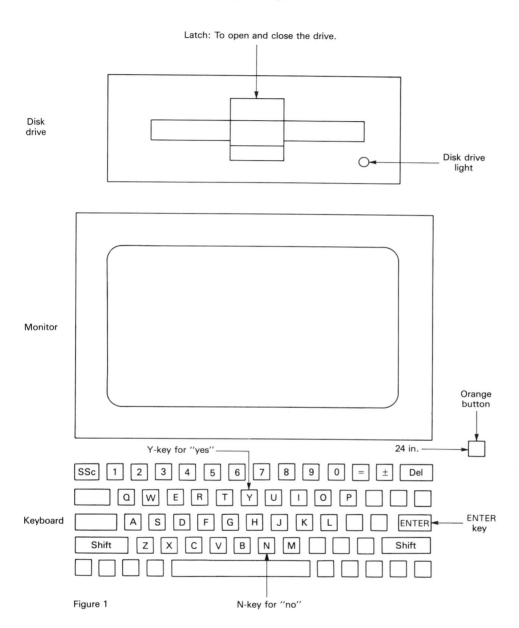

Figure 1

Turning on the computer requires only two tasks and several observations:

1. The data to be accessed and depicted on the monitor screen are contained on one of the hard disks located in the disk cabinet of the Marketing Department's computer room. Each disk is labeled alphabetically by company name. The user retrieves the appropriate disk and slides it into the disk drive. The slot on the disk should be facing up. The disk drive is located at the workstation. The disk drive door should be shut before proceeding to task 2.

2. The user locates the orange button approximately 24 inches to the right of the CRT, presses the button, and waits to observe several things happening on the screen.

Observations

• The CRT screen will be filled for 3 seconds with random numbers, letters, and symbols (this tells you that the computer is checking its memory).

• Next, the disk drive light will come on and a soft, clicking noise will be heard, indicating that the computer is loading data from the disk into its memory.

• Finally, after approximately 10 seconds, the disk drive will stop clicking and the message "System Operating and Logon Procedure Invoked" will appear on the CRT screen.

ENTERING THE USER IDENTIFICATION CODE

After the expression "Enter User ID" appears on the screen, the user types in the eight-digit User Identification Code assigned by the Marketing Department and presses the ENTER KEY (Located below the orange ON key) to enter the code into the computer memory.

ENTERING THE USER PASSWORD

When the computer has accepted the User Identification Code, the expression "Enter User Password" will appear on the CRT screen. The user types in the six-letter password assigned by the Marketing Department and then presses the ENTER key. If the password is valid and has been correctly entered, the main menu of data options will appear on the CRT screen.

SELECTING INFORMATION

Each item on the Data Menu is a possible choice the user may wish to access. To select a single item, the user should press the appropriate number (the one beside the item) and press the ENTER key. To select multiple items, the user can press up to three numbers and then press ENTER. The computer will provide submenus as needed—items on these are accessed in the same way that Main Menu items are accessed. The computer will also request additional information as necessary. These requests will consist of YES/NO answers. To respond YES, the user should press the Y key; to respond NO, the user should press the N key.

After reading through your document, you note that it lacks substance. Something is missing, so you ask Mr. Anderson to read it over and make suggestions. Let's look at this from Mr. Anderson's viewpoint. In reviewing the document, what would he be most interested in critiquing? What does he want the document to do? Consider how he might respond to the following:

Style: Is the objective style appropriate for Mr. Anderson's purpose: to get a simple version of computer operation for the Marketing Department?

Organization: Is the organization of material appropriate for Mr. Anderson's needs? Should some facts be placed differently in the document? Is the introductory explanation effective? Is the sequence of steps logically organized?

Format: Is the format the best one to use for this type of document? Should there be more lists and fewer paragraphs? Should there be more visual reinforcement of information? Graphs? Charts? Tables? Drawings? Photos?

Content: Is the description complete? Can you think of additional information that should be included?

Now that you have had a chance to answer these critical questions, what is your overall criticism of the document? How should it be revised?

CONSIDERING COST

How does a company account for money spent on project teams? In the examples above, you worked as an employee for the Mapple Corporation. You worked part-time with the Monitor Team and part-time for Mr. Anderson's department. How does Mapple account for the cost of the work you did? How much did Mapple pay for your reports?

As we have learned, the cost of your reports is to a large degree determined by their effectiveness. If your CRT report helps the team make a good decision and your description of the computer system operation enables Marketing to be more productive, Mapple will earn a good return on opportunity cost it has invested in you. Actual cost is largely the percentage of your time devoted to the reports multiplied by your salary.

Two other concepts you should know about are hard and soft dollars. **Hard dollars** are additional expenses a company must incur to get work done. **Soft dollars** are an accounting of how companies use the personnel already on staff. In the Mapple cases, your reports would be expensed as soft dollars. Your salary was already an expense—the company incurred no additional expenses because you wrote the reports. If an outside consultant had written them, they would be expensed as hard dollars.

CHAPTER ASSIGNMENT

Write either an operator or a nonoperator process description for readers in the range 3 to 5, such as Mr. Anderson and the nontechnical team members. Create a professional environment such as the Mapple Corporation in which to write your document. Imagine yourself as a new employee, and create a writing situation. Use the following outline to help you get organized.

Description of the professional situation you have imagined:

Your Role

Your Audience

Type of Writing You Have Been Asked to Produce

Type of Document You Will Produce to Fulfill Audience's Needs (report, long memo, article in corporation magazine, other)

Be sure to discuss your choices with your instructor. Consider the consistency of your ideas. Do they seem to fit together logically?

Despite the type of document you choose to write, use the following outline to organize your information.

Introduction
How would you define the process?
Who performs it, or in what type of machine is it performed?
What is the purpose of the process?
What is the principle of operation? (if necessary)
What are the principal steps in the process?
Why are you describing the process?

Equipment and Materials
List all equipment and materials used to perform the process and be sure to include them in the actual description of each step.

Step-by-Step Description
Each step must be introduced and broken into substeps.
The reader needs to know:
What is done
How it is done
The reader should be able to visualize the process while reading the description.

Conclusion
Emphasize the results received from successful completion of the process.

Good luck on your assignment. In Chapter Six we will study instructions and operations manuals.

SIX

Writing Instructions and Manuals

PREVIEW

Manuals and instructions inform users how to use and operate products properly. They use the step-by-step organization also used in process descriptions. They differ from process descriptions in style and audience: instead of the objective style, they use the imperative and friendly styles; and instead of an audience of managers, they have an audience of workers and customers who actually perform the tasks described.

While a set of instructions is simply a list of steps that tell a user what to do, a manual also includes a parts list, maintenance suggestions, troubleshooting advice, service center information, and a description of correct operation. Your assignment in this chapter will be to write either a set of instructions or a brief manual.

THE BASICS

The major difference between process descriptions and instructions is the audience. Instructions are for workers to perform tasks. Process descriptions are for managers and researchers who want to know what workers do, or in the case of a researcher, how and why a process occurs. Remember, the audience in this chapter is the worker who follows instructions and performs operations. Many situations call for instructions and manuals: computer operators following instructions for new job tasks, auto mechanics referring to manuals to discover how to repair new models, and consumers using instructions to put together a product.

ESTABLISHING THE WRITING SITUATION

Manuals do more than provide instructions. They include parts lists, maintenance suggestions, troubleshooting advice, lists of service centers where a product can be fixed, and descriptions of correct product operation.

You should distinguish a manual from a simple set of instructions. A set of instructions is a list of commands accompanied by a visual depiction of parts and steps. Instructions are usually just part of a manual. Instructions can be separate documents for retail products such as bookcases, ceiling fans, and toys, but when they are, the document is a simple one- or two-page list of commands with a labeled drawing.

Identify instructions and operations manuals that you have either used or seen. Include the product, product type (industrial or retail), intended audience, and the style. See Example 1, and then fill in information for Examples 2, 3, and 4.

Example 1

Product	ceiling fan
Product Type	retail/household/low price/simple
Audience	homeowner/apartment dweller
Style	imperative/visual aids

Example 2

Product
Product Type
Audience
Style

Example 3

Product
Product Type
Audience
Style

Example 4

Product
Product Type
Audience
Style

Discuss with your instructor how to use this information to define a writing situation to develop instructions or a manual.

DECIDING ON A DOCUMENT TYPE

Four documents you should know about are owner's manuals, technical manuals, user's manuals, and a plain set of instructions.

Owner's Manual

Manuals include descriptions of parts, maintenance advice, troubleshooting tips, service center locations, and correct operating and usage information. If necessary, they also include operating and assembly instructions. You are probably familiar with owner's manuals. They contain the following sections:

- Introduction (often a congratulations to the purchaser and a brief overall description of important product characteristics)
- Mechanism description of the basic parts of the product

- Process description of how the product operates
- Instructions on how to perform various operations
- Troubleshooting suggestions
- General maintenance advice

Examine an owner's manual and see if it contains all these sections.

Technical Manual

A technical manual usually has more job-related technical information; it is intended for professional users. For example, a service manual for an automobile or a computer contains far more technical information than that in an owner's manual. It is filled with technical specifications, charts, drawings, and schematics that do not make much sense to average consumers. Technical manuals leave out the introductory matter found in owner's manuals. They concentrate instead on technical information about parts, operations, troubleshooting, and maintenance.

User's Manual

A third type of manual is the user's manual. It can be for a professional or the consumer audience. As its name implies, it explains how to use a product. It is sometimes referred to as an operator's manual or an instruction manual. It contains instructions on how to operate a piece of machinery or a product, such as a computer or a copying machine, and it may contain a section on troubleshooting.

Instructions

The fourth type of document is a plain set of instructions. Instructions may consist of assembly, operating, installation, maintenance, or troubleshooting procedures. They can be single sheets for simple products or small pamphlets for complicated products. Remember, instructions can appear in many documents in addition to manuals. You will find them on the packaging of products, in letters, in articles of magazines such as *Workbench* and *Popular Mechanics,* and do-it-yourself books such as the Time–Life series on home maintenance.

DEVELOPING AN APPROPRIATE STYLE

The style used in manuals and instructions depends on readers' needs. Consider consumer-oriented documents first.

Automobile owner's manuals include several styles. The friendly style in the introduction persuades purchasers that they have made a wise purchase. The imperative and objective styles used in the body quickly and clearly explain procedures and facts. Drawings and charts make understanding important points a lot easier. The introduction in this automobile owner's manual is in friendly style to compliment readers for purchasing products:

Thank you for choosing a NISSAN. We are sure you will be happy you did. This manual has been prepared to help you understand the operation and maintenance of your vehicle so that you may enjoy many miles of driving pleasure.

The manual covers areas of the product the consumer will be involved with daily:

> Economy Hints
> Safety Checks
> Starting and Operating
> Comfort and Convenience Features
> Emergency Procedures
> Emission Control System
> Maintenance Schedule
> Do-It-Yourself Tips (Oil and Coolant Changing)
> Appearance and Interior Care
> Specifications (Gas-Tank Capacity, etc.)

The "Economy Hints" section of the manual is written in the imperative style (Figure 6-1). Other sections of the manual contain visual reinforcement

Economy Hints

Normal driving saves fuel and money.

Severe driving wastes fuel and money.

Operational economy is one of the outstanding features of your NISSAN. By developing the following good driving habits, even greater economy may be attained.

1. Do not pump the accelerator. Gently depress until the desired speed has been attained and then try to maintain that speed.
2. Always drive your vehicle in the gear which properly suits driving conditions.
3. Maintain moderate speeds on the highway. Speeds above 50 MPH (80 km/ h) will considerably increase fuel consumption.
4. Maintain a safe distance behind other vehicles. Avoid sudden stops. This will reduce wear on brake linings and pads and save fuel, as extra fuel is required to accelerate back to driving speed.
5. Excessive engine revving while the vehicle is stopped increases fuel consumption.
6. Keep the tires at the recommended inflation pressures for longer tire life and fuel economy.
7. Keep your engine tuned-up and follow the recommended periodic maintenance schedule. This will increase the life of all parts and lower operating costs.
8. Check your tires regularly for abnormal wear. Wheels that are out of alignment cause the tires to drag, resulting in premature tire wear and additional fuel consumption.
9. Use the air conditioner only when necessary. When cruising at highway speeds, it is more economical to use the air conditioner and leave the windows closed to reduce drag.
10. 4 × 4: When driving on a dry, paved road, it is recommended that the transfer control lever be set at "2H." Driving in "4H" or "4L" will cause additional fuel consumption and noise, as well as unnecessary tire and component wear.

FIGURE 6-1 Example of Imperative Style (Courtesy of Nissan Motor Co., Ltd., Tokyo, Japan.)

RADIO

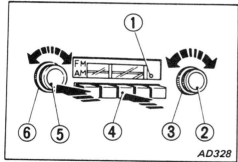

① ST AUTO indicator (AM-FM stereo radio only)
② Manual tuning control knob
③ Speaker balance control (AM-FM stereo radio only)
④ Band selector (2 band radio only) and tuning push button
⑤ On-Off and volume control knob
⑥ Tone control knob

The radio has five selector buttons for station and band selection. Other stations may be selected by the manual tuning knob.
The ignition key must be in "ON" or "ACC" position.

AM-FM stereo radio
The ST (stereo) AUTO indicator will be illuminated during FM stereo reception.

When receiving a stereo broadcast in mountainous areas, etc. where FM is weak, the radio will automatically change from stereo to monaural to prevent static from entering the radio. At this time, the ST AUTO indicator shuts off. (AM-FM stereo radio only)

SETTING PUSH BUTTONS

1. Pull the selector button straight out until it stops. Tune in the station you want with the manual tuning knob of the radio dial.
2. After the station is clearly tuned in, push the selector button straight in until it stops, then release it.
3. Repeat steps 1 and 2 for the remaining station selector buttons.

FIGURE 6–2 Combination Imperative/Objective Style (Courtesy of Nissan Motor Co., Ltd., Tokyo, Japan.)

and a combination of the imperative and objective styles (Figure 6–2). The manual concludes with charts on dimensions, weight, and related subjects (Figures 6–3 and 6–4).

Some manuals assume that readers are uninformed, whereas others assume that readers have some technical expertise. Automobile manufacturers want owners to understand and use manuals to reduce breakdowns from improper operation during the warranty period. They put readers in the lower end of the 3 to 5 scale by including obvious information about reading the speedometer and using the pushbutton radio to avoid any possibility of owners' misunderstanding.

Gas Station Information

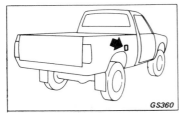

GS360

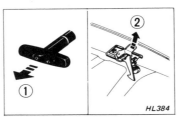

HL384

THL012

FUEL FILLER CAP

It is located at right rear side of the vehicle.
Do not forget to replace the filler cap after refilling.

FUEL RECOMMENDATION

	Outside temperature	Fuel	Octane (Gasoline)/Cetane (Diesel) number (minimum)	
			AKI (Anti-Knock Index) number $\frac{R+M}{2}$	Research octane number RON
Gasoline engine	–	Unleaded gasoline*1	87	91
Diesel engine	above 20° F (–7°C)	2-D Diesel fuel or equivalent blended diesel fuel*2	42	
	below 20° F (–7°C)	1-D Diesel fuel or equivalent blended diesel fuel*2		

*1: Refer to "Oil and fuel recommendation" in "Do-it-yourself" for gasolines containing alcohol.
*2: Check with the service station operator to be sure you get the properly blended fuel.

Do not use a fuel other than that specified above. The fuel filler opening of the gasoline engine models is designed for use with an unleaded fuel nozzle [nozzle diameter less than 0.84 in (21.3 mm)] only.

HOOD RELEASE

Pull the hood lock release handle ① located below the instrument panel; the hood will then spring up slightly. Move the lever ② at the front of the hood with your fingertips and raise the hood.

Insert the hood stay into the hole in the underside of the hood to support the hood while it is open.

When closing the hood, disengage the stay while supporting the hood, then slowly close the hood and make sure it locks into place.

RECOMMENDED TIRE INFLATION PRESSURE

● **Tire pressure should be checked when tires are COLD.**

Unit: psi (kPa, kg/cm²)

Tire size		Load		Moderate	Heavy
4×2	P195/75R14	Front		24 (165, 1.7)	24 (165, 1.7)
		Rear		24 (165, 1.7)	32 (221, 2.25)
	P205/75R14	Front		24 (165, 1.7)	24 (165, 1.7)
		Rear		24 (165, 1.7)	28 (196, 2.0)
	LT195/75R14	Front	(Single tire)	36 (245, 2.5)	36 (245, 2.5)
		Rear	(Dual tire)	65 (441, 4.5)	65 (441, 4.5)
				36 (245, 2.5)	36 (245, 2.5)
4×4	P185/80R14	Front		27 (188, 1.9)	27 (188, 1.9)
		Rear		27 (188, 1.9)	27 (188, 1.9)
	P215/75R15	Front		28 (196, 2.0)	28 (196, 2.0)
		Rear		28 (196, 2.0)	28 (196, 2.0)
	P225/75R15	Front		28 (196, 2.0)	28 (196, 2.0)
		Rear		28 (196, 2.0)	28 (196, 2.0)

14-1

FIGURE 6-3 General Service Information (Courtesy of Nissan Motor Co., Ltd., Tokyo, Japan.)

OIL APPLICATION CHART FOR ALL NISSAN MODELS

To provide proper lubrication during all weather conditions, the charts shown below should be closely followed.

LUBRICANTS

GEAR OIL SPECIFICATIONS

Manual Transmission/ Transaxle	All models except those below	API GL-4
	300ZX Turbo (BW T-5)	API GL-4 (SAE 80W-90) or Type Dexron ATF
	Diesel models with transmission (not for trans-axle)	API GL-3 (SAE Viscosity number 90 or 140) or API GL-4
Differential	All models	API GL-5

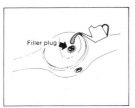

Filler plug

ENGINE OIL SPECIFICATIONS

Non-Turbo Engine	API SF (Energy Conserving Oils)**
Turbo Engine	API SF/CC or SF/CD***
Diesel Engine	API SE/CC, SF/CC, SE/CD, SF/CD or CD

** Non-energy conserving oils or API SE grade oils can also be used in 1982 and before models.
*** API SE grade oils can also be used in 1983 and before models.

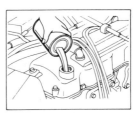

SAE VISCOSITY NUMBER

GEAR OIL   DIESEL ENGINE OIL   *GASOLINE ENGINE OIL

SPECIAL CAUTIONS:

- Using incorrect viscosity motor oil could lead to poor lubrication during cold weather, resulting in engine damage.
- Viscosity modifier type oil additives *should not* be used in any Nissan engine.
- When changing grades of oil (i.e., 5W-30 to 10W-30), it is recommended that the oil filter be replaced at the same time.

FIGURE 6-4 General Service Information (Courtesy of Nissan Motor Co., Ltd., Tokyo, Japan.)

Other manuals assume that readers are knowledgeable. They put readers in the upper end of the 3 to 5 range. The following documentation of a computer printer requires familiarity with the computer:

The Apricorn 80-Column Video Display is a plug-in circuit board for the Apple 11e computer that provides the capacity to expand the standard 40-column display to a full 80 columns. The 64K version provides 80-column display capability as well as 64 bytes of additional RAM (random access memory). This extends the RAM capacity of your Apple 11e from 64K to 128K. A unique feature of the 80-column video display/1K version is that it can be upgraded to the 64K version with our 64K Upgrade Kit.

The 80-Column Video Display can greatly enhance your Apple 11e computer. Word processing now becomes easier because you can see on the screen exactly what will be printed. Financial spreadsheet programs can display twice as much information on the screen at one time. Applesoft and Integer BASIC users will find additional editing features useful for their program development. The 40- and 80-column video displays can easily be switched back and forth under keyboard or program control.

The reader must know computer-related terms and applications to understand the documentation. The writer assumes that purchasers of an 80-column card will own a computer and be familiar with hardware as well as software such as word processing and spreadsheet. This manual does not contain the friendly style because informed readers want facts explained in the objective style.

Installation instructions are presented in the imperative style, but the writer assumes here that readers know virtually nothing about the internal operating parts of a computer:

---

1. Turn off the power to your Apple 11e. The power light on the lower left corner of the keyboard should not be illuminated.
2. Remove the cover on your Apple 11e by pulling up on the rear corners of the cover until a slight pop is heard. Pull up enough to separate the fasteners, then stop.

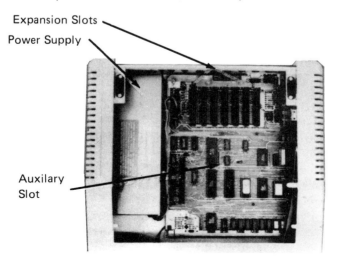

Expansion Slots

Power Supply

Auxilary Slot

3. Slide the cover rearward away from the Apple 11e. You should now be able to see the interior of your Apple 11e (Figure 1). Check inside to be sure that the red light in the back is *not* on. If it is, the power is still on and should be turned off.

4. Position your Apple 11e computer comfortably in front of you with the keyboard nearest you. Familiarize yourself with the various components of the Apple 11e computer. See Figure 1 for details. These will be referred to in later installation steps.

Using imperative style and supporting visuals, the writer carefully guides the (now-assumed-to-be) uninformed readers along.

Simple products have brief documentation, usually just a set of instructions on installation or operation. These include a numbered parts list and an exploded drawing (Figure 6–5), assembly and (if necessary) operations instructions (Figure 6–6), and precautions, all amounting to a total of one or two pages. Brief documentation quickly enables consumers to assemble, install, and make products operational.

Documents for professionals give technical details of products because these readers are knowledgeable about product technology. Writers of these target the top rung of the 3 to 5 range. Instructions, descriptions, explanations, and visuals have to be clear, thorough, and accurate. Automobile service manuals provide a good illustration of documents for the professional.

Service manuals are written for professional mechanics, not for car owners, although owners may purchase them if they like. The introduction of the service manual is strikingly different from the owner's manual introduction:

This service manual has been prepared primarily for the purpose of assisting service personnel in providing effective service and maintenance. This manual includes procedures for maintenance, adjustments, removal and installation, disassembly and assembly of components, and troubleshooting.

All information, illustrations, and specifications contained in this manual are based on the latest product information available at the time of publication. If your NISSAN model differs from the specifications contained in this manual, consult your NISSAN/DATSUN dealer for information.

Using the objective style, the writer includes a "General Information" section with information on dimensions, model variation, identification number, lifting points and towing, special service tools, and tightening torque of standard bolts—areas of concern primarily to professionals.

The writer organizes the main body of the manual according to the parts and systems of the automobile, including engine, clutch, differential, transmission, suspension system, brake system, electrical systems, steering system, body and frame, and heater and air conditioner. Some sections of the manual also include diagnostic flowcharts which instruct the mechanic how to diagnose symptoms in the automobile (Figure 6–7). Each section contains illustrated instructions on how to perform tasks of adjustment, installation, removal, and diagnostic procedures (Figure 6–8).

Manuals for professionals employ objective and imperative styles. Manuals for consumers also use objective and imperative styles, but they soften information with the friendly style because they are sales documents.

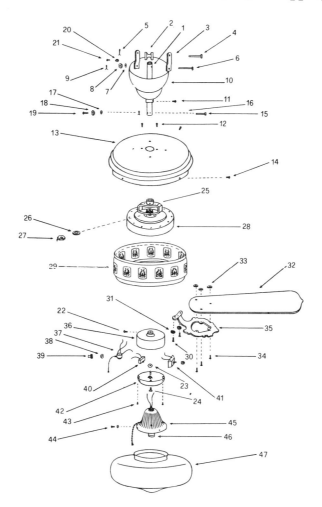

DECORATIVE CEILING FAN PART LIST

Part No.	Description	Qty.	Part No.	Description	Qty.	Part No.	Description	Qty.
1.	downrod	1	17.	lock-washer	1	33.	nut	12
2.	rubber wheel	1	18.	nut	1	34.	screw	12
3.	downrod shackle	2	19.	securing bolt	1	35.	blade holder	4
4.	pin	1	20.	ground wire cup	1	36.	switch housing	1
5.	split-pin	1	21.	ground wire screw	1	37.	on/off switch (REVERSE)	1
6.	securing bolt	1	22.	screw	1	38.	nut for switch	1
7.	lock-washer	1	23.	nut	1	39.	screw for switch	1
8.	nut	1	24.	plug	1	40.	condenser	1
9.	split-pin	1	25.	yoke	1	41.	motor speed control	1
10.	upper canopy	1	26.	lock-washer	1	42.	cap switch housing	1
11.	screw	1	27.	nut	1	43.	screw	2
12.	screw	2	28.	motor	1	44.	screw and nut	3
13.	top housing	1	29.	bottom housing	1	45.	lower canopy	1
14.	screw	3	30.	screw	8	46.	light kit	1
15.	pin	1	31.	lock-washer	8	47.	globe	1
16.	split-pin	1	32.	blades	4			

FIGURE 6–5   Parts List/Exploded Drawing

ASSEMBLY INSTRUCTIONS

(use parts list for number reference)

MOTOR HOUSING ASSEMBLY

1. Remove two bolts from top of yoke (#25). Remove securing pin (#15), and down rod securing bolt (#19).

2. Attach top housing (#13) to top of yoke with two bolts that were removed. Tighten bolts!

3. Attach bottom housing (#29) to top housing with three small screws (#14), which will be found in screw and bolt packaging kit.

MOTOR HOUSING ASSEMBLY IS COMPLETED

DOWN ROD ASSEMBLY

1. Slide down rod (#1) through hole of upper canopy (#10) as pictured in parts.

2. Insert end of down rod (#1) into hole at top of yoke (#25). Line up holes of yoke with holes in lower down rod and insert down rod pin (#15) and secure with carter key. Then secure further by screwing in and tightening down rod securing bolt (#19).

DOWN ROD ASSEMBLY IS COMPLETED

BLADE AND BLADE HOLDER ASSEMBLY

Connect blades (#32) to blade holders (#35) with screws and nuts found in screw packaging kit.

Do not attach blades and blade holders to fan until fan has been securely hung to ceiling. This eliminates the risk of breaking blades during installation.

FAN IS READY TO INSTALL IN CEILING

FIGURE 6-6 Assembly and Operations Instructions

INSTALLING FAN TO CEILING

1. Screw the screw hook which comes packaged with the universal hanging kit securely into joist at selected point of installation. A J-Hook with locking washer and bolt may be optionally used when installing fan in electrical junction box that is well secured in ceiling. Electrical power source should be off during this procedure.

2. Hang rubber wheel at top of down rod on J-hook. Connect color coded wires of ceiling fan to wires of power source and secure with wire nuts.

3. Push upper canopy (#10) up flush with ceiling surface, and tighten securing screw (#11).

4. Attach blade holders to motor of fan using enclosed screws, washers, and nuts. (#30, #31, #33)

YOU MAY NOW TURN ON POWER SOURCE AND OPERATE FAN.

HERES HOW YOUR TRADITION FAN IS OPERATED

1. Pull the ON-OFF chain on switch (#36), and fan will begin to turn. Pull the chain again and the fan will be turned off.

2. REVERSE FEATURE — Every other time that fan is turned on, it will be turning in reverse air motion. This allows you to circulate warm air flow up circulating warm air off of ceiling and down into living area of room. This feature can be used as a energy saving procedure during cool weather.

3. VARIABLE SPEED CONTROL SWITCH — can be found on side of switch housing. This allows you to control the R.P.M. of fan blades. The Tradition fan can also be turned off by variable control switch.

LIGHT KIT INSTALLATION

1. Remove plug (#24) from switch housing cap (#42). Remove the switch housing cap (#42). by removing two small screws on bottom of cap.

2. Thread wires of lower canopy (#45) through hole left by removal of plug. Screw threads at top of lower canopy into plug hole of switch housing cap.

INJECTION PUMP CONTROL SYSTEM

TROUBLE DIAGNOSES AND CORRECTIONS

TROUBLE-SHOOTING CHART

Case 1

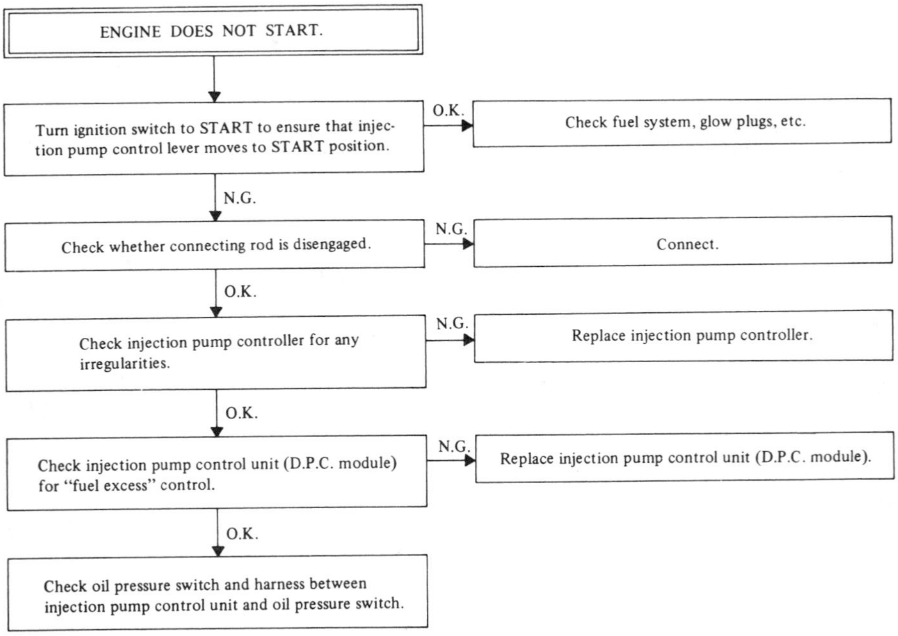

FIGURE 6-7 Diagnostic Flowchart (Courtesy of Nissan Motor Co., Ltd., Tokyo, Japan.)

CHARGING SYSTEM

DISASSEMBLY

1. Remove vacuum pump (Diesel engine model only).

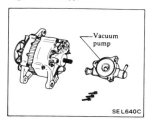

2. Remove through-bolts and the separate front cover and rear cover.

Gasoline engine model

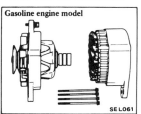

Diesel engine model

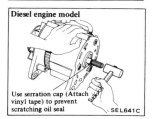

Use serration cap (Attach vinyl tape) to prevent scratching oil seal

3. Remove pulley and fan.
(1) Place rear cover side of rotor in a vice.
(2) Remove pulley nut.

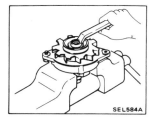

4. Remove setscrews from bearing retainer.

5. Remove attaching nuts and take out stator assembly.

Rotor

Pull rear bearing off from rotor assembly with a press or bearing puller.

Once removed, bearing cannot be reused. Replace with a new one.

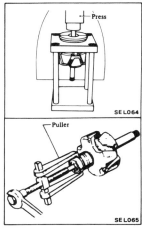

Stator

Disconnect stator coil leas wires from diode terminals

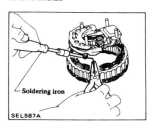

Soldering iron

Replacement of oil seal
(Only diesel engine model)

If oil leaks from oil seal or any abnormalities are found after inspection, replace oil seal.

1. Pry off oil seal.

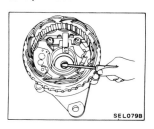

2. Apply engine oil to seal and install oil seal in position.

FIGURE 6-8 Diagnostic Flowchart (Courtesy of Nissan Motor Co., Ltd., Tokyo, Japan.)

MAKING IT FIT: SITUATION, DOCUMENT, AND STYLE

Let's resume your situation in Chapter Five—you are a new Mapple Corporation employee who wrote a process description of a cathode ray tube (CRT) for a Monitor-Project Team. Also, Mr. Anderson, the vice president of marketing, asked you to write a process description of a new computer system for his department. You had to revise both reports, but afterward, your readers liked them. You are starting to like writing.

You have now been employed with Mapple for three months. The Monitor Project Team has adopted the CRT instead of the LCD for the Mapple 111. Mr. Anderson's Marketing Department is using your computer system procedures report to train themselves on the new computer system.

Now you learn that Mapple's chief competitor, Data Specific Corporation, is planning to release its new computer to market three weeks before the Mapple 111 will be introduced. This is a shock to your company because it had no knowledge that Data Specific was so close to completing its new model. The executives at Mapple are in a panic. Fortunately, the Mapple 111 is complete except for user documentation.

You attend an emergency meeting of the Mapple 111 Documentation Team. You learn that Mapple will try to beat Data Specific to market with its new model. The Documentation Team is playing a key role in this goal. All documentation will have to be produced as soon as possible. You are assigned to write the chapter in the Mapple 111 Owner's Manual that introduces major parts of the Mapple 111 system to owners. You are excited at the opportunity to write such an important document.

You make a prewriting checklist:

> *Audience:* uninformed end user in the low-to-middle 3 to 5 range
> *Placement:* after Chapter 1, entitled "System Assembly"
> *Style:* second person, plain English, defined computer terms
> *Length:* similar in length to Chapter 1
> *Format:* explanations, listings, visuals
> *Organization:* step by step and part by part

Next you go to the Mapple 111 prototype, examine its parts, and read through the engineering operations manual. You operate the machine and take notes. From notes, you develop sections for your future document. You ask yourself: What information will end-users need to understand how the system operates? After thinking this over for a while, you develop a list of subject headings for the chapter:

> *Parts of the system*
> Description of how parts operate
> Suggestions on care for parts
> Instructions on how the user should operate parts

Now you divide the parts of the system into two types: ones the user interacts with directly and ones the user interacts with indirectly:

> *Parts the user directly interacts with:*
> Keyboard
> Monitor
> Disk drive
> Floppy disks
>
> *Parts the user interacts with indirectly:*
> Microprocessor
> Main memory
> Speaker

You decide to emphasize items in the first list, but you feel that items in the second list should be explained throughout the chapter as well. Now you decide to begin the chapter with a brief definition/description of the parts of the computer, emphasizing the keyboard, monitor, disk drive, and floppy disk, and mentioning the importance of the microprocessor, main memory, and speaker. After a little more fine-tuned thinking, you realize the major headings of your chapter:

> Parts: Definition and Description of Functions
> Instructions for Using the Disk Drive
> Starting the System
> Keyboard Use
> Monitor Use
> Care and Maintenance of Parts

You know that the chapter will begin with a description of parts, but you are not sure of the best order of other topics. Should the sequence be in the same order the user will follow when operating the system? Are there topics the user will need to be informed about, such as care and maintenance of parts, before attempting to operate the system—should these elements precede the others? You decide that users should know about care and maintenance procedures before trying to operate the system. After care and maintenance, you will sequence topics in the order the user will follow to operate the system. You make a new list of topics:

> Parts: Definition/Description of Functions
> Care and Maintenance of Parts
> Disk and Disk Drive Operation
> Starting the System
> Keyboard Operation
> Monitor

You decide that the last two items overlap. Keyboard operation includes monitor use because each time a key is hit, users look for some output on the monitor screen. You decide to blend these two sections:

> Keyboard/Monitor Operation

You continue examining your list of topics, making decisions about them until you form the following outline:

> 1. Parts: Definition/Description of Functions
>   Most important parts for the user to know:
>   Disk drive
>   Floppy disk
>   Keyboard
>   Monitor
>   Other important parts:
>   Microprocessor
>   Main memory
>   Speaker
> 2. Care and Maintenance of Parts
>   Care of hardware
>   Care of software
> 3. Disk and Disk Drive Operation
> 4. System Startup
> 5. Monitor/Keyboard Operation
>   Monitor: turning it on and cursor control

Keyboard: upper and lower case, standard keys, special function keys

After reviewing the outline, you decide to write the rough draft of the manual chapter.

Main Parts of the Mapple III System

The four most important parts of the Mapple III system are:

Disk Drive—a machine that stores and transmits information generated on the computer

Floppy Disk—a spherical, record-like recording medium, encased in a square paper envelope, which "holds" the information deposited on it from the disk drive

Keyboard—typewriter-like keys that enable you to program the computer and interact with computer programs by pressing certain appropriate keys

Monitor—a cathode ray tube (which looks like a television screen) that creates visual output from the keyboard and the disk/disk drive.

Three other important parts of the Mapple III you need to understand, even though you will not be using them directly, are the following:

Microprocessor—the electronic device that actually translates keyboard commands into instructions the computer can carry out

Main Memory—another electronic device, which works closely with the microprocessor to store data in the computer while it is running programs. Unlike the disk/disk drive system, which stores data permanently, the main memory can store data only while the computer is turned on

Speaker—a third electronic device, which emits sounds such as beeps in response to correct or incorrect use of the keyboard.

Besides these seven basic parts, there are other peripheral devices, such as printers, modems, and certain component cards (such as interface and expansion devices), that you may need to know about later. But for now, you need only a general understanding of these seven parts, especially the first four.

Care and Maintenance of the Parts

Hardware

Except for the floppy disks, all the parts mentioned above are called hardware—the electronic devices that comprise the computer system. Software comprises the data contained on floppy disks (and other input media, such as magnetic tape and hard disks), which enable the computer to function. There are a few simple care and maintenance procedures that you should follow to ensure the safety and longevity of the system hardware:

1. Avoid placing your computer in direct sunlight or near extreme heat or cold.

2. Keep moisture away from all hardware.
3. Hook up your system to a grounded outlet, preferably connected to a surge protector; avoid circuits loaded with appliances or other electronic devices.
4. Keep air vents on the sides of your computer open to freely circulating air.
5. Make sure that your system is not exposed to impurities such as dust or dirt.

Software

Here are a few tips on caring for your software:

1. Hold floppy disks by their protective jackets; don't touch the disk itself.
2. When labeling disks, use a felt-tip pen and avoid pressing down too hard.
3. When storing disks, avoid bending them or attaching them with paper clips; store them upright in a disk holder and away from sunlight, moisture, and extremes of heat and cold.
4. Keep disks away from magnetic or electrical devices, especially telephones, television sets, and large motors.

Disk and Disk Drive Operation

Before you can operate your computer, you must know how to load a floppy disk into your disk drive:

1. Make sure that the red light on the front of your disk drive is OFF before loading or unloading disks.
2. Lift up the door to the disk drive and be sure that the drive is empty before loading the disk: if it is not, remove the disk that is in the drive by carefully sliding it out.
3. Remove from its envelope the disk you wish to insert into the drive, and holding it by its jacket, locate the label and oblong slot on the floppy disk.
4. With the oblong slot in front and the label up, carefully slide the disk into the disk drive: do not force or bend the disk.
5. After the disk has been inserted into the drive, close the drive door until it ''clicks'' shut.

System Startup

After you have loaded your disk drive, you can start up the computer system by following these procedures:

1. Turn on your monitor and allow it time to warm up.
2. Refer to the hardware diagram in Chapter 1 to locate the ON switch; press the switch to the ON position.
3. Listen for the ''beep'' which indicates that the system is on, and observe the red light on your disk drive glow as the computer loads information from the floppy disk into its memory; when the whirring stops and the light goes out, the computer has successfully loaded the software from the disk.

4. Look at the monitor screen to read the prompt for the software you have loaded.

Keyboard Operation

The most important keys on the Mapple 111 keyboard are the following:

RETURN *key:* Moves the cursor to the next line
Indicates the end of a written command

Space bar: Generates a space in the text of the program

DELETE *key:* Erases information from a program moving right to left

CAPS LOCK key: When pressed, it makes all alphabetical characters come up on the screen in upper case; all other characters function in lower case

SHIFT key: When held down, forces all keys to function in upper case (SHIFT keys do not lock)

LEFT ARROW key: Moves the cursor to the left

RIGHT ARROW key: Moves the cursor to the right

DOWN ARROW key: Moves the cursor down

UP ARROW key: Moves the cursor up

TAB key: Moves the cursor to the next tab setting

CONTROL key: Used in combination with other keys to perform important program functions such as printing, copying, saving, and deleting data from programs

ESC key: Used in combination with other keys to exit or stop programs quickly

---

After reading through your draft, you feel you have done a decent job, but you want an objective evaluation. You think of Mr. Anderson, the Marketing VP for whom you wrote the brief computer manual, and decide to ask either him or one of his marketing people for suggestions on how to edit and revise for improvement.

You understand the importance of having an uninformed reader review the material, so Mr. Anderson or someone in his department seems a logical choice. However, you realize that you must provide a list of questions to help the reviewer focus on pertinent aspects of the chapter. Mr. Anderson agrees to have one of his employees review the chapter. You provide him with the following list of questions to guide the review:

1. Do the content and format of the chapter provide a clear explanation of how to use the basic parts of the Mapple III computer? In what sections of the chapter do improvements need to be made in either area? If there is a general problem with the format and/or scope of content in the chapter, can you identify what it is?

2. Does the information in this chapter seem appropriate considering that it follows the chapter on assembling the Mapple III system? What specific information seems inappropriate? What information seems most appropriate?

3. Is the style understandable? Are computer terms defined adequately? Is the level of language too simplistic or overly complex? What suggestions do you have for improvements in the level of language? Is the second-person perspective effective?

4. Is the length of the chapter about right? Can you think of additional information that needs to be included? Is information presently included in the chapter that should be edited out or excluded?

5. Specifically, what aspects of the format need to be improved? Are explanations presented in a clearly structured manner? Are the listings of instructions clear and in parallel form? Where in the chapter should visuals be placed?

6. Are the step-by-step and part-by-part explanations effective in communicating desired information? Can you suggest any improvements in wording or sequencing of facts?

Now play the role of reviewer by answering the foregoing questions about the Mapple III chapter on introducing the basic parts of the computer system to the uninformed owner. After answering the reviewer questions, read through the chapter rough draft and consider each of the questions in the spaces provided below.

1. Content and format: clear on use of Mapple III parts?

2. Information: all appropriate? any inappropriate?

3. Language: understandable for the uninformed reader?

4. Details: sufficient or insufficient?

5. Structure: headings and subheadings parallel?
   properly sequenced?
   visuals well placed?

6. Explanations: wording and sequencing of steps clear?

You may wish to provide some additional suggestions for improvements.

CONSIDERING COST

Companies may use several methods to decide how much to spend on instructional documentation. Some products require at least a basic set of instructions or manual to ensure proper use. Beyond this basic cost, companies may decide to use manuals and instructions as promotional devices.

Competing brands of the same product may use elaborate instructional material to differentiate each other to boost sales. Management may look at the type of documentation that has traditionally accompanied their products and decide to stick with it. Some companies may simply look at their budgets and spend as much as they can afford. A final method is spending a percentage of sales revenue on documentation.

In most cases instructional documentation cost is a very low percentage of actual product cost and sales revenue (probably well below 5%). Customers buy products for benefits derived from product features. Good instructional documentation is important in the purchase decision of many products. But it is not the most important reason that people buy certain products.

CHAPTER ASSIGNMENT

For your assignment, choose a consumer product and write a short manual for an uninformed end user audience. Try to provide visuals of parts and steps of operation or assembly. Use the following outline to get started:

Identify the product, specific audience, purpose, and document type:

Product (Explain thoroughly)

Audience (Specify the characteristics of the typical user)

Purpose (Explain what the end user should learn)

Document Type (Specify the type of manual and explain its characteristics)

Establish your outline:

Introduction (Establish a rapport with the reader by congratulating him or her regarding purchase and provide brief introduction to the product)

Points of congratulations:

Most important points about the product:

Body

Mechanism Description: Describe major parts

Process Description: Explain central steps in operation

Instructions: List steps involved in assembly and operations, in command style

Troubleshooting: Explanation of common problems and methods for fixing them

General Maintenance Suggestions: Describe procedures for maintaining the product

Conclusion: Summarize main points about the product

Point 1

Point 2

Point 3

Now it is time to begin writing your rough draft. Here are a few tips to keep in mind:

1. Use the friendly style early in the document to develop a positive rapport with readers. Emphasize benefits that the product provides.

2. Explain only the major parts of the product in the mechanism description, and emphasize characteristics that you believe the consumer will need to know about. Include limitations of the product in this section, and any potential negative information as well as positive. Use a blend of friendly and objective styles. For example, address the consumer using the friendly style, and then describe the product using the objective style.

3. Emphasize in the process description major steps that you feel readers need most to know about. Describe steps in the objective style. Mention limitations or problems that users may have either understanding the process or completing the steps.

4. Provide thorough instructions on product assembly, installation, and operations. Use the imperative style, and include necessary cautions for readers to complete instructions safely.

5. Consider providing a troubleshooting chart that illustrates potential problems and suggested solutions.

6. Include a schedule of maintenance checks and procedures and a checklist of maintenance suggestions.

SEVEN

Memos and Letters

PREVIEW

Memos and letters communicate a central idea. Memos are written to employees about everyday business matters such as promotions, meeting announcements, and company policies. Letters are written to readers outside the company. Letters follow several formats. Major types are inquiry, reply, instructions, order, sales, claims, and adjustment. The styles used in both memos and letters are determined by the relationship of writer and reader and the writing situation.

In addition to communicating information to an intended reader, memos and letters are documents that communicate to any and all who read them how well an individual (writer or reader) is fulfilling job-related responsibilities. As you write, keep in mind political and legal implications of memos and letters.

Letters convey an image in addition to facts. Letters are part of public relations. Those outside judge company quality in part by the quality of documentation. All communication with customers and business associates should convey desired image. Since memos are internal, image is not as important a feature. Clear, concise communication is important in memos and letters.

THE BASICS

Letters and memos are frequently written on the job. Both are formal communications. Letters are written to readers outside a company. Memos are written to readers within a company. Both express messages with a single purpose.

MEMOS

Memo format consists of a heading and the message. Since both correspondents are members of the same company or department, letter elements such as inside and return address, salutation, and complimentary close are not included. The heading resembles the following:

INTEROFFICE MEMORANDUM

TO: cc:

FROM:

SUBJECT:

DATE:

The writer places the intended reader's name, and title if necessary, beside the "TO:." Beside the "cc:" the writer puts the names of people who will receive a copy. Quite often, the writer provides copies to supervisors. The writer's own name and title are placed beside the "FROM." Writers often handwrite their initials beside their typed name to authenticate memos.

The subject of the memo obviously goes beside "SUBJECT": it should be concisely written, but detailed enough for the reader to understand the exact subject clearly prior to reading the entire message. Some memos include a reference line (REFERENCE:) in addition to a subject line. The reference line contains a specific explanation of the subject line. All memos are dated.

ESTABLISHING THE WRITING SITUATION

Writing situations for memos always involve internal communications about company business. Messages are usually routine. Here are some examples:

Price increases: A purchasing manager writes a memo to an operations manager indicating that recent price increases require replacing a part currently used in manufacturing operations with a different, less expensive part.

New Employee: A personnel manager writes a memo to members of the Research and Development Department to introduce a new R&D employee.

Promotion: A company president issues a memo to the company to announce the promotion of an employee to a high administrative position.

Policy change: A department manager issues a memo to inform the staff of changes in salary raises.

DEVELOPING AN APPROPRIATE STYLE

Be prepared to answer the following questions about memos listed below:

• Are the subject and intended message in each clear?
• Is the relationship between writer and reader(s) evident?
• Does the style of writing in the memos reveal anything about the relationship between writer and reader?
• What improvements would you suggest in any of these examples, and how would your improvements achieve better communication?

The first memo announces a promotion—it is an outline of professional experience and credentials.

TO: Company Staff
FROM: G.D. Poindexter
SUBJECT: Management Announcement
DATE: April 5, 1989

I am pleased to announce the promotion of Gregory Hines to the position of Director of Finance at our Cleveland office.

Mr. Hines, as many of you know, has been Director of New Accounts for the past three years. Prior to that, he served as Associate Director of New Accounts for two years. Greg joined our organization as a manager trainee and quickly moved into the New Accounts division as an account representative.

Greg's credentials include an MBA, with a concentration in finance from the University of Pittsburg. He earned a bachelor of science in business administration degree from Boston College.

Join me in congratulating Greg on his latest success.

Message clear?

Evident relationship?

Style?

Improvements?

The second is a meeting announcement—it is a terse message consisting of date, time, and room.

TO: Marketing Communications Department
FROM: Bob Richards
SUBJECT: Departmental Meeting
REF: The Addison Account
DATE: September 26, 1989

We have scheduled a meeting as follows:

FRIDAY, OCTOBER 7, 1989

1:00 PM

CONFERENCE ROOM 3

Please be there.

Message clear?

Evident relationship?

Style?

Improvements?

The third is a request for article submissions—it is a two-part message: the preface is a thank-you note for past accomplishments and an announcement of future mailings; the second part is the request for submissions.

```
TO:        All Correspondents and Contributors
FROM:      Kevin Roseberry
SUBJECT:   Next Edition of Viewpoint
REF:       Needed Submissions
DATE:      November 15, 1989
```

Thanks for helping make 1988 a successful year. Articles throughout our latest volume have been very high in quality. Our penultimate issue for this volume is just off the presses and should be to you in two weeks.

I need more articles for our year-end issue, and quite frankly, I am running out of time. Anything you can send me on activities in your departments will be of great value. Include black-and-white pictures and any biographical information you can muster on authors and subjects.

Can I have something from you by November 29?

Message clear?

Evident relationship?

Style?

Improvements?

Discuss your evaluations of each memo with your instructor. Does each serve its situation well?

LETTERS

You have all written letters to your friends and parents, so the general format of letters should be familiar. The format for business letters is not very different. The format for a business letter consists of the following items:

>*Heading:* Return address and date.
>
>*Inside Address:* Name and address of the reader.
>
>*Salutation:* Make the salutation as specific as possible—address the person by title and name. When the name is not known, address the person by title: Dear Customer, Dear Doctor, Dear Consumer. Avoid the sexist expression "Dear Sir." Use "Dear Person:" or "Ladies and Gentlemen:" instead.
>
>*Body of the letter:* Main paragraphs of information.
>
>*Enclosures line:* Indicates number of items enclosed with the letter.
>
>*Complimentary closing:* Sincerely; Respectfully; Sincerely yours; or whatever is appropriate.
>
>*Signature:* author's name handwritten.
>
>*Typed name of the writer.*
>
>*Author's title:* President, Manager, etc.; this is optional.

The parts of the business letter may be positioned as demonstrated in the example on page 131.

Another arrangement is to align all elements on the left. Aligning everything on the left is easier to format on a word processor.

You may include a subject line (SUBJECT:) above the salutation to prepare the reader for your message. If you give copies of the letter to anyone else, you should include a copy line (cc:) at the bottom of the page aligned to the left. Paragraphs may be indented, but current practice is to skip lines between paragraphs instead of indenting them.

ESTABLISHING THE WRITING SITUATION

Seven major types of letters include the following:

1. *Inquiry:* The writer composes a letter to request information from a company.
2. *Reply:* A company employee composes a letter in response to an inquiry.
3. *Instructions:* A company employee provides instructions for a company product or service.
4. *Order:* The writer places an order for company goods or services by writing a letter.
5. *Sales:* A company salesperson or marketing department composes a letter offering a product or service for sale.
6. *Claim:* The writer has a claim against a company and writes a letter to explain the circumstances of the claim. (This may be an insurance claim or a claim based on a poorly made product or poorly delivered service.)
7. *Adjustment:* The company responds to a claim letter by issuing an adjustment letter that explains how the claim will or will not be satisfied.

HEADING

Return Address
Date

INSIDE ADDRESS

Name and address of the reader

SALUTATION

Dear Person: (Use a more specific name or title if possible)

Body: Concise and courteous message

CLOSING

Sincerely yours,

SIGNATURE
Typed Name of Writer
TITLE (optional)

Enclosures:2

BUSINESS LETTER FORMAT

DEVELOPING AN APPROPRIATE STYLE

The seven types of business letters have a checklist of requirements. The letter of inquiry should contain the following information:

- A statement of the purpose of the inquiry in the first sentence
- Concrete and specific questions regarding the inquiry
- A statement of appreciation for information requested

An example:

444 Triplet Street
Roxanne, TX 42111
August 25, 1989

Frank L. Beard, President
Alpha, Incorporated
125 Megahertz Drive
Phoenix, AR 70004

Dear Mr. Beard:

I would like to know the following characteristics about spatial light modulators (SLMs) manufactured by your company:
　　　—design type
　　　—percentage of reflectivity of the dielectric mirror
　　　—color range of performance within the light spectrum
　　　—wattage of input response

Please include schematics, if possible. I appreciate your help.

Sincerely,

Edward Douglas

LETTER OF INQUIRY

Correspondents want to fulfill each other's needs: Beard's need is to sell an SLM; Douglas's need is to buy one. The letter is concise, specific, and conventionally polite.

A reply letter contains the following:

- Reference to the date and subject of the inquiry letter
- Clear and explicit responses to the items requested by the inquirer

An example:

Alpha, Incorporated
125 Megahertz Drive
Phoenix, AR 70004
September 4, 1989

Mr. Edward Douglas
444 Triplet Street
Roxanne, TX 42111

Dear Mr. Douglas:

Thank you for your letter of August 25 inquiring about our spatial light modulators (SLMs). Since we have so many different models, it is impossible for me to include the information you requested for all of them in one mailing. However, I have included information and schematics on several popular models. Here are the specs on our most popular model, the Alpha One:

    —liquid crystal design
    —99.995% reflectivity in the dielectric mirror
    —performance within the blue-green region of the light spectrum
    —input response range of 0.01 to 1.5 watts

I hope that you find this information useful. I look forward to hearing from you again when you have decided which one of our SLMs best suits your needs.

Sincerely,

Frank L. Beard, President
Alpha, Incorporated

REPLY LETTER

Again, note the polite, yet concise style of writing. Beard refers to Douglas's earlier letter, provides requested information, and uses polite, concise writing style.

A letter of instruction, a type of reply letter, is written to a customer who cannot understand how to operate a product after purchasing it. It contains the following:

- Explanation of the situation requiring the instructions
- Clear, detailed, and definite instructions
- Important additional information

An example:

Mapple Corporation
Silicon Drive
San Diego, CA 55223
October 15, 1989

Mr. Robert Smith
2235 Elm Street
Norwood, MA 02062

Dear Mr. Smith:

Thank you for your letter of September 28 requesting information on how to print hard copies of BASIC programs from your Mapple 11 computer. The procedure is quite simple to follow:

—Press PR#1 on your Mapple 11 keyboard to activate your printer
—Press PR#6 to activate the disk drive
—Use the standard BASIC PRINT command to print a hard copy
—Use PR#0 to disable the printer when you have finished

I hope these instructions provide you with the information you need. If not, please contact me personally 992-351-7263.

Yours truly,

Elliot Goldsmith,
Customer Service Representative

LETTER OF INSTRUCTION

Order letters place an order for a product or service. They should contain the following:

- Precise description of the product or service desired (catalog number, color, weight, size, model number, finish, type of service and number of times it is to be provided)
- Mode of payment (check, money order, COD, charge account, credit card)
- Transportation (parcel post, U.S. mail, railway, air express, trucking, padded van, courier)

An example:

6335 Morse Road
Columbus, OH 43215
December 15, 1989

Camel Industries
156 Northbrook Terrace
New York, New York 10010

Dear Salesperson:

Please send five Hudson Blankets: catalog number 2374-A, two in red, two in blue, and one in yellow. Be sure to send me the jumbo size (100 × 120).

Bill me as soon as possible, and I will remit a check in the full amount.

After you receive my check send the blankets prepaid, preferably by United Parcel Service.

If you have difficulty filling this order, please contact me at once.

Sincerely,

Miriam Daly, Proprietor
Sun Valley Sleep Shop

ORDER LETTER

Claims letters either express dissatisfaction with a product or service, or issue an insurance claim. They contain the following:

- Explicit statement about why you are writing
- Specific action you expect to be taken to resolve the problem
- Explanation of what you will be forced to do if the problem is not resolved

Here is an example of a claims letter:

113 Richland Road
Chicago, IL 67980
July 24, 1989

Mr. Ronald Phillips
Director of Employee Benefits
The Bisco Company
5000 Michigan Avenue
Chicago, IL 68532

Dear Mr. Phillips:

I need to find out what happened to my retirement check for the month of July 1989. I never received it.

I have called your office several times, but I have been unable to contact you. I am sure that you understand the financial bind a missing retirement check causes somebody like me who is on a fixed income.

I would like the check and an explanation immediately. If I do not receive a response from you within a week, I will take my case to our local legal aid agency, and I will call the local newspapers, television stations, and radio networks with a human interest story they may find quite interesting.

May I hear from you by July 28?

Respectfully,

Gladys Germaine

CLAIM LETTER

Gladys's style of writing is firm and concise. She fulfills requirements for claims letters. Is her threat too inflammatory? Or is it what Mr. Phillips needs to get motivated to take care of the problem?

Phillips contacts Gladys immediately, first by phone and then by letter to confirm their phone conversation. His letter is an adjustment letter. Adjustment letters should be written promptly, and they should contain the following two points of information:

- An explicit reference to the claim letter
- Clear statement of action to be taken on the claim

An example:

THE BISCO COMPANY

Division of Employee Benefits
5000 Michigan Avenue
Chicago, IL 68532

July 26, 1986

Ms. Gladys Germaine
113 Richland Road
Chicago, IL 67980

Dear Ms. Germaine:

We have examined our records for your missing check for July mentioned in your letter of July 24 and in our phone conversation on July 26.

Check #1956782 that was issued to you for July is still outstanding. We can only assume that the check was misplaced or misdelivered.

We will be happy to reissue your July check. I have already taken appropriate steps to have that done. It should be posted tomorrow, so you should receive it by July 29. If you do not, please contact me personally at 843-6912.

I regret any inconvenience.

Sincerely,

Ronald Phillips,
Director of Employee Benefits

ADJUSTMENT LETTER

The last type is the sales letter. It should contain the following:

- Statement to attract the reader's attention
- Explanation of the benefits of the product
- Method for purchasing the product

Sales letters are mailed out by the millions. See if you can find some in your own mail. They attract attention with a note of congratulations and provide a detailed list of product benefits, and a phone number for easily ordering a product.

MAKING IT FIT: SITUATION, DOCUMENT, AND STYLE

Let's produce letters and memos in a real business situation. You work part-time and summers for an electronics supply house to support yourself in college. Your manager is on summer vacation. It is a slow period, and you are in charge. On your second day in charge, you pick up the mail and read the following letter of inquiry:

5001 South Broad Street
Dayton, OH 48765
July 13, 1986

Jetson Electronics Supply
1350 Alum Creek Drive
Columbus, OH 43209

Dear Salesperson:

I would like to know if you have the Intel 8085a microprocessor in stock in a quantity of 600. My future plans are contingent upon your response.

Please call me at 1–513–699–7400 if you do have them.

Sincerely,

Joseph Stevens, President
Stevens Computer Mart

You check the computerized inventory and see that there are 750 8085a's in stock. You inform Stevens by phone that you can fill an order for 600 8085a's. He is pleased. He tells you that Jetsons is the first electronics supply house to respond to his letter. He promises to mail a check for the amount immediately, so you will receive it within two days. Two days later the following letter accompanied by a check arrives from Stevens:

5001 S. Broad St.
Dayton, OH 48765
July 15, 1986

Jetson Electronic Supply
1350 Alum Creek Drive
Columbus, OH 43209

Ladies and Gentlemen:

In confirmation of our phone conversation of July 15, I would like to order 600 Intel 8085a microprocessors. I have enclosed a certified check drawn on the First National Bank of Dayton for the amount you quoted over the phone.

Please send the shipment prepaid via United Van Couriers in Columbus. I have arranged for insurance of the shipment with this carrier. Please send out the order no later than July 25. I will appreciate an earlier shipment.

Let me know when the order leaves your warehouse. Be sure to include a shipping order and receipt of payment with the microprocessors. If there are any problems or delays, contact me immediately at 1–513–699–7400.

Sincerely,

Joseph Stevens, President
Stevens Computer Mart

You begin to prepare Steven's shipment by first phoning instructions to the warehouse, and then sending a follow-up memo:

TO: Warehouse Supervisor
cc: Gregg Sullivan, Director of Operations
FROM: Sales Department
SUBJECT: Shipment of 600 Intel 8085a microprocessors
DATE: July 17, 1986

Prepare 600 Intel 8085a microprocessors for shipment to the following customer and address:

> Mr. Joseph Stevens, President
> Stevens Computer Mart
> 5001 South Broad Street
> Dayton, OH 48765

Send the shipment prepaid. Be sure to use United Van Couriers here in Columbus. Mr. Stevens has arranged for insurance coverage with them. The shipment must go out before July 25—if there are any delays, notify the Sales Department at once. And please notify us immediately when the shipment does go out.

Two days later, on July 19, you receive a phone call from the warehouse that the shipment is about to leave. You call Mr. Stevens and inform him. As soon as the shipment goes out, you call purchasing and inform them that the inventory on 8085a's has been depleted from 750 to 150 due to Stevens's order. You reinforce your phone call with a follow-up memo:

TO: Purchasing
cc.: Gregg Sullivan, Director of Operations
FROM: Sales Department
SUBJECT: Depletion of Intel 8085a microprocessor inventory
DATE: July 19, 1986

Our inventory for Intel 8085a microprocessors has been depleted from 750 to 150 because of an order from Stevens Computer Mart in Dayton. We sell 8085a chips at a rate of about 200 per month.

If Mr. Stevens becomes a regular customer, we will need to expand our stock of 8085a's. Despite Mr. Stevens's future business, we will need at least an additional fifty 8085a's to supply our customers over the next month.

CHAPTER ASSIGNMENT

Let us assume that Mr. Stevens is not completely happy with his shipment of Intel 8085a's. You receive a claim letter from him stating that 53 of the 600 microprocessors are defective. You tell him by phone that before you can adjust his account, you have to settle the claim with Intel.

Intel requests that you "put the claim in writing." You write your own claim letter to Intel on behalf of Jetsons. Intel responds with an adjustment letter stating that Jetsons will be credited for fifty-three 8085a's as soon as Intel receives the defective products.

You write an adjustment letter to Stevens that he will be credited either in cash or on his next order for fifty-three 8085a's as soon as they are returned to Intel. You then draft a memo to the Accounts Payable Department informing them that Intel's account will be debited and Jetson's credited for fifty-three 8085a microprocessors.

The following documents are required to deal with this claim from Stevens:

> Stevens's claim letter to Jetsons
> Your claim letter to Intel
> Intel's adjustment letter to Jetsons
> Your adjustment letter to Stevens
> Your memo to Accounts Payable

Work with your instructor to develop a chapter assignment from this information.

EIGHT

Reports

PREVIEW

Reports state facts important to decision making. They are written in the objective style. Proposals and evaluation reports also use the conditional style to explain hypothetical situations. Proposals identify problems and suggest plans for solving them. They may be internal or external documents. They can be letters, memos, or reports. Progress reports keep management informed about work completed, work in progress, work planned, and changes in original project plans. Evaluation reports show the feasibility of ideas, plans, or theories. Reports persuade through facts and demonstration of expertise.

THE BASICS

Reports state facts that are used by management to make decisions. They are organized to communicate quickly the main idea first and supporting details afterward. The most important part of a report is the executive summary. It contains the purpose, main points, and recommendations in short form:

THE APPLICATION OF ARTIFICIAL INTELLIGENCE IN THE FINANCIAL SERVICES INDUSTRY

EXECUTIVE SUMMARY

Artificial intelligence (AI)—expert systems—knowledge engineering—natural language—advanced programming—just about every business journal contains articles that make reference to these new developments in computer science. Managers in the financial services industry are paying increased attention to this surge of activity because they realize that this technology can have far-reaching consequences for their businesses. As a result, questions are being asked and issues raised regarding developments in expert systems, or what AI practitioners call knowledge-based systems (KBS); questions such as:

- How will AI and KBS developments affect my business?

- Do these developments represent real breakthroughs and hence significant opportunities?

- What applications are possible for financial services?

- What are the development and maintenance costs of such applications?

- What are the payoffs?

- How can I get some hands-on experience using AI technology such as KBS?

- How can I incorporate KBS opportunities into the strategic planning process for my company?

To provide answers to these questions, Battelle professionals in financial services research and artificial intelligence have developed a timely, comprehensive research program for companies interested in assessing possible new business opportunities in KBS. In brief, the Battelle program will provide you with the following products and services:

- A two-day workshop in AI principles and knowledge-based systems, and an up-to-date report and analysis of industry activity in KBS program development (end of month 1)
- A one-day workshop structured to guide client members in identifying, assessing, and selecting potentially high payoff KBS applications in the financial services area (end of month 3)
- Development and demonstration of a KBS prototype system for a financial application
- A business forecast for KBS suitable for use in corporate strategic planning
- A comprehensive technical report that integrates the program results
- A two-day workshop consisting of an opportunity for hands-on use of the KBS prototype developed and presentation of the final report (end of month 9)

Since the need for information regarding potential applications of KBS is industry-wide, this research program has been structured for multiclient support. Each subscriber will receive the results of the entire program (estimated to cost between $150,000 and $200,000), but will only pay a share of the total cost—$10,000.

The program will provide you with useful research information by the time of the first workshop; a final report is scheduled for completion in nine months. The program offers to subscribers a rare opportunity to tap into Battelle's many years of experience with and knowledge of the financial services industry and artificial intelligence. The results of the program will provide a strong technical and practical base from which individual subscribers can determine their own direction for adapting the enormous potential of AI to their businesses.

Some short reports consist of only a management summary. Long reports inform about complicated topics with supporting details that persuade management to accept recommendations in the executive summary.

Additional report elements include the following:

Introduction: This follows the executive summary. In the introduction explain the purpose of the report, its scope (the breadth of information included), the sequence of main points, and provide enough background for the reader to understand information presented.

Discussion: This section produces data to support the purpose. The type of report determines exact elements of the discussion section. Proposal, progress report, and evaluation report each have special discussion sections that you will see below.

Conclusion: General findings and recommendations complete the report. The conclusion shows readers how the purpose has been fulfilled in the discussion. It states general points that readers should know upon finishing the report.

ESTABLISHING THE WRITING SITUATION

Three useful report types are proposals, progress reports, and evaluation reports. **Proposals** suggest a plan of action to solve a problem. Internal proposals recommend improvements within organizations. External proposals present plans to solve problems for outside organizations (companies and government) for a fee. **Progress reports** provide information about the status of a project, including the current emphasis of the project, as well as scheduling and budgeting. **Evaluation reports,** also called feasibility studies, examine the usefulness of proposed ideas or theories. For example, when a new product is proposed, an evaluation report is completed to determine its real chances for success.

Describe below in spaces provided situations at school, work, and your community that may require a proposal, progress report, or evaluation report.

School

Description of the situation:

Type of report needed:

Work

Description of the situation:

Type of report needed:

Community

Description of the situation:

Type of report needed:

Discuss with your instructor the possibilities of developing your ideas into report assignments.

DECIDING ON A DOCUMENT TYPE

Each report type has unique characteristics.

Proposal

The goal of all proposals is to secure a contract, grant, or permission to proceed. Good proposal writing convinces readers through persuasion and expertise.

Proposals persuade by showing favorable cost/benefit ratios for solutions. Successful proposal writers stress effective and efficient use of assets to solve problems while containing costs. They stress benefits (see page 164). However, the least expensive method is not always the best. Companies will pay more for higher-quality work, especially when guaranteed with maintenance and warranty agreements. Government proposals, in addition, should demonstrate knowledge of procedures and willingness to comply.

You do not have to be a business executive or an engineer working for IBM to come up with relevant proposal topics. If you really think about some areas of your school, work, or community life that need improvement, you can probably form a good argument for writing a proposal.

Proposals are separate documents, but they are not all alike. Formal proposals contain all the following elements:

Executive Summary

Content: nontechnical summary of the proposal for management
Purpose: to sell top management on features competing firms cannot provide and to summarize benefits

Introduction

Content: summary of analysis of problem and proposed solution
Purpose: demonstrates real understanding of the problem

Technical Approach to the Solution

Content: evaluation of objective, proposed approach, and anticipated result
Purpose: demonstrates why each specific method has been chosen to produce each specific desired result

Program Organization

Content: program organization chart, qualifications of program supervisory staff, procedures used to control schedules and costs, schedule chart for project completion
Purpose: demonstrates a feasible plan for completing work and identifies qualified people who will do the work

Key Personnel

Content: professional qualifications of each team member
Purpose: demonstrates qualifications of each team member to perform assigned tasks

Related Experience

Content: examples of other projects completed
Purpose: demonstrates the ability of the proposer to complete similar projects successfully

Facilities

Content: description of facilities (equipment, facilities, machinery) to be used, including visuals
Purpose: demonstrates that the proposing organization has the necessary resources to complete the project

Proposing Organization

> *Content:* brief description of the company and its capabilities
> *Purpose:* calls attention to the unique combination of skills, facilities, and personnel that the proposing organization can offer

However, proposals do not have to be so full-blown. In the example below, the proposal consists of a one-page letter that specifies three tasks:

505 King Avenue
Columbus, Ohio 43201
January 17, 1980

Mrs. Terri Huffman
Coordinator
Operation Feed Food Bank
980 Parsons Avenue
Columbus, Ohio 43206

Dear Terri:

I've been thinking about what I might do to help you get your operation started and I propose to provide the following:

- A plan for a small-scale marketing effort

- Text for an introductory letter (or letters) to food brokers, grocery stores, and farmers (initial effort should be directed to the brokers)

- Text and layout for a modest descriptive brochure suitable for general distribution and as an enclosure for letters.

My efforts will not include compilation of mailing lists, reproduction of letters or other printed materials, or addressing and mailing of letters. However, to the extent that I can help with suggestions, I'll be glad to do so.

At the outside, this work should be completed by March 31, 1980.

Do you have letterhead stationery? If not, the first thing we should do is design some.

If this plan is acceptable, please sign the copies of this letter and send one to Linda Willis at United Way and return one to me. If you would like to make any changes, please call me and we will do so.

Sincerely,

_____

Terri Huffman

Date: _____

Adalene Flechtner
424–4937

Proposals can also be memos. The following one suggests an inexpensive plan for purchasing videotaped programs.

TO: William Jones, Vice President

cc.: Bob Reynolds, Susan O'Brien

FROM: Professors Steve Smith and Gary Phillips, Columbus School

RE: Licensing of Video Programs Taped on Public Airways

When we recently contacted Mr. Dan Gregg of PBS Video in Washington, DC, for information regarding possible purchase of Bill Moyers' *A Walk Through the Twentieth Century* videotape series for my history class, we learned that PBS will sell any school or person a license to legally show a taped version of a broadcasted PBS program as a public performance. Licenses purchased to show independently taped programs cost initially about 1/3 the purchase price of a videotape of a program purchased from PBS; additional licenses can be purchased for additional copies of the program for a nominal fee. Let us illustrate what we mean with an example. Each show in the Moyers series retails for about $350; however, if an institution tapes its own copy of a broadcasted show, PBS will sell the institution a license to legally show the program for about $110; in addition, PBS will license each additional copy of the program for about $50 or less. Mr. Gregg indicated that all of the PBS programs could be licensed in a similar manner.

Considering Roger Cohen's August 6 memo regarding infringement of copyright laws by showing unlicensed videotapes of broadcasted programs in classrooms, we propose that a system be established whereby broadcasted programs that are desirable for classroom use are first, taped by personnel, second, licensed for multiple copies through PBS or the appropriate agency, and finally, distributed to schools nationwide. Such a system would ensure that tapes of broadcasted programs shown in the classroom are licensed. In addition, each school would own an individual and licensed copy of each program shown. According to Mr. Gregg, such licensing arrangements are common practice throughout the industry and not germaine to PBS so desirable copies of programs shown on other networks could be licensed for multiple distribution at similar savings. To illustrate, taping and licensing one episode in the Bill Moyers' series for distribution throughout the system would cost:

Videotape	$ 11.00
First license	$110.00
Ten additional licenses (10 at $50)	$500.00
Total..$621.00	

(A per-school price of $56.50)

Purchasing the same videotape at the retail price for all schools in the system would cost $3850.00. The implications for this type of independent taping and subsequent licensing of taped programs is great for all curricula and courses in the system. A network of communication among schools could be set up to share preferences for programs in various courses and to provide the initial taping and copying of videotapes for licensing and distribution to interested parties. One of the really beautiful aspects of this approach to purchasing the rights to show videotapes is that programs can be carefully selected for taping, and even after a program is taped, it need not be licensed if it fails to meet expectations or if the quality of the tape is poor.

External proposals fall into two categories: sales and government proposals. They both offer to solve problems for a fee.

Expensive and large projects require formal, detailed proposals to justify cost and inconvenience. Sometimes they are written in response to a request for a proposal. Sometimes they are issued to companies who are known to need products and services offered. The following proposal (page 148) was sent to companies who may want to share the cost of an insulated arctic pipeline research project.

Government proposals must adhere to strict guidelines set down in bid invitations and proposal requests issued by government agencies. Bidders agree to perform tasks following guidelines for a competitive fee. The following bid invitation (page 149) to print a newsletter entitled *Thunderbolt* illustrates tight regulations required of bidders.

This proposal is a bid sheet (page 150) filled in to assure compliance and to record the bid.

Large government proposals can be very complex and are often huge documents because they have a huge scope.

See the Proposal Criteria Matrix on page 168.

Progress Report

Progress reports are issued at regular intervals throughout the life of a project. They summarize work accomplished, work in progress, work remaining, changes from earlier budgets and forecasts, and plans for the upcoming reporting period. Progress reports keep projects running smoothly because they indicate when management should reassign workers, adjust schedules, allocate funds, or purchase supplies and equipment.

Progress reports may be formal or informal. If submitted in a series, each should be uniform. External reports are usually in report or letter form. Internal progress reports are memos. Content should be organized similar to the outline below:

> **Introduction:** The first progress report should identify important information about the project (project name and ID number, methods, materials, and completion date) to ensure that the reader understands to which project the report refers. The introductions to later progress reports should review briefly the previous progress report and summarize work completed or begun since that report.

> **Body:** Important details of work completed or begun should be explained carefully and thoroughly. There should be a logical organization, such as the following:

>> Tasks completed
>> Materials used
>> Personnel activities
>> Equipment status
>> Materials and equipment ordered

> **Conclusion:** Information and recommendations about changes in scheduling, equipment, personnel, techniques, materials, and other areas should be clearly summarized, and an estimate of future progress (in terms of the original proposal) and the date of the next progress report should be included.

Battelle
Petroleum Technology Center

A Research Proposal

Prediction of Damage and Degradation of Insulation for Offshore and Arctic Pipelines

MANAGEMENT SUMMARY

Problem

The structural integrity or economic operation of arctic and offshore pipelines is frequently contingent upon the proper design of a thermal insulation system. For an insulated arctic pipeline carrying petroleum at elevated temperatures, increases in subsea soil temperatures of only a few degrees may lead to thaw-settlement of subsea permafrost strata and subsequent damage to the pipeline. For offshore pipelines in nonarctic applications, thermal insulation may be required to maintain the crude above its pour point or to prevent the formation of hydrates. In either case, a method is needed to estimate the rate of deterioration of the insulation due to water intrusion to ensure adequate design life.

At present, there are no demonstrated methods for predicting the long-term thermal conductivity increases of typical pipeline insulation materials under mechanical loads and sea water permeation. In addition, there is an absence of basic thermal property data for typical pipeline insulating materials.

Solution

Battelle's Petroleum Technology Center is proposing a comprehensive research program to: (1) develop an analytical procedure for prediction of moisture intrusion into foams, (2) develop experimental techniques for comprehensive measurement of the thermal properties of foam, and (3) generate an extensive data base on the thermal properties of pipeline insulating foam.

Because the design and selection of insulating systems for arctic and offshore applications is a problem that is common to many pipeline designers and operators, as well as insulation manufacturers, this program is being offered for multiclient support. All participants will receive the results of a major study for a fraction of its total cost.

Approach

The research will be conducted in six tasks, split into two phases. The phases will run sequentially with the results of the first phase being used to direct the work of the second phase.

Phase I—Analytical and Experimental Methodologies

    Task 1: Literature Survey
    Task 2: Development of Analytical Model
    Task 3: Evaluation of Experimental Procedures
    Task 4: Validation of Model
    Task 5: Long-Term Thermal Simulations

Phase II —Insulation Foam Properties

    Task 6: Development of Data Base.

At this time, only Phase I is being offered.

Benefits

The benefits to be derived by the program participants from the proposed research are:

- Minimization of pipeline construction costs
- Reliable pipeline designs for long-term performance
- Relaxed monitoring requirements due to assurances of pipeline integrity
- Minimization of the need for pipeline repair or replacement contingencies
- Performance specifications, both thermal and mechanical, for foam manufacturers and installers.

Time and Costs

The price for Phase I is $35,600 per member and it will require 14 months to complete. The first three tasks, Literature Survey, Development of Analytical Model, and Evaluation of Experimental Procedures, will be initiated when 7 companies have joined. The remaining two tasks of Phase I, Validation of Model and Long-Term Thermal Simulations, will be added as additional memberships are obtained.

For more information

Mr. R. J. Olson
Battelle Petroleum Technology Center
1100 Rankin Road
Houston, Texas 77073
Telephone: 713-821-9330

2

148

SECTION 2.- SPECIFICATIONS

SCOPE: These specifications cover the production of a saddle-wire stitched newspaper requiring such operations as composition, film making, printing, binding, packing and delivery.

TITLE: Thunderbolt.

FREQUENCY OF ORDERS: Bi-monthly (every two months).

QUANTITY: Approximately 8,500 copies per order.

NUMBER OF PAGES: 24 pages per issue.

TRIM SIZE: 8-3/8 x 10-7/8 inches.

SAMPLE: The sample submitted is considered to be typical of the product(s) which will be ordered under these specifications. However, it cannot be guaranteed that future orders will correspond exactly to this sample.

GOVERNMENT TO FURNISH: Manuscript copy. Camera copy consisting of glossy and matte finish, photoprints for halftones, artwork for line illustrations. Film negatives. Camera copy for standing masthead and mailing indicia. Dummy for page makeup, reproduction proofs and reprint copy to be used as camera copy.

Identification markings such as register marks, ring folios, rubber stamped jacket numbers, commercial identification marks of any kind, etc., except GPO imprint, form number, and revision date, carried on copy or film, must not print on finished product.

CONTRACTOR TO FURNISH: All materials and operations, other than those listed under "Government to Furnish," necessary to produce the product(s) in accordance with these specifications.

COMPOSITION:

The entirety of each category of composition (text, tabular, and display) must be identical throughout the product(s) ordered under these specifications.

Composition must be hot metal or photocomposition.

Composition Methods Defined:

(a) Hot Metal—typesetting produced by casting the characters in metal.

(b) Photocomposition—typesetting produced by photographically creating the characters on sensitized film or paper.

The contractor will be required to set all type from manuscript copy according to the following specifications.

Format: The general format will be 48 x 57 picas, including running bottom folio, made up of two 22-1/2 pica columns, three 16 pica columns, or one 48 pica column, or combinations thereof. Photographs may bleed to page edge side and bottom. The Department will furnish a rough layout with the manuscript and illustration copy, and the contractor will be required to make up pages according to layouts.

Typefaces and Sizes: The contractor is required to furnish the following:

Text: News Gothic - 8, 9, 10 or 12-point. Leaded 1, 2-point or solid.

Display: News Gothic w/Italic and Condensed - 14, 18, 24, 30, 36 and 42-point.

Legends: Same as display.

While the above typefaces are preferred, suitable alternates of comparable weight, face, and size will be considered. Each bidder shall list in the bid the name of the alternate typeface(s) and composing machine to be used.

The GPO reserves the right to require samples and to judge the suitability of any alternate typeface offered in order to make an award which is deemed to be in the best interest of the Government.

In addition, the successful bidder must provide the ordering agency with specimens or a complete listing of typefaces and sizes which are available for use under this contract.

Overset Matter: There may be a small portion of type matter surplus to a certain issue, some or all of which may be ordered held for use in subsequent issues. The contractor will receive payment for setting such matter whenever it is used in a particular issue, is ordered killed, or otherwise disposed of at the direction of the GPO.

A proof of all overset matter for which payment is requested must be submitted with the contractor's voucher.

Note: "Overset Matter" applies to both composition and illustration negatives and will be paid for on a "per line" or a "per illustration" basis.

Upon termination of this contract, a proof of all overset matter remaining in the contractor's plant must be approved and signed off by the ordering agency and then submitted to the GPO.

The contractor will then destroy all overset matter unless he is again the successful bidder, in which case he will hold the overset matter as directed above.

FILMS: The contractor must make all films required. All halftones are to be 133-line screen or finer. Reproduce camera copy at various focuses. There will be approximately 18 halftones and 3 line illustrations per issue.

Films may be opaqued on either the emulsion or non-emulsion side.

GPO Form 910
(R6-85)
Part 3
BIDDER'S COPY
(Retain for your files)

U.S. GOVERNMENT PRINTING OFFICE
200 North High Street
Federal Building, Room 614
Columbus, Ohio 43215

09672

BID

By submission of bid, the bidder agrees to all of the provisions of the following: (i) Government Printing Office Contract Terms No. 1 in effect at the time the offer is submitted, (ii) the specifications, (iii) Representations below and (iv) Certifications on the reverse. Solicitation instructions and Conditions are Part I of Contract Terms No. 1.

As per your inquiry of _____, 19 ____, *we submit a bid herewith* **based on delivery at ordered destination, free of all charges to the Government for boxing, cartage, and freight unless otherwise required in the specification.**

Shipment(s) will be made from: City_____, **State**_____

(The city(ies) indicated above will be used for evaluation of transportation charges when shipment f.o.b. contractor's city is specified. If no shipping point is indicated above, it will be deemed that the bidder has selected the city and state shown below in the address block and the bid will be evaluated and the contract awarded on that basis. If shipment is not made from evaluation point, contractor will be responsible for any additional shipping costs incurred.)

JACKET NO. _____ **PROGRAM NO.** _____

QUANTITY	TITLE OR FORM NUMBER	NET AMOUNT
	ADDITIONAL_____ RATE_____	

Discounts are offered for payment as follows:_____percent,_____calendar days. (See provision entitled, "Discounts", in Part I of Contract Terms No. 1.)

REPRESENTATIONS (Check or complete all applicable boxes.) The bidder represents as part of the offer that:
R-1. Small Business. Bidder ☐ is, ☐ is not, a small business concern. (See definition in Part I of Contract Terms No. 1.)
R-2. Minority Business Enterprise. Bidder ☐ is, ☐ is not, a minority business enterprise. (See definition in Part I of Contract Terms No. 1.)
Bidder hereby acknowledges amendment(s) number(s)_____

In compliance with the above, the undersigned agrees, if this bid is accepted within_____calendar days (60 calendar days unless a different period is inserted by the offeror) from the date for receipt of bids specified herein, to furnish any or all items upon which prices are offered at the price set opposite each item, delivered at the designated point(s), in exact accordance with specifications, within the time specified in the schedule.

Bidder _____ **Address** _____

_____ *(Please Type or Print)*

City _____ , **State**_____ **ZIP**_____

Name _____
(Please Type or Print)

Phone _____

By _____
(Signature of person authorized to sign this bid)

Title _____

Date _____

NAME AND ADDRESS OF BIDDER AND JACKET OR PROGRAM NUMBER MUST BE ENTERED ON FACE OF BID ENVELOPE.

HAVE FIRM NAME ENDORSED – PEN SIGNATURE. YOUR BID MUST BE FORWARDED IN THE ADDRESSED ENVELOPE SENT HEREWITH.

Bidders are invited to be present at the opening of bids.

Sealed bids for above items will be received until **3 P.M.** prevailing Columbus, Oh., time *8-1-86* , **and no later.**

Evaluation Report

Evaluation reports study the feasibility (workability) of ideas. Ideas are evaluated by criteria such as efficiency, cost/benefit ratios, and increased production capacity. Evaluation reports can be internal or external. They can be written as memos between departments of the same company, or as reports between two different companies.

At the conclusion of an evaluation, you should be able to recommend an option: using the idea, modifying the idea, or discarding the idea as unfeasible and suggesting an alternative for further evaluation. The conclusion of the evaluation report is crucial because it is the most carefully read section. Contents of evaluation reports are organized similarly to the following outline:

> Summary of evaluation and conclusions
> Background description of the situation
> Guidelines or criteria
> Investigation/study details and methods
> Evaluation results
> Conclusions and recommendations

The example of an evaluation report (pp. 153–155) illustrates how this outline is actually used.

DEVELOPING AN APPROPRIATE STYLE

Reports state facts, so report writers use the objective style. Proposals and evaluation reports require limited use of the conditional style to explain hypothetical situations and to state recommendations. Progress reports are usually concise.

Reports should use facts to persuade. Instead of stating: "Our Company is best and we can do the job for you!" writers convincingly describe and illustrate capabilities, facilities, experience, and personnel. The examples below illustrate the persuasive objective style that is used for report writing.

The introduction authoritatively describes the situation:

A clear statement of objectives, benefits, and the technical approach follows:

INTRODUCTION

Development of offshore and arctic petroleum reserves requires a reliable and economic means of transporting oil and gas. Offshore gathering lines and pipelines offer an all-weather, year-round means of bringing production to shore or offshore storage and loading facilities. However, such pipelines may need to be insulated to maintain proper thermal operational conditions.

For an insulated arctic pipeline carrying petroleum at elevated temperatures, increases in subsea soil temperatures of only a few degrees, over extended periods of time, may lead to the thawing of subsea permafrost strata. The resulting soil subsidence and pipe settlements can imperil the integrity of the pipeline.[1]* In this situation, the integrity of the pipe depends directly on the integrity of its insulation. Unlike thermal insulation deterioration on subsea pipelines on thermally stable soils, the damage and degradation of even short lengths of pipe insulation in a region of subsea permafrost can result in subsidence-induced pipe stresses which can jeopardize the useful life of the line.

For offshore pipelines or subsea flowlines in nonarctic applications, thermal insulation may be required to ensure that the crude remains above its pour point.[2] For gas or oil pipelines, thermal insulation may also be necessary to prevent the formation of hydrates.[3,4] In either case, the deterioration of thermal insulation on these pipelines can affect the economics of the transport or the physical ability to move the product, but rarely does it endanger the integrity of the line itself.

The development and evaluation of insulated flowline and pipeline designs for the arctic and offshore requires an accurate, engineering method of estimating the rate

---

*Superscript numbers in brackets correspond to the list of references at the back of this proposal.

of deterioration of pipeline thermal insulation. However, no demonstrated method for predicting the long-term deterioration of insulation under mechanical loads and sea water permeation is currently available.

Consequently, the pipeline designer and thermal analyst are severely limited in their ability to assess the sensitivity of pipeline insulation systems to damage and the long-term degradation of thermal properties. A proven methodology and the necessary insulation property data for predicting the long-term degradation of pipeline thermal insulation are essential both to evaluating alternative insulated pipeline designs and to selecting insulation system materials to ensure adequate design life.

OBJECTIVES

The objectives of this proposed research project are: (1) to develop predictive techniques to estimate long-term performance of insulation systems when exposed to moisture, on the basis of insulation characteristics and operating conditions, (2) to collect experimental data on the degradation of thermal and mechanical properties of typical pipeline insulation foams, and (3) to assess the long-term impacts on a sensitive permafrost soil caused by thermal insulation degradation.

BENEFITS

The benefits to be derived by the program participants from the proposed research are:

- Minimization of pipeline construction costs
- Reliable pipeline designs for long-term performance
- Relaxed monitoring requirements due to assurances of pipeline integrity
- Minimization of the need for pipeline repair or replacement contingencies
- Performance specifications, both thermal and mechanical, for foam manufacturers and installers.

Through the use of the analytical model, the experimental procedures, and data generated in this program, the installation and operational costs for insulated subsea and arctic pipelines will be reduced. By accurately simulating the degradation of the insulation due to water permeation, pipeline owners, designers, and fabricators can optimize the insulation design, thereby minimizing pipeline costs.

For foam manufacturers, the results of this study will provide a means for designing and evaluating the performance of various foams without the need to resort to an extensive laboratory test program. This could substantially shorten the design time for a high-performance foam, which is directly translatable into enhanced return on investment or a competitive market advantage.

TECHNICAL APPROACH

The development of the methodology for predicting damage and degradation of insulation for arctic and offshore pipelines will be conducted in two phases, consisting of six closely interrelated tasks:

Phase I—Analytical and Experimental Methodologies

        Task 1. Literature Survey
        Task 2. Development of Analytical Model
        Task 3. Evaluation of Experimental Procedures
        Task 4. Validation of Model
        Task 5. Long-Term Thermal Simulations

Phase II—Insulation Foam Properties

        Task 6: Development of Data Base.

These six tasks form a comprehensive program of analysis and experimental evaluation of insulating foams, coupled with state-of-the-art assessment and practical application of the program results. Thus, they provide all of the analysis tools and data needed to design practical pipeline insulation systems for the offshore or arctic environment.

III - 19.5

Example of an Evaluation Report:

```
FEASIBILITY REPORT

ON

REPLACING THE COMPANY PRINTER

by

Barry Bird

for

XYZ Company

March 10, 19--
```

III - 19.6

PURPOSE

The purpose of this study is to determine whether XYZ Company should replace its printer to meet projected increased printing volumes.

SCOPE

This study looks at the projected print volumes for the company, alternate printers as compared to the present printer, operator times and costs, and special features of printers.

THE STUDY

Printing Projections

Printing volumes have increased 29% in the past year, from 140,000 pages to 180,000 pages per month. New contracts will increase pages-per-month demand to 200,000 by the end of this year. Projections based on new contracts and market surveys indicate a growth in print volume to 300,000 pages per month by the end of the next three years.

Current Printer Capacity and Status

The present company printer, an IBM 1403, has a capacity of 150,000 pages per month when operated eight hours per day.

The machine is two years old and has needed no major repairs in that time. A maintenance fee that covers all repair costs is paid monthly. Estimated machine life is five years. Surveys of other users have supported this estimate:

1. Grilch Corporation—This company has operated the IBM 1403 on a full-time basis for the past four years with no major repairs.
2. Quay International—This company recently replaced their IBM 1403 after six years of full-time service with one major repair.
3. Quinby and Associates—The IBM 1403 at this company has been operated full time for three and a half years with no major repairs needed.

Running the IBM 1403 on an overtime basis would proportionally lower its estimated machine life. Running 200,000 pages per month would add overtime usage that would decrease the approximately three years of remaining machine life to two and a quarter years.

The IBM 1403 model printer has been discontinued and cannot be replaced with the same model.

Operator Overtime

Operator salary rates are currently $9.78/hour, with overtime paid at time and a half, or $14.67/hour. Operators currently work approximately two hours of overtime a day to meet print-volume demand of 180,000 pages per month. Overtime will increase to more than two and a half hours a day by the end of the year when the new contracts increase print volume to 200,000 pages per month.

Other Printers

Two alternate printers were investigated as replacements for the IBM 1403. They are the IBM 3211 and the Xerox 8700. These two printers represent the latest improvements in printing technology within a medium price range. They were selected by the purchasing department of the company after industry surveys.

Both printers are capable of printing 200,000 pages per month without operator overtime. A comparison of the monthly basic operating costs of all three printers is presented in Table 1.

Table 1—Monthly Printer Operation Costs at 200,000 Pages/Month

ITEM	IBM 1403	IBM 3211	Xerox 8700
Lease Cost	$ 568	$1108	$3733
Paper	1820	2060	550
Meter Charge	None	None	2100
Maintenance	1187	1269	0[1]
Tape Drive	418	344	0[2]
Operator Salary	1721	1686	1084
Operator Overtime	860	---	---
Sales Tax	39	0[1]	0[1]
Totals	$6613	$6467	$6972

1 Included in lease cost.
2 Not required at this printing volume.

Paper Costs

The two IBM printers use pin-fed, fan-fold computer paper at a cost of $9.10 per thousand sheets for the IBM 1403 and $10.30 per thousand sheets for the IBM 3211. The Xerox 8700 can use any standard 8½-by-11-inch precut paper at a cost of $5.00 per thousand sheets.

The Xerox printer can also print on both sides of the paper; the IBM printers cannot. Ninety percent of the company's printing can be done using both sides of the paper, reducing paper usage to 550 sheets on the Xerox printer for every 1000 sheets on the IBM printers. This ratio is reflected in Table 1.

Paper costs have risen 28% over the summer and are predicted to rise by 25% by year's end. With a 25% increase in paper costs inserted into Table 1, the new monthly operation costs would be as follows:

IBM 1403	IBM 3211	Xerox 8700
$7068	$6982	$7110

Indications are that paper costs will continue to rise. Another increase of 25%, which could occur as early as the first quarter of 19--, would cause the monthly cost of operating either IBM printer to be higher than that of the Xerox printer.

Special Features

When equipped with a logo font, the Xerox 8700 printer is capable of printing specially designed forms with the company logo. The logo font's purchase price is $1,000.

Neither IBM printer has the capability to print the company logo. Current company practice is to use outside printing contractors for these forms.

Last month's charges from outside printing contractors for forms with the company's logo were $235. Internal company demand for these forms has increased steadily over the past year.

Spreading the cost of the logo font over the five-year estimated life span of the Xerox 8700 would bring this cost to approximately $16.70 a month. Further adjusting monthly operation costs by this amount and by last month's cost of printing the logo forms on the outside produces the following monthly costs:

IBM 1403	IBM 3211	Xerox 8700
$7303	$7217	$7127

Operator Time

Table 2 shows the number of operator hours required to print both 200,000 and 300,000 pages per month on the three printers.

Table 2—Daily Operator Time
for Set Print Volumes

ITEM	IBM 1403	IBM 3211	Xerox 8700
For 200,000 Pages/Month	10.6 hrs.	7.8 hrs.	5 hrs.
For 300,000 Pages/Month	15.9 hrs.	11.7 hrs.	7.5 hrs.

With operator time down to five hours a day on the Xerox 8700 at 200,000 pages per month, a full-time printer operator could spend the remaining three hours each day inputting data. Present workloads for input operators already include overtime.

Table 2 also shows that the Xerox 8700 alone would still not require operator overtime even at the predicted 300,000 pages per month print volume.

Printer Quality

The Xerox 8700 is a laser Xerographic printing device. Since it does not use a ribbon as the IBM impact printers do, print quality remains sharp and clear no matter how many pages are printed.

CONCLUSIONS

The Xerox 8700 is lowest in operating costs when the factors of paper cost increases and internal logo form printing are added to basic operating costs. The Xerox 8700 has the additional advantages of higher quality printing and higher printing speed, speed which would free printer operators to help reduce input operator overtime.

RECOMMENDATION

I recommend the company lease the Xerox 8700 by year's end.

Each area of the technical approach section consists of a description of the objective of each task, a technical discussion of how the task will be performed, and a description of results:

Objective

The objectives of Task 1 are to conduct a state-of-the-art assessment of insulating foam thermal characteristics, and to catalog existing data on the thermal and mechanical performance of insulating foams.

Technical Discussion

The accurate characterization of the most significant properties of foam insulations, as they affect long-term performance, requires data on the structural, thermal, and physiochemical properties of candidate pipeline insulation foams, as well as an indication of the anticipated variation in these properties. Such data are essential to the selection process for a particular offshore application and are a key to developing and verifying a computational model for deterioration of insulation due to water permeation.

Technical data will be compiled from the current literature on insulating materials. The data will include changes in thermal conductivity with increases in entrained water content, mechanical compaction, and variations in closed-cell ratios. Data on water absorption rates as a function of temperature, pressure, and mechanical stress will be compiled from the open literature, manufacturer's published data, and nonproprietary materials data bases.

In addition, information on the structural/mechanical strengths of candidate insulating materials will be reviewed to define the state of knowledge on strength and mechanical failure limits for these materials. Literature on insulation performance under a wide range of applications will be reviewed to establish a broad base for future study. Insulation materials of primary interest will be those most suitable to subsea pipeline applications and will include high-density polyurethane and polyvinyl chloride foams which have adequate structural strength.

Results

The results of this task will provide baseline data on the range of variation in insulating foam material properties, as well as definition of the deterioration mechanisms which are most significant for the use of insulating foams subsea. These data will then form the basis for development of a water permeation model, design of thermal property data-collection experiments, analytical model verification, and the selection of foam properties to be used in long-term pipeline thermal performance simulations.

MAKING IT FIT: SITUATION, DOCUMENT, AND STYLE

Let's return to the Mapple Corporation. The Mapple III is competing well against Data Specific. Your manual chapter is successful. You have been rotated out of Documentation into Research and Development. All outdated Mapple 11 computers have been stored away and Mapple IIIs have replaced them. You are developing software for a hardware development system. R&D work is going slowly right now because of delays in engineering.

Mr. Anderson wants to donate the Mapple II computers to the Central Institute of Technology. He believes that Central graduates familiar with Mapple equipment may recommend that their companies purchase Mapple computers instead of other types. Mr. Anderson learns that R&D isn't keeping you busy enough, so he suggests that you work with him writing a proposal to Central explaining why the school should accept the Mapple II computers. He explains that accepting the computers will require Central to maintain them and to establish an area where they can be used.

After a few phone calls to the school, you arrange a meeting with a Professor Steve Smith, who wants to use the computers to teach professional writing. You and Mr. Anderson suggest that Professor Smith write a proposal convincing the school administration to accommodate a study of using the computers to teach writing. After collaborating with you and Mr. Anderson, Professor Smith produces the proposal:

PROPOSAL FOR
PILOT PROGRAM USING MAPPLE COMPUTERS
IN WRITING INSTRUCTION

Prepared for
Mr. William Jones
President of Central Institute of Technology

By
Professor Steven Smith

ABSTRACT

A tremendous need exists for graduates with good writing skills. Computer technology is an important part of new trends in professional communication. This proposal suggests an inexpensive effective system to enable students to use Mapple computers to produce writing assignments. The pilot will provide a model for other instructors who may wish to use computers in their teaching.

PURPOSE

This report proposes developing and using a system of twelve donated Mapple computers to teach writing.

PROBLEM

Several recent surveys indicate that graduates will spend 25 to 30 percent of workdays writing. Effectively teaching students to write well-organized, grammatically correct documents is essential to career success. Using computers will help to achieve this goal. Students will be confronted with computer technology after graduation. Instructing to write using word-processing systems will help them produce well-written reports, letters, and memos and make them computer literate at the same time.

SCOPE

A proposed system for using Mapple computers in teaching writing is presented, followed by sections on hardware, software, personnel, capabilities, costs, and conclusions.

PROPOSED SYSTEM

The proposed system includes instruction in word-processing software by spending class time composing, editing, and revising assignments at computer terminals. Students will also be encouraged to complete homework and out-of-class activities on computers.

Students will be supervised. Data disks containing student assignments will be checked periodically for evaluation of assignments. Reports will be submitted for grades in hard-copy form as well. Students will have opportunities to improve grades by editing graded work to produce improved final copies.

EVALUATION

Teachers and students will evaluate the success of the proposed system. The instructor will report on strong and weak points of the project. Evaluations will include descriptions of how the system helps students to produce assignments, explanations of influences on students motivation to produce written work, and analysis of such student problems as availability of computer time and software difficulties.

Students will respond to a questionnaire on how word processing has helped to improve writing skills. Selected students will be interviewed for in-depth information. Results of student evaluations will be included in instructor reports.

HARDWARE AND SOFTWARE

The Mapple Corporation will provide twelve Mapple II computers at no cost. Equipment will consist of keyboards, disk drives, and monitors. Eight will be placed in the Learning Resources area and four in the Language Skills Lab. Special times for using them will be reserved for writing students. The Central Institute of Technology will provide two printers, one in each area.

Word-processing software packages (including disks and instruction manuals) will be placed at each station. These will be provided by the Central Institute. Mapplewriter II software is inexpensive and offers flexible word processing such as moving blocks of information within and between files. It can be learned quickly by following simple instructions.

PERSONNEL AND CAPABILITIES

Personnel will include one instructor (teaching a normal load) and a student assistant. Associate Professor Steven Smith will instruct the pilot program. Professor Smith holds an M.A. in English education. He has taught writing for five years, the last three at the Central Institute. He is knowledgeable about word processing on the Mapple II. A student assistant will be chosen at a later date.

SCHEDULING

Mapple indicates that the twelve donated computers can be installed by July 1. If approved, the pilot program can begin in the summer term. If approval is delayed, the summer term will be used to develop course materials.

COSTS

12 Mapplewriter II packages at $25 each	$300.00
Sales tax	16.50
1 Student assistant 10 hr/wk × 15 weeks × $4/hr	600.00
Total estimated costs	$916.50

CONCLUSIONS

1. Updating writing instruction using word processing will improve the writing skills of Central graduates.

2. This pilot program will increase computer literacy among students and faculty.

3. The benefits of the proposed program far outweigh costs.

After reading through this proposal, compare its elements to the list of elements listed above. How do the elements differ? Is this proposal on setting up the computer lab appropriately written? What changes would you recommend?

1. Do you find this proposal to be convincing? Why? Why not? Convincing proposals are usually very informative. If you are not convinced, some information may be missing. What additional information, if any, would you include?

2. Is the writing style of the proposal appropriate?

3. Should more or fewer technical terms be included?

4. Is the vocabulary too sophisticated or too simple?

5. Are sentences of a suitable variety?

6. Considering the intended audience, the president, do content and expression suit the purpose of the document?

7. What changes would you suggest in the writing style? Writing style is inappropriate when it is too difficult for readers to understand or so simple that they are insulted.

8. How does the style of this proposal compare to the style of the other internal and external proposals included above?

9. Is it too formal or too casual?

10. Is it detailed enough—what information would you suggest adding or deleting?

11. Is it persuasive? The writing style should be consistent with topic, content, and audience.

Smith's proposal is accepted. The computers are donated. Smith conducts an informal study of how students perceive computers as an aid in technical writing. He has mailed you the following report for your comments and suggestions prior to submitting it to President Jones:

PROGRESS REPORT FOR
PILOT PROGRAM USING MAPPLE COMPUTERS
IN WRITING INSTRUCTION

Prepared for
Mr. William Jones
President of Central Institute of Technology

By Professor Steven Smith

INTRODUCTION

Purpose & Progress Made

This report summarizes progress made on the proposal to institute a program using Mapple Computers to teach Writing. The result of meetings during May was the May 24 memorandum (attached) issued to the Academic Dean, proposing the conversion of TV studio space into a Mapple Computer Room. After cost estimates ($3600 approximately), the proposal was accepted and furniture and equipment were ordered and staffing was arranged.

Use of the Lab in Writing

Due to delays in shipping of some items, the lab was not operational until the seventh week of the summer term, the week of August 20–24. At that time, I brought two classes into the lab and explained to them the facilities. I did not require students to use the lab. Instead, I encouraged them to use it for writing their final required reports. During the last week of the term I handed out questionnaires (attached) in class and requested that students fill them out. The questionnaires consist of questions about how word processing has helped students.

Results of the Questionnaire

Five (5) areas of student response on the questionnaire that seem most important to writing include the following:

1. Areas where word processing has made writing reports easier.
2. Word processing systems and software preferred.
3. Percentage of time saved on writing reports using word processing.
4. Areas of writing where most time is saved using word processing.
5. Areas where word processing improves the quality of reports.

Summary of Data of the Five Areas

Two groups were questioned. Both were technical writing classes in afternoon schedules. Class sizes were: 50 (class A) and 41 (class B).

Percentage of return of questionnaires: Class A: 74   Class B: 68

Percentage of questionnaires returned with some informed responses:
Class A: 89   Class B: 79

	Percentage of Positive Responses on Questionnaires Returned	
	Group A	Group B
Area 1		
Developing Ideas	27	14
Outlining	27	3.5
Composing Rough Drafts	35	7
Editing	40.5	43
Composing Final Drafts	40.5	28.5
Area 2		
Mapple Software		
Mapplewriter II or IIe	11	3.5
Magic Window	43	25
Screenwriter	3	3.5
Magic Window II	8	3.5
PFC Writer	0	3
IBM Software		
WordStar	8	7
Bankstreet	3	0
Commodore		
Easywriter	3	0
Atari		
Atari-Writer	3	0

	Percentage of Positive Responses on Questionnaires Returned	
	Group A	Group B
Area 3		
10%	3	3.5
15%	0	3.5
20%	0	3.5
25%	5.5	0
30%	3	0
50%	22	11
60%	3	0
75%	0	11

Area 4

Initial Composing	13.5	3.5
Editing	40.5	36
Revising	40.5	43
Composing Final Draft	19	36

Area 5

Grammar	16	14
Writing Style	8	7
Clarity of Expression	5	7
Paragraphing	19	7
Sentence Structure	8	3.5
Wording	13.5	0
Spelling	19	14
General Appearance	35	21
Organization of Ideas	5	3.5
Subheadings	16	11
Visuals	11	7
Content	5	3.5

Summary of Results

Area 1

In both groups, the highest percentage of students indicated "editing" and "composing final drafts" as areas in which word processing has helped the most. For both groups percentages were also high for "developing ideas." Percentages in group A were above 25% in all areas, while those in group B were low for "outlining" and "composing rough drafts." Comments made by students on the questionnaire indicate they were considering the editing and recording aspects of all these areas. For example, a comment by a student under "developing ideas" was that the word processor allowed him to record ideas, rearrange them, and then retrieve them when needed.

Area 2

The highest percentage in both groups on preferred software was for Magic Window. I suspect that many students considered both Magic Window I and II in this area, because a few students indicated Magic Window II below "other."

Area 3

The highest statistics in both groups were for 50% as the percentage of time saved by using word processing. In group B, 11% of the sample indicate 75% as amount of time saved.

Area 4

The highest statistics in both groups were for editing, revising, and composing final draft as areas of greatest time-savings. Except for the 19% in group A for composing the final draft, statistics in these areas are consistently between 36–43%.

Area 5

In both groups statistics are highest for general appearance. They are also consistently higher for grammar, spelling, and subheadings. In group A statistics are also higher in areas of paragraphing, wording, and visuals.

Discussion of Data

Some of the data indicate areas that might be of interest to departments considering word processing programs. Students preferences on this questionnaire indicate the following:

1. Students perceive word processing to be a helpful tool for composing written assignments in many areas, but to a greater degree in areas of editing, revising, and composing final drafts.
2. Students seem to prefer Magic Window I and II over other types of software.
3. Students indicate that time savings using word processing ranges from 10% to 75%. The most popular estimate is 50% time savings.
4. Students indicate the quality of reports has improved in general appearance areas such as subheadings and visuals; quality is also improved in writing mechanics such as grammar, spelling, paragraphing, and wording.

The percentage of returned, informed questionnaires indicates that more than 60% of the students in group A and more than 50% in group B were informed about word processing. Data on the questionnaires indicate students' perceptions of the usefulness of word processing for saving time and controlling the quality of their writing.

After reading the progress report, what recommendations will you give to your friend the professor about the organization, content, and style of the document? Consider the following questions in arriving at your recommendations:

1. Is the report formal enough? Too formal?

2. Does it follow the guidelines suggested above for progress reports?

3. Is it clearly written? Why or why not?

4. What revisions would you suggest?

Discuss your conclusions with your instructor.

After analyzing this progress report, you realize that it is really two reports in one. In addition to reporting on the progress of the implementation of the computer lab, it also reports on the feasibility of using word processing to teach technical writing based on the questionnaire results, so it is partially an evaluation report. Isolate the sections of the report that constitute an evaluation report. Suggest a structure, content, and style for developing a separate evaluation report.

Evaluation Report Changes

Information Summary

Structure

Content

Style

When writing proposals be aware that features of a product or service being proposed are only important if their benefits to the customer are evident.

Features or Benefits?

We are always advised to point out benefits in our proposals and presentations. But we frequently get benefits mixed up with features. A feature is an attribute of the object being sold (in our case, the research project); the benefit is the result of the feature; it solves or avoids a problem for the customer.

The following is an excellent example of how benefits result from features. It is from the 1966 Sears Spring Through Summer Catalog, and describes a plastic trash can.

Sears best....because of these important reasons:

● Because it is all heavy-weight plastic. There will be no noisy metallic clang if it is dropped...it won't break.

● Because handy bottom grips plus side handles and lid handle for easy portability. No hand-cutting bail handle here.

● Because friction-fit top stays on without twisting, fits snugly without getting stuck.

● Because no seams. Holds water, won't leak. The utility area stays cleaner...won't be as likely to attract pests.

● Because stands boiling water, "boiling" hot sun... "boiling" hot concrete. Made to withstand the weather.

● Because treated with SANI-GARD to retard odor and bacteria. Won't pick up odors ... resists the growth of fungi, mildew and bacteria that cause them.

Note how each feature (plastic, bottom grips, etc.) is followed by one or more benefits for the customer.

(Courtesy of Adalene Flechtner)

CONSIDERING COST

What does it cost to produce a report? The best way to estimate this is to ask: What does it cost *not* to produce it? If a proposal is not written, the company has saved certain labor and material costs, but it has also created the expense of lost opportunity. A proposed improvement or contract will never have a chance of being completed. If a progress report is not written, the company will remain uninformed about the status of a project. Is the risk of remaining uninformed worth the cost savings? If an evaluation report is not written, the company will not know the feasibility of options. Reports produce information vital to making knowledgeable decisions. The cost of not producing reports will be much greater than the cost of producing them.

In Chapter Eight you have learned to write three major types of reports. In Chapter Nine you will be learning how to conduct a research project.

CHAPTER ASSIGNMENT

Your assignment in this chapter is to write a proposal similar in length and breadth either to the "Pilot Project Using Mapple 11 Computers in Writing Instruction" or to a memo proposal such as "Licensing of Videotaped Programs Taped on Public Airways." You may write to an internal or an external audience about conditions at work, in school, or in your community.

Avoid topics that are complex or too technical. If you choose to write about a technical topic, address it to a manager rather than to a technical expert so that you will have an opportunity to explain clearly your technical ideas to a nontechnical reader. Before attempting to write your proposal, fill in the following outline to organize your thoughts:

Introduction

Description of the problem

Summary of the proposed solution

List of benefits derived from proposed solution

Specific aspects of the problem solved by the solution

Body

Description of tasks involved in the solution of each aspect of the problem

Task 1 (as it applies to aspect 1)

Task 2 (as it applies to aspect 1)

Task 3 (as it applies to aspect 1)

Task 4 (as it applies to aspect 1)

etc.

Conclusion

Summary of benefits provided by the proposed solution (*Note:* Do not confuse benefits with features)

Findings or recommendations

After completing your rough draft, ask the following questions about your proposal and revise it according to your responses.

1. Is the topic appropriate for our chapter assignment? Or is it too complex or too simple? Why?

2. Are details of the proposed solution fully and clearly explained? Why? Why not?

3. Are benefits and concluding recommendations and findings suitably written? Why? Why not?

4. Rate this proposal using the following proposal rating sheet. Describe your results below.

Based on your evaluation of this proposal, what improvements would you suggest?

INQUIRY SUMMARY
PROPOSAL CRITERIA MATRIX

R&E No/Job No. _____
Client/Title: _____
_____
RFP No. _____ Due Date: _____

CATEGORY		CRITERIA	WEIGHTED DECISION FACTORS			RATING	
			Positive 10-9-8-7	Neutral 6-5-4-3	Negative 2-1-0	BD Representative Rating	Grp./Dept. Manager Rating
RESOURCES		1. Experience	Strong/ In-House Experience	Average/ Plan to Import	Weak/ New Areas		
		2. Technical Capability	Superior	Capable	Limited/ Qualified		
		3. Ability to Respond	Can Meet/ Exceed Every Requirement	Understand Problem/ Able to Respond	Don't Know/ Have a Better Idea		
		4. Proposal Team	Best and Available	Good/ May Impact Some Members	Second String		
	OTHER	5. Subcontractors/Consultants	Available and/or Assessable	No Impact	Inadequate Support Available		
		6. Associates	Available and/or Assessable	No Impact	Inadequate Support Available		
MARKET CONDITIONS		7. Marketing Intelligence	Inside Track/ Good Work-Up	Generally Up-To-Date	Surprised by RFP		
		8. Client Report	Good Working Relationship	Known— But Not Cultivated	Unknown		
		9. Competition	Sole-Source or Excellent Chance	Open/ Unknown	Wired for Competitor		
		10. Price Strategy	Realistic/ Within Funding Limits	Reasonable/ Competitive	Must Cut Corners		
STRATEGY		11. Importance	Key/Strategic	Of Some Strategic Importance	Minimal/No Strategic Importance		
		12. Potential for Controversy	No Impact	Somewhat Controversial	High Potential for Controversy		

MAIN: STRENGTH/WEAKNESS:

PROBABILITY OF:
(1) PROJECT PROCEEDING ____%
(2) AWARD TO R&E ____%
(3) NET PROBABILITY ____%
    (1) × (2) =

COMMENTS:

NINE

Researching Information for Reports

PREVIEW

Research is a process of testing a hypothesis against facts to form a thesis. A plan of action for producing a research report should consist of having a hypothesis and testing it by identifying sources, taking notes, forming a thesis, outlining, drafting, and producing the final draft. A research report supports a thesis with facts taken from reputable sources. Readers must be provided with a list of all sources, so that if they choose, they can verify facts. A bibliography and references in the report text provide this information.

THE BASICS

Research reports summarize, paraphrase, quote, and form conclusions about published information. They can include information gathered through questionnaires and surveys. Businesses hire consultants to write research reports to aid executives in decision making. They are organized as reports, written in objective style, and include references that show readers sources of information. Crediting sources of information is very important. Using facts without crediting where they came from is plagiarism.

ESTABLISHING THE WRITING SITUATION

A vice-president of marketing is assigned to determine the marketability of a new product idea before going into production. Instead of guessing about the marketability of the product, the VP hires a consultant to do a research study of similar products. Another case is a production manager considering a new manufacturing process—making a decision will require research.

Research reports are assigned in school because they are also written in business. In addition, research reports are educational: doing them teaches you to read critically, to document information, to argue, and to organize logically.

Doing research reports teaches you the importance of consulting published sources of information when forming ideas and opinions. Research requires you to base ideas, conclusions, and judgments on facts from published sources, on interviews with experts in the field, or from actual research in the form of lab experiments, surveys, or observation.

THE RESEARCH DOCUMENT

The quality of a research document depends on the quality, quantity, and breadth of sources consulted in arriving at conclusions, findings, and recommendations. Other criteria are content, organization, format, and the physical appearance of the document.

Remember, a research paper is an extensive presentation of facts and ideas in a highly organized format. Its purpose is to inform or convince through logic, ideas, and quality of presentation. The format strongly supports main ideas with pertinent information. The components of the research document should prove that a comprehensive research project has been completed:

TITLE PAGE   The first page of the report should give the report title, the report number (sometimes required in companies), the author's name, the company (or school, class, and instructor) for which the report was produced, and the date on which the report is submitted. Other information can be added as necessary.

ABSTRACT or SUMMARY   This section may serve as the entire report for some readers. It can be either a tightly condensed, one- or two-paragraph version of the actual information contained in the body of the report, or a description of what the body of the report covers.

TABLE OF CONTENTS   The table of contents should list all the components of the report except for the title page and abstract. If subheadings are used in the body of the report, the table should list these as well. Corresponding page numbers are listed across from each component or subtopic.

LIST OF ILLUSTRATIONS   If more than four illustrations are used in the body of the report, the number and title of each should be listed along with the corresponding page number. Both figures and tables are considered here to be illustrations. Figures include drawings, photographs, schematics, diagrams, bar and pie charts, computer programs, and graphs. Tables include all data arranged in columns or rows.

INTRODUCTION   As the first of the three main components of the report—the body and ending are the other two—this section <u>introduces</u> the reader to the body of the report. It should tell the reader

1.   what the report is about (subject and scope),
2.   why the report was written (purpose), and
3.   how the body of the report is developed.

To achieve the first objective, announce the subject of the report and give a definition or description of it if necessary. Then set the scope of your report: explain how broad or limited your coverage of the subject will be.

The scope of your coverage will be linked to the second objective—why you wrote the report. For example, if your company asked for a report on recent developments in an area of technology, you would report only on those that are related to the company's business. Your subject would be "recent developments in ABC technology," but your scope would be "those developments that would assist or improve the company's operations." This is because your purpose (second objective) is "to investigate whether there <u>are</u> any ABC developments the company might be interested in."

For the third objective, list the major subtopics of the body of your report in the order of their presentation. The list can be presented within a sentence or two, or as a vertical list.

Since this section <u>introduces</u> your report, you may want to include some background here on the subject itself or on the circumstances that led to your doing the report. If you think readers may need a lot of background, however, place it in the body of the report instead. You can also use the introduction to comment on the significance of your subject—why it is important enough to report on.

BODY   The body of the report <u>is</u> the report. All the other components are there to support and lend organization and credibility to this section.

How you develop and format the body depends on the type of report you are producing. To decide, think of your purpose and your readers. For example, if you are trying to convince the readers of something, present your argument in such a way that you build point on point. In this case you may want to avoid abrupt subheadings and let the argument flow without a break. If you're analyzing something, however, subheaded sections on each aspect of the subject would be most appropriate and effective. Use the organization and format that make the most sense to you.

Most technical reports do establish a series of subheaded sections. Each section presents not only information on the subtopic but also ties the subtopic in with the purpose of the report. To establish the subtopics, you may need to provide definitions and background information for each.

The body may also include illustrations if you decide these are helpful. If you use an illustration, make sure you number it and refer to it by number in your text before it appears.

ENDING   How you end your discussion again depends on the type of report you are preparing. The following four are useful and common endings.

1. Summary—If the purpose of your report is to inform, providing a summary of the important points would be most helpful to the reader.
2. Conclusions—If your report analyzes something, you would logically reach conclusions about cause and effect. Restating your conclusions at the end helps emphasize them.
3. Recommendations—If the point of your report is to evaluate something or to provide the company with information so it can make a decision, give your own recommendations here.
4. Graceful exit—Sometimes no purpose is served by using any of the three preceding endings. In that case, a general comment on the subject of your report would be a graceful way to exit and would leave the reader with the feeling that the report is complete.

NOTES PAGE   Instead of providing footnotes at the bottom of pages within the body, endnotes can be listed on a separate page at the end. They should be numbered and sequenced to match the body, just like footnotes.

BIBLIOGRAPHY   All sources of information that you consulted in preparing your report should be listed in alphabetical order here.

APPENDICES   For large diagrams and graphs, flow charts, computer programs, and other data that are not easily incorporated into the body of the report, sections labeled "Appendix A," "Appendix B," etc., can be added at the end and referred to in the body.

DEVELOPING A PLAN
FOR THE RESEARCH PROJECT

The word "research" means to examine information sources with a mind to discovering new knowledge. It is a "re-looking" at situations, concepts, and facts in a creative way to make new, interesting, and meaningful statements. Research may involve different types of sources:

> Published sources from the library in the form of books, periodical articles, pamphlets, and reference works
>
> Interviews with knowledgeable people
>
> Observation of events
>
> Laboratory experimentation

There are several steps in the research process. First, develop a hypothesis. This is an unproven thesis, a guessed at conclusion. It is based on experience or knowledge of the topic. It is arrived at in a creative, spontaneous flash of intuition.

Next, try to disprove the hypothesis. That's right, disprove it. If during your research, you discover evidence that contradicts your hypothesis, logic dictates that you must either reject the evidence or reject your hypothesis and form a new one in line with the evidence. The entire research project consists of "re-looking" at evidence to disprove or support your hypothesis. During the research process, you should be able to form your hypothesis into a thesis, a statement of opinion that is supported by facts.

Remember that the research document is the end product of the research project. Your grade on the research project will probably be derived solely from your paper. However, to produce an acceptable research report, you will have to perform successfully and carefully all the steps in the research project that lead up to it. You should devote approximately five weeks to the production of a research project and report.

Week 1: Develop a hypothesis that is focused but complex enough to be of interest to you and the readers. Also, plan to use published sources as most of the evidence. Check availability of sources—a good suggestion is to have available at least twenty sources that you can consult.

Week 2: Create a working bibliography by recording authors, titles, and publication information on 3 by 5 cards.

Week 3: Collect notes of information related to your hypothesis. Develop a thesis before, during, or after you collect notes—you may have to loosen or tighten your thesis as you collect more data, or you may have to question or reject some data.

Week 4: Organize collected notes into an outline by deciding which information to place in particular sections of the report. Compose a rough draft from the outline.

Week 5: Refine the rough draft and produce a typed or word-processed final draft.

Next, examine each of the five stages of the research project in more detail:

Topic Selection

Make it easy on yourself by selecting a familiar topic that interests you. Avoid topics that are:

Too broad: You won't be able to present any in-depth information.
Too difficult: Neither you nor your reader will understand.
Too trivial: You will only bore yourself and your reader.
Dominated by a single source: Your findings will be biased.

Just to be safe, keep narrowing your topic until you think that you won't be able to find quite enough information to fill up a research report—start there. Instead of trying to develop a hypothesis on computers, try doing one on speech synthesis; instead of electronics, try active filter applications; instead of corporations, try an analysis of income statements of the three top Fortune 500 companies. Be specific and focused.

Working Bibliography

During the research process, examine your sources at least twice: once to collect bibliography sources and again to take notes. Examine and collect all sources before actually taking notes. Although some researchers prefer to collect sources and take notes simultaneously, there is one big advantage to keeping the activities separate. Collecting sources first lets you see and judge all of them. You can decide which sources are most important for taking notes. Prepare a 3 by 5 bibliography card for each source you choose to use by placing on it the following information:

Name(s) of the Author(s)   Library and Call Number

Title of Work

Facts of Publication

Page(s) of Information

Description of Source

The Title and Facts of Publication differ according to the type of source. In general, underline or italicize independently published items such as books, pamphlets, or monographs, and place quotes around titles of articles or other sources that appear within another published source. When using articles, be sure to provide also the title (and author, if applicable) of the book, journal, or magazine from which it comes.

Facts of publication differ for each type of source. Books include publishing company, city of publication, date of publication, edition number (if there is more than one), and page numbers. Most journals and magazines include volume, number, month, year, and page numbers. For magazines and journals that do not contain all this information, include everything that is available. If the source has no author (such as in an encyclopedia article or news magazine article), include all other pertinent information.

The information on the bibliography cards must be complete, comprehensive, and accurate because the reference notes and final bibliography will be composed from the cards. Take the time to do them right—or else you may have to spend time looking some of them up again to write the final bibliography.

Tell your teacher and librarian your hypothesis so that they can give you help locating sources. To get started, look up your subject in encyclopedias, the card catalog, and periodical indexes. Check with the librarian on using each of these. When selecting sources for future note taking, here are a few tips to keep in mind:

1. To determine which sources to read thoroughly, examine them with your hypothesis in mind. Check the subject index at the back of a book, and read its table of contents, preface, and foreword. Also, read abstracts of articles and contents summaries of articles. Finally, skim paragraphs and scan pages by reading topic and concluding sentences.

2. Apply your hypothesis to primary and secondary sources. Primary sources are original or firsthand documents. The Declaration of Independence is a primary source. Secondary sources are commentary, criticisms, and analyses of primary sources. Secondary sources are often useful because authors have already done the groundbreaking work. As a researcher you can agree, disagree, or react to them.

3. Use high-quality sources to test your hypothesis. Avoid questionable sources such as gossip sheets and comic books. Check the credentials of authors (these are usually provided at the front or back of books, journals, and magazines). Prefer authors with the best credentials. Compare your hypothesis with views of different au-

thors or sources on the same subject. If one view seems uninformed or extreme, question its validity. Compare your own views with those of the leading experts. Be prepared to change your mind if the evidence you uncover warrants this. Do not get tangled up in statistics. Be sure that you absolutely understand the original purpose and use of any statistical evidence you use. Do not use statistics outside the original context.

Note Taking

After you have completed your working bibliography, be prepared to take notes. Read through your bibliography cards and form a plan for taking notes by deciding which sources are most important. Also, decide what sequence you wish to use when taking notes. You should probably spend most of your time early in the week taking notes from the most important sources. Use any system you wish, but you should have a plan. Do not take notes haphazardly because you may not have time to cover all your sources. Once you have established a plan, use your bibliography cards to locate your sources.

There are four types of notes:

1. *Summaries* are the most useful notes because they condense longer pieces. Summarize information whenever possible. *Note:* These must be carefully documented.
2. *Paraphrases* are also useful. Use your own words to record information in the same degree of detail. *Note:* These must be carefully documented.
3. *Quotations* are of limited use because it is difficult to locate large numbers of quotations that will say what you wish to say in support of your thesis. Use quotations only when a brief verbatim statement from another source states your own thoughts perfectly. *Note:* These must be carefully documented.
4. *Personal notes* are opinions, comments, criticisms, and insights that you have about the information you are recording. Do not hesitate to write personal notes because often they will be major portions of the final document.

Plagiarism is misrepresenting another's ideas as your own. It is a form of stealing and cheating. Be sure to cite in your final document (provide a footnote, endnote, or parenthetical note) the author and source of summaries, paraphrases, and quotations. Follow these guidelines to avoid plagiarism:

- Personal notes, generally, do not require citations unless they contain summaries, paraphrases, or quotations.
- All ideas borrowed from another source must be documented.
- Quoted material must be placed within quotation marks.
- A bibliography entry should be included for every source consulted.

Note Cards

Place the author and page number at the top of each note card. The author's name will lead you to the corresponding bibliography card, and this, as you now know, contains information for writing proper notes and a bibliography.

Your note cards should be arranged as follows:

```
                Author's Name         Subject Heading



                Body: Summary, Paraphrase

                Quotation, or Personal Note
```

Devote one idea, fact, observation, or description to each card. Do not cram your cards full of information because later you will not be able to understand them. Devoting one card to one unit of information lets you separate facts into individual categories as different piles of cards. Composing rough and final drafts will go smoothly as you refer to categories and retrieve information from each card. Having several facts on each card requires you to make new cards or cut up portions of old cards to divide facts up for the various sections of your paper.

Thesis Development

During the note-taking process, you should be able to transform your hypothesis into a thesis. It will be an informed version of your hypothesis expressed as a one-sentence statement that indicates *the* central idea you are trying to communicate. The thesis should be specific, concrete, and clearly opinionated. Do not confuse your topic or main points with your thesis. See the examples of bad and good theses below:

Bad thesis: focuses on two topics instead of one

Telecommunications is a fast-growing business in which fiber optics are used because they are so efficient and inexpensive.

Improved thesis: focuses on only one topic

The efficiency and low cost of fiber optics are changing the field of telecommunications.

Bad thesis: confusing wording

BASIC programming was once the New England Primer of computer science students.

Improved thesis: clear and detailed wording

Learning BASIC programming once prepared computer science students to master other computer languages, such as Pascal, JCL, and COBOL.

Bad thesis: too vague

A personal computer is a handy machine.

Improved thesis: more specific

A personal computer can be useful at home and on the job because it can store and compile virtually any type of information.

Your thesis should focus on a single topic and employ clear and specific language. It should indicate major divisions within the research paper. In all of the improved versions included above, divisions are indicated. Readers can expect sections on efficiency and effectiveness in the first thesis; sections on Pascal, JCL, and COBOL in the second one; and sections on home and job use in the third.

Outline

Now begin developing an outline for using your notes to support your thesis in the final document. Three types of outlines are topic, sentence, and paragraph. A typical outline orders points in the following hierarchy:

Thesis

   I. Main Idea in support of thesis
   A. Sub-idea
   B. Sub-idea
      1. Division of sub-idea
      2. Division of sub-idea
         a. Minor idea
         b. Minor idea
  II. Second main idea in support of thesis

The thesis is the main point of the entire paper. Several main points support the thesis, several sub-ideas support each main point, and several minor ideas support the sub-ideas. In a topical outline, each item in the hierarchy is a word or phrase; in a sentence outline, each item is a complete sentence; and in a paragraph outline, each main idea in support of the thesis is a topic sentence with sub-ideas, divisions of sub-ideas, and minor ideas forming either clusters of sentences or individual paragraphs supporting the topic sentence.

Begin with a topic outline to organize main points and supporting details. Use a sentence outline to develop a "feel" for the paper. If your note cards contain paragraphs as they may appear in the paper, try the paragraph outline. Higher-level outlines (sentence or paragraph) save time composing rough drafts. Arrange your note cards in the sequence of your outline and have your bibliography cards at hand for writing the rough draft.

Rough Draft

You have finally arrived at the writing stage in your project. To compose the rough draft, copy from the note cards information (summaries, paraphrases, quotes, and personal notes) to create sections of your report according to the

Example of a Formal Report (in schematic form):

Peter Graves, a research assistant at the ABC Corporation, discovered a need for a device similar to those manufactured by his company but altered to suit handicapped people. Peter made the modifications and came up with a workable device. He was asked by his supervisor to prepare a report on his project. Peter's supervisor felt that ABC's executive management should be informed about the technical capabilities and the manufacturing feasibility of the device, as well as its similarities to devices currently manufactured by the company. Peter's report is presented here in partial, schematic form.

← TITLE PAGE

MICROPROCESSOR-CONTROLLED RADIO ANTENNAS

FOR THE HANDICAPPED

by Peter Graves
Research Assistant
Research and Development Department

for ABC Corporation

October 11, 19--

ABSTRACT

A survey of handicapped radio operators in the area showed that a need and a market exists for a radio-antenna controller with special adaptations. The problem most mentioned in the survey....

Peter chose to condense the information in his report here, including his evaluations, so that all executives would at least get the gist of his ideas even if they didn't read the whole report.

TABLE OF CONTENTS

Peter listed the report components—including the five subheaded topics in the body of the report—and their page numbers here.

LIST OF ILLUSTRATIONS

Though not shown here, Peter listed two tables that showed manufacturing costs, three schematics, and a drawing of his device.

INTRODUCTION

Many handicapped people use amateur radio equipment for communication but often do not have the strength or coordination to aim the antenna with conventional antenna controllers. This report describes the usefulness, design, and manufacturing costs of [subject] a newly designed radio-antenna controller that is operated by a microprocessor. It also compares this controller to those currently produced by ABC Corporation. This information is presented to determine whether the invention of this device presents a manufacturing opportunity for ABC.

The report presents survey information on handicapped radio operators; a discussion of the problems and needs of handicapped operators; the design of the microprocessor-operated controller, including schematics and specifications; a comparison of the design to controllers presently manufactured by ABC Corporation; and manufacturing costs of the new design.

Peter decided to provide background in the first sentence of his introduction. In the second sentence, he combined part of his scope statement with the subject of the report. The third sentence also deals with the report's scope, and the last gives Peter's purpose, or why he wrote the report.

In the second paragraph, Peter explains how the body of the report is developed.

Only the subheadings and beginning statements of each subtopic are reproduced here from the body of Peter's report.

A Survey of the Handicapped
A conversation with a handicapped friend illustrated the special problems and needs of handicapped radio operators, and led to the idea of using the capabilities of a microprocessor to replace human motor skills. A survey of 87 handicapped radio operators was conducted by phone to.....

Needs of Handicapped Operators
The most frequently cited problem in the survey was difficulty in applying the amount of pressure necessary to hold down the switches on conventional antenna control-lers.....

The Design of the Controller
By utilizing a 6508 microprocessor, a 2716 EPROM, a 6522 Versatile Interface Adapter (VIA), a 7574 Analog-to-Digital (A/D) Converter, a stepper motor, and an application program.....

Design Comparisons to ABC Controllers
Adaptations needed to convert presently manufactured antenna controllers to microprocessor operation are minimal.....

Manufacturing Costs of the Controller
The costs of components used in the microprocessor-operated controller are shown in Table 1.....

Peter decided to end his report with his own conclusions about whether his device presented a manufacturing opportunity for the company. He listed the positive aspects of his design—marketability, low manufacturing costs, and compatibility to current manufacturing operations—and concluded that an opportunity did indeed exist.

CONCLUSIONS
Based on the informal surveys conducted during the design of the radio-antenna controller presented here, marketability of the design appears.....

Peter used facts and quotes from five magazine articles, two data manuals, and two books in his report.

NOTES
1. Alex Gunther, The Special Needs of Special People (New York: Putnam Books, 1984), p.108.
2. Shelley Nankin...

Peter listed alphabetically all the sources he had consulted in researching his report.

BIBLIOGRAPHY

Peter used two appendices: Appendix A for his survey questions and Appendix B for his application program. Both had been referred to in the body of the report.

APPENDIX A
Survey of Handicapped Radio Operators
1. How long have you been operating...

plan of your outline. A sketch of a formal report developed from an outline and rough draft is provided on pages 177–178.

Use bibliography cards to insert proper citations in the body of your rough draft. Remember to indicate in your rough draft the source of each fact or idea not your own. These citations can be numbers, parenthetical insertions, or bibliographical entries written in a space to the side on the rough draft. Numbers and parenthetical insertions should refer clearly to bibliography cards and page numbers.

Documentation

Information from bibliography cards has to be transferred into the text in two ways. One is a list of all sources used; this, the bibliography, is arranged in alphabetical order using the author's last name. The author, if there is an author identified, is the first item listed in each bibliographical entry. Following is an example of a bibliography from a student research paper.

BIBLIOGRAPHY

Brady, Rosemary, "Up in Smoke," *Forbes,* volume 131, June 20, 1983, p 88.

Breecher, John. "King Coal's Lobbying War (Slurry Pipelines to Cross Railroad Tracks)," *Newsweek,* volume 102, October 3, 1983, p 76.

"Business Backs Further Away from Synfuels (Pullout by Standard Oil from Coal-to-Gasoline Plant in Wyoming)," *Business Week,* November 8, 1982, p 39.

Curtis, Carol E. "End of the Line for Coal Slurry? (Railroads Kill Eminent Domain Bill)," *Forbes,* volume 133, January 30, 1984, p 94.

Lappen, Alyssa A. "Will Coal Finally Clean Up Its Act?" *Forbes,* volume 136, July 29, 1985, pp 78+.

Long, M. E. "Wrestlin' for a Livin' with King Coal," *National Geographic,* volume 163, June 1983, pp 792–819.

Perry, Harry. "Coal in the United States: A Status Report," *Science,* volume 222, October 28, 1983, pp 377–84.

Peters, Alexander R. "A Long-Lost Synfuels Process (Low-Temperature Carbonization)," *Nation,* volume 234, April 24, 1982, pp 487–9.

"Rail Rates Could Send Coal Exports down the Chute," *Business Week,* May 16, 1983, pp 27–8.

Raloff, J. "Washington Deals Synfuels a Big Blow (Great Plains Coal Gasification Project)," *Science News,* volume 128, August 10, 1985, p 87.

Rudolph, Barbara. "Shattered Hopes for Synfuels (Great Plains Project)," *Time,* volume 126, August 19, 1985, p. 35.

Shiels, Merrill, and others. "Coal's Future Burns Bright," *Newsweek,* volume 95, March 10, 1980, pp 73+.

Tracey, Eleanor J. "Appalachian Coal Turns Green," *Fortune*, volume 104, July 27, 1981, pp 72–5.

"What Coal Companies Fear from the Railroads (Higher Rail Rates)," *Business Week*, January 31, 1983, p. 30.

"What Happened to the Coal Boom?" *U.S. News and World Report*, volume 94, March 14, 1983, p 22.

Can you distinguish books from magazine and journal articles? What does the information about each entry indicate about the source? *Hint:* Book and periodical titles are underlined or italicized and articles appear in quotes.

The second use of the bibliographical information is to show to the reader the sources of each fact used in the text. This is achieved by placing a number, raised one-half a space, in the text next to a paraphrase, summary, or quote. Bibliographical information corresponding to the number is located on a page at the back of the report and titled Endnotes. Readers simply locate the same number on the endnote page to discover the source of the information. Numbers are arranged throughout the text in the same sequence in which the information appears. When using the endnote system, no number is repeated. Bibliographical information is arranged slightly differently in endnote entries than in bibliographical entries. Following are examples of endnotes.

ENDNOTES

[1] Len Deighton, *Blitzkrieg: From the Rise of Hitler to the Fall of Dunkirk* (New York: Alfred A. Knopf, Inc., 1980), p. 99.

[2] *Blitzkrieg: From the Rise of Hitler to the Fall of Dunkirk*, p. 61.

[3] Norman Rich, *Hitler's War Aims* (New York: W. W. Norton & Company, Inc., 1973), p. 121.

[4] *Blitzkrieg: From the Rise of Hitler to the Fall of Dunkirk*, p. 11.

[5] Brigadier Peter Young, *The World Almanac Book of World War II* (New York: World Almanac Publications, 1981), p. 54.

[6] Brigadier Peter Young, *World War II, Illustrated*, (New York: H.S. Stuttman, Inc., 1978), p. 11.

[7] *World War II, Illustrated*, p. 11.

[8] *Blitzkrieg: From the Rise of Hitler to the Fall of Dunkirk*, p. 65.

[9] *Blitzkrieg: From the Rise of Hitler to the Fall of Dunkirk*, p. 66.

[10] Telford Taylor, *The Breaking Wave* (New York: Simon and Schuster) p. 109.

[11] *Blitzkrieg: From the Rise of Hitler to the Fall of Dunkirk*, p. 65.

[12] *The World Almanac Book of World War II*, p. 36.

[13] *Hitler's War Aims*, p. 106.

[14] *Blitzkrieg: From the Rise of Hitler to the Fall of Dunkirk*, p. 101.

[15] Patrick Turnbull, *Dunkirk, Anatomy of Disaster* (New York: Holmes & Meier Publishers, Inc., 1978), p. 45.

[16] Hanson Baldwin, *The Crucial Years 1939–1941* (New York: Harper & Row, Publishers, Inc., 1976) p. 87.

[17] *The World Almanac Book of World War II*, p. 51.

[18] *The World Almanac Book of World War II*, p. 51.

[19] *The World Almanac Book of World War II*, p. 51.

[20] *The World Almanac Book of World War II*, p. 51.

[21] *Blitzkrieg: From the Rise of Hitler to the Fall of Dunkirk*, p. 82.

[22] *Hitler's War Aims*, p. 67.

[23] *Blitzkrieg: From the Rise of Hitler to the Fall of Dunkirk*, p. 180.

[24]Colonel A. Goutard, *The Battle of France 1940* (New York: Ives Washburn, Inc., 1959) p. 78.

[25]*The World Almanac Book of World War II*, p. 54.

[26]*Blitzkrieg: From the Rise of Hitler to the Fall of Dunkirk*, p. 205.

[27]*Blitzkrieg: From the Rise of Hitler to the Fall of Dunkirk*, p. 200.

[28]*Blitzkrieg: From the Rise of Hitler to the Fall of Dunkirk*, p. 250.

[29]*The World Almanac Book of World War II*, p. 59.

[30]*The Crucial Years 1939–1941*, p. 272.

[31]*The Crucial Years 1939–1941*, p. 272.

[32]*The Crucial Years 1939–1941*, p. 279.

[33]*The Crucial Years 1939–1941*, p. 278.

[34]H. R. Trevor-Roper, *Blitzkrieg to Defeat—Hitler's War Directives 1939–1945* (New York: Holt, Rinehart and Winston, Inc., 1965), p. 106.

[35]*Blitzkrieg to Defeat—Hitler's War Directives 1939–1945*, p. 109.

[36]*Blitzkrieg to Defeat—Hitler's War Directives 1939–1945*, p. 110.

There are two other methods of achieving this second use of bibliographical information. The simplest of all methods is to place the author's last name, along with a page number, in parentheses after the paraphrase, summary, or quote that needs to be cited. Readers look up the author's last name, which will be located in alphabetical order, in the bibliography and use the page number to establish the precise location of the source.

This system can be troublesome if the same author has two sources cited or two different authors have the same last name. In these cases brief additional information, such as the date of the source or the first word or two of the title (properly punctuated) can be included in the parenthetical insertion. Following are a few examples of parenthetical-insertion citations.

According to Carol E. Curtis, coal slurry pipelines would mean cheaper transportation costs for coal users, but they are staying with the railroads. The reason for this is that the railroads are purposely turning in low bids to win contracts and put slurry pipeline companies out of business. Curtis, p 94)

Transportation is a major factor concerning the downfall of the American coal industry, but it cannot be given all the blame for the decreased popularity of American coal. Another major issue concerning the decline in coal use involves the harmful effects that coal burning has on the environment. According to Harry Perry, it is more expensive for coal users to comply with the laws concerning air and water pollution than for the users of any of the other fossil fuels. (Perry, p 382) Compared to coal, oil and natural gas burn with very little smoke. Also, in addition to the large quantity of smoke produced, coal burning creates harmful gases. One gas created from coal burning that is harmful to the environment is sulfur oxide. Studies show that sulfur oxide may be a cause of acid rain. It also damages plants and is believed to be a major factor contributing to the acidification of lakes. (Perry, p 382)

The high costs concerning pollution steer most large companies away from coal use. According to Eleanor Tracy, many large industries presently using oil would switch to coal if it were not for the costly switchover process and the many standards set by the Environmental Protection Agency related to air and water pollution. (Tracy, p. 72)

One of the advantages of using parenthetical insertions is that it eliminates the need for an endnote page. Readers use the bibliography to locate sources.

A third method, a different type of parenthetical note, has the same advantage. In this method the bibliography entries are numbered and the number is used in the parentheses instead of the author's last name. An example follows.

BIBLIOGRAPHY

1. Prepared by Lawrence Mass, M.D., "Medical Answers about A.I.D.S.," Published by Gay Men's Health Crisis, New York, Copyright June 1984.
2. Matt Clark, "A.I.D.S.," Newsweek Magazine, Published by Newsweek Inc., Copyright Aug. 12, 1985.
3. Kenneth H. Mayer, MD., *The A.I.D.S. Fact Book,* Published by Bantam Books, Copyright Sept. 1983.
4. Jean Seligmann, "A.I.D.S.: Fears and Facts," Newsweek Magazine, Published by Newsweek Inc., Copyright Aug. 8, 1983.
5. Janice Hopkins Tanne, "The Last Word in Avoiding A.I.D.S.," New York Magazine, Copyright Oct. 7, 1985.
6. Jonathan Lieberson, "A.I.D.S.: What Is to Be Done?" Harper Magazine, Published by Harper Magazine Foundation, Copyright Oct. 1985.
7. Claudia Wallis, "A.I.D.S.: A Growing Threat," Time Magazine, Published by Time Inc., Copyright Aug. 12, 1985.
8. William A. Check, Ph.D., *The Truth about A.I.D.S.,* Published by Holt, Rinehart and Winston, Copyright 1984.
9. Victor Gong, M.D., *Understanding A.I.D.S.,* Published by Rutgers University Press, Copyright 1985.
10. Robert Rodale, "Protecting Ourselves against A.I.D.S.," Prevention Magazine, Published by Prevention Inc., Dec. 1985.
11. Janet Baker, *A.I.D.S.,* Published by R and E Publishers, Copyright 1983.

This method, sometimes referred to as scientific notation, also eliminates the possibility of confusing different sources by the same author or different authors with the same last name. In this system numbers can be used more than once in parenthetical notes because the same bibliographical source can be used often throughout the document. If you need more specific information on documentation techniques and styles, consult a style manual or ask your instructor.

You probably can understand now why doing the bibliography cards properly is so essential and why they are necessary in composing your rough draft. If you leave the sources of information out of your rough draft, you will have a very difficult task trying to relocate sources after completing the rough draft.

Your report should consist of 60 to 80 percent referenced paraphrases, summaries, or quotes (very few quotes). And the sources you reference in your text should be well balanced—some may be referenced slightly more often than others, but in general, all sources should be used several times. Placing sources where they do not belong will show up in uneven and contradictory use.

If you have done a thorough job on the rough draft, composing the finished draft should consist of cleaning up the rough draft and typing or word-processing the final copy. Following is a checklist of items to consider when editing and revising your rough draft.

The Editor's Checklist: Does Your Document Have the "Write" Stuff?

1. What is the author's stated purpose? Is it clearly identified? Does the document fulfill this purpose?
2. What is the intended audience? Will everyone understand what you say and how you say it? (Be careful of being too technical.) Is there enough background to orient all anticipated readers?
3. Does the author follow a logical organization? Does the author make this organization immediately clear to the reader?
4. Does the author conform to the required or appropriate format?
5. Is there a liberal sprinkling of headings and subheadings to guide the reader along?
6. Is the transition from point to point clear, smooth, and logical?
7. Is there any extraneous information?
8. Is there enough information such that the author's points and overall message are clear?
9. Are the facts relevant, clear, and correct?
10. Are the illustrations relevant, clear, and properly placed?
11. Is the style readable, understandable, and clear? Do the words and ideas flow smoothly from sentence to sentence and paragraph to paragraph? Check for wordiness, nominalizations, passive voice, sentence length, etc. The ultimate test is to read it aloud.
12. Are spelling, grammar, and usage correct?
13. Does the document create the desired impact or impression?

Next is shown an example of the finished draft of a student research paper.

MEMORANDUM

TO: Mr. Steve Smith
FROM: William Rase
DATE: February 19, 1986
SUBJECT: Research Paper

The attached report, entitled "Phoneme Synthesis," is submitted in accordance with your requirements for Technical Writing 401.

The research paper examines how phoneme synthesis is used to generate artificial speech. The paper also discusses the advantages of this method.

The rough drafts of the report and the note cards are included.

PHONEME SYNTHESIS

Prepared for
Dr. Steve Smith
Technical Writing TW-401
Central Institute of Technology

By
William Rase
4DP

TABLE OF CONTENTS

ABSTRACT

Phoneme synthesis is one of the two basic approaches to generating artificial speech. This report examines how phoneme synthesis is used to generate speech and discusses its advantages.

Phoneme synthesis depends on the basic principles of language. This method divides speech into its basic units of sound, allophones. Combining allophones in the proper sequence creates speech. This is very similar to the way speech is produced by man.

The electronic circuitry used with this method is modeled after the human vocal tract. Random sound sources are shaped by time-varying filters to produce speech sounds. These filters control the frequency content of the sound. By approximating the frequency content of natural speech, the basic speech sounds are produced.

Phoneme synthesis is easily implemented. Data rates are low and memory requirements are not large. Phoneme synthesis offers the additional advantage of an unlimited vocabulary.

INTRODUCTION

PURPOSE

The purpose of this report is to explain a method of generating artificial speech known as phoneme synthesis. The advantages of this method over other approaches will be discussed.

PROBLEM

Artificial speech has become an important part of the interface between man and machine. (Ciarcia, "Unlimited," p. 168) Computerized speech frees an operator from constant attention to a terminal screen. In industrial applications, artificial speech allows warning messages and status reports to be given without interruption of the worker's routine. (Witten, 1)

Other applications include a variety of consumer products and toys. There are talking microwave ovens and story-telling dolls. Learning aids that teach spelling and math are commonplace. Artificial speech also plays an important role in electronic devices designed to aid the blind. (Sclater, 20–24)

The widespread use of artificial speech requires a simple, economical means of implementation. Phoneme synthesis offers such a method. It is easy to implement and offers an unlimited vocabulary. The speech produced by this method is very intelligible and has only a slight mechanical accent. (Ciarcia, "Low-Cost," 134)

SCOPE

Section I of this report explains how phoneme synthesis is used to generate speech. Section II deals with the actual reproduction of sound. This section compares how speech sounds are produced by man and by the phoneme synthesizer. Section III discusses the advantages of phoneme synthesis over other possible techniques of generating speech.

SECTION I: PHONEME SYNTHESIS

Phoneme synthesis is a method of generating artificial speech by which basic units of sound are strung together to form words. These basic units of sound are commonly called "phonemes." This section of the report deals first with the principles behind this method. It continues with the application of this method to produce speech.

PRINCIPLES

Speech is spoken language. Over the range of possible sounds, there are a limited number used in speech. Within the language itself, there are a limited number of linguistic constructions which result in these sounds. Phonemes are the basic units of language that result in these sounds. (Morgan, 26)

Phonemes are logical units that are defined in terms of the language itself. They are not sounds in themselves. (Witten, 3) The table in Figure 1 lists the phonemes of the English language. One second of average speech contains ten to fifteen phonemes. (Sclater, 25)

Phonemes may be pronounced in different ways. The actual sound of the phoneme is affected by its position in a word and by the phonemes that are adjacent to it.

A single phoneme may result in several variations of sound. For example, although the "k" sound of both "key" and "caw" is a single phoneme, two different sounds are required to voice this phoneme. These variations in sounds are called allophones. One phoneme may have several allophones. (Witten, 36)

Allophones are the basic building blocks of speech. They are small segments of sound unique to speech. Phoneme synthesis actually utilizes the production of allophones to create speech. Words are formed by producing the correct sequence of allophones. (Sclater, 26)

APPLICATIONS

Phoneme synthesis uses integrated circuitry that is capable of producing the sound of individual allophones in response to an input code. Through the selection of the proper sequence of codes, the individual sounds are linked together to form a word.

The allophones available with one popular speech synthesizer are listed in Figure 2. Words must first be translated into the basic sounds, the allophones. Then the corresponding codes for these allophones are used to control the speech synthesizer.

Phonetic translations of words are easily made. For example, the basic sounds of a word are identified.

cat	3 sounds	K AE T
five	4 sounds	F AH E V
starve	5 sounds	S T AH R V

Next the variations of these phonemes are considered. The specific allophone or combination of allophones is chosen to best represent the desired sound.

cat	K AE T	K AE1 AE1 T
five	F AH E V	F AH1 EN3 E1 V
starve	S T AH E V	S T AH1 UH3 R V

These adjustments are usually made with the vowel phonemes. (Gargagliano and Fons, 187)

Once individual words are coded, the phonetic translations can be saved and used when needed. Storing the coded phonetic translations requires only 20% more memory than storing just text. (Gragnon, 178)

Phoneme synthesis uses a set of unique language sounds to produce speech. Section II describes how these unique sounds are reproduced.

SECTION II: PRODUCING SOUNDS

Phoneme synthesis uses an electronic model of the human vocal tract to produce the sounds of the allophones. (Witten, 95) To better understand how this model functions, we must first understand how the sounds of speech are produced in man.

HUMAN SPEECH

Sound is the fluctuation of air pressures. Humans produce sound by forcing air from the lungs, through the vocal tract, and out the mouth.

The vocal chords determine two types of speech sounds. When the vocal chords are held open, the sound produced is unvoiced. When the vocal chords are allowed to vibrate, the sound produced is voiced. The difference between the sounds "sss" and "eee" is the difference between unvoiced and voiced sounds, respectively. The vibration of the vocal chords is the pitch of the voiced sound. These two types of sound may be combined. (Morgan, 12)

The rest of the vocal tract and the mouth shape these basic sounds in much the same way that an organ pipe shapes a musical note. The shape of the chamber strengthens certain frequencies while attenuating others. This is the acoustic principle of resonance. The resonant frequency of the organ pipe is the musical note it sounds. (Witten, 25-26)

Three main resonant frequencies of speech are determined by the vocal tract and by the shape of the mouth. These frequencies will vary due to changes of the mouth and vocal tract. The spectrogram shown in Figure 3 is helpful in understanding the frequency content of speech.

A special frequency analyser is used to make a three-dimensional graph of speech called a spectrogram. Time is plotted along the horizontal axis and frequency, along the vertical axis. The darker areas of the graph indicate frequencies of greater strength. (Witten, 26)

Each specific segment of speech has a specific frequency content. Certain frequencies are stronger, others are weaker. As time varies, the frequency content of the sound changes. The pattern in which the frequency content changes is unique for each allophone.

ELECTRONIC SPEECH

A phoneme synthesizer uses a series of time-varying filters to control the frequency content of the sound it produces. The filters act like the resonant chambers of the vocal tract. (Teja, 7) Figure 4 is a simplified block diagram of a phoneme synthesizer. Its operation is as follows.

The phoneme controller receives a 6-bit input indicating that a specific allophone be produced. The controller determines which of the two sources is required for the specific sound. These two sources represent the two types of basic sounds determined by the vocal chords, voiced and unvoiced. (Gargaliano and Fons, 164)

The phoneme controller also determines the required filter parameters. The filter determines the frequency content of the sound. The filter parameters are varied to approximate the actual changes in frequency content of the sound of the allophone. (Ciarcia, "Unlimited," 134)

The frequency characteristics of speech change more slowly and smoothly than do other characteristics because frequency content is dependent on physical attributes. The phoneme controller varies the filter parameters which shape the frequency content of the sound source. The filter shapes the sound to resemble the allophone that was requested. (Sclater, 29)

SECTION III: ADVANTAGES

The production of artificial speech by phoneme synthesis offers several advantages over other methods. Phoneme synthesizers are designed for easy connection to computers and other electronic devices. They provide a low-cost method of implementing speech with an unlimited vocabulary.

Because phoneme synthesis generates speech from the basic sounds of speech, only a few codes per second are required to operate the circuitry. One second of speech contains ten to fifteen phonemes. If a six-bit code is needed to describe the phoneme, one second of speech requires approximately 100 bits of data. This is the data rate.

The other major approach to speech synthesis utilizes techniques similar to those of digital audio recording. These digital techniques reproduce the sounds in terms of pressure fluctuations. These pressure fluctuations change very rapidly. More information and a higher data rate are required to operate the devices using these techniques than are required for phoneme synthesis. (Slater, 29)

The data rate for these digital techniques can exceed 100,000 bits per second. To transfer data at these rates requires complicated circuitry. The size of the memory needed to store data for more than a few seconds of speech becomes prohibitively large. (Ciarcia, "Unlimited," 135) Phoneme synthesis offers a low-cost alternative to this technique.

Digital techniques demand that the speech to be produced must first be recorded. Phoneme synthesis offers "complete freedom in the choice of possible output utterances." (Gagnon, 177) Words to be spoken do not have to be recorded. The sounds that the phoneme synthesizer produce are the basic sounds of speech. Words are constructed with the phoneme synthesizer as easily as words are constructed in natural speech.

Phoneme synthesis is well suited to text-to-speech conversion. Computer programs are used to make a phonetic translation of a written text. The phonetic translation is then coded in terms of the allophones that the phoneme synthesizer is capable of producing. Applications include reading machines for the blind. (Gagnon, 177)

CONCLUSION

Phoneme synthesis generates speech by producing the basic sounds of speech. These basic sounds are allophones. Allophones are strung together to form words.

Integrated circuits supporting this technique are easy to use. A binary code is used to determine which allophone is produced. Through use of the proper sequence of codes, the phoneme synthesizer can be activated to produce a series of allophones that form a word.

Phoneme synthesis is an efficient and low-cost method of implementing speech for a wide variety of applications. In 1984 the addition of speech to a product raised the price of that product by about $20. (Morgan, 7) Today the cost is less.

APPENDIX: ILLUSTRATIONS

CREDITS:

FIG. 1 TABLE OF PHONEMES (Radio Shack, 12-15)
FIG. 2 TABLE OF ALLOPHONES (Ciarcia, "Unlimited," 172)
FIG. 3 SPECTROGRAM (Witten, 27)
FIG. 4 PHONEME SYNTHESIZER (Gargaliano and Fons, 165)

CONSONANT PHONEMES OF ENGLISH

		LABIAL	LABIO-DENTAL	INTER-DENTAL	ALVEO-LAR	PALA-TINE	VELAR	GLOTTAL
Stops:	Voiceless	PP			TT		KK	
	Voiced	BB			DD		GG	
Fricatives:	Voiceless	WH	FF	TH	SS	SH		HH
	Voiced		VV	DH	ZZ	ZH*		
Affricates:	Voiceless					CH		
	Voiced					JH		
Nasals	Voiced	MM			NN		NG*	
Resonants	Voiced	WW			RR,LL	YY		

VOWEL PHONEMES OF ENGLISH

	FRONT	CENTRAL	BACK
High	YR IY IH*		UW# UH*#
Mid	EY EH* XR	ER AX*	OW# OY#
Low	AE*	AW# AY AR AA*	AO*# OR#

FIGURE 1 : TABLE OF PHONEMES

Hexadecimal Phoneme Code	Phoneme Symbol	ASCII Character	Duration (ms)	Example Word
00	EH3	@	59	jacket
01	EH2	A	71	enlist
02	EH1	B	121	heavy
03	PA0	C	47	no sound
04	DT	D	47	butter
05	A2	E	71	make
06	A1	F	103	pail
07	ZH	G	90	pleasure
08	AH2	H	71	honest
09	I3	I	55	inhibit
0A	I2	J	80	inhibit
0B	I1	K	121	inhibit
0C	M	L	103	mat
0D	N	M	80	sun
0E	B	N	71	bag
0F	V	O	71	van
10	CH	P	71	chip
11	SH	Q	121	shop
12	Z	R	71	zoo
13	AW1	S	146	lawful
14	NG	T	121	thing
15	AH1	U	146	father
16	OO1	V	103	looking
17	OO	W	185	book
18	L	X	103	land
19	K	Y	80	trick
1A	J	Z	47	judge
1B	H	[	71	hello
1C	G	\	71	get
1D	F	]	103	fast
1E	D	↑	55	paid
1F	S	←	90	pass
20	A	(space)	185	tame
21	AY	!	65	jade
22	Y1	"	80	yard
23	UH3	#	47	mission
24	AH	$	250	mop
25	P	%	103	past
26	O	&	185	cold
27	I	'	185	pin
28	U	(	185	move
29	Y	)	103	any
2A	T	*	71	tap
2B	R	+	90	red
2C	E	,	185	meet
2D	W	–	80	win
2E	AE	.	185	dad
2F	AE1	/	103	after
30	AW2	0	90	salty
31	UH2	1	71	about
32	UH1	2	103	uncle
33	UH	3	185	cup
34	O2	4	80	bold
35	O1	5	121	aboard
36	IU	6	59	you

Hexadecimal Phoneme Code	Phoneme Symbol	ASCII Character	Duration (ms)	Example Word
37	U1	7	90	J*u*ne
38	THV	8	80	*the*
39	TH	9	71	*th*in
3A	ER	:	146	b*ir*d
3B	EH	;	185	r*ea*dy
3C	E1	<	121	b*e*
3D	AW	=	250	c*a*ll
3E	PA1	>	185	no sound
3F	STOP	?	47	no sound

FIGURE 2 : TABLE OF ALLOPHONES

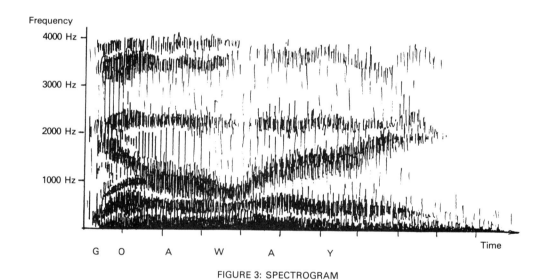

FIGURE 3: SPECTROGRAM

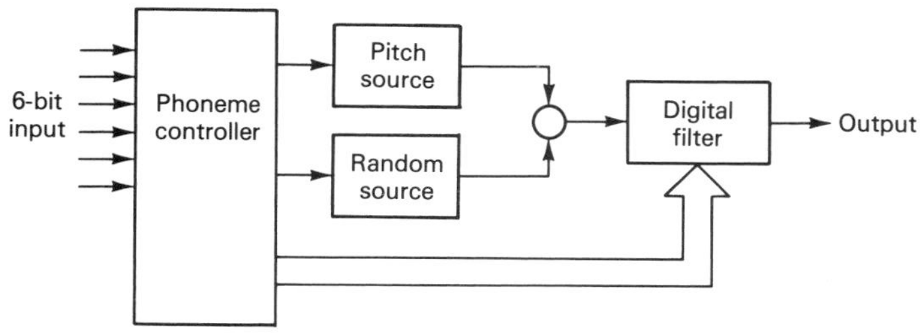

FIGURE 4: PHONEME SYNTHESIZER

BIBLIOGRAPHY

Ciarcia, Steve. "Build a Low-Cost Speech-Synthesizer Interface." *Byte.* June 1981. Reprinted *Ciarcia's Circuit Cellar.* Vol. III. Peterborough, New Hampshire: Byte/McGraw-Hill, 1982

———. "Build an Unlimited-Vocabulary Speech Synthesizer." *Byte.* Sept. 1981. Reprinted *Ciarcia's Circuit Cellar.* Vol. III. Peterborough, New Hampshire: Byte/McGraw-Hill, 1982

Fons, Kathryn and Gargagliano, Tim. "Articulate Automata: An Overview of Voice Synthesis." *Byte.* Feb. 1981

Gagnon, Richard. "Phonetic Synthesis Using Analog Filters." *Electronic Speech Synthesis.* Ed. Geoff Bristow. New York: McGraw-Hill Book Co., 1984

Gargagliano, Tim and Fons, Kathryn, "Teach Your Robot to Speak." *Robots Age,* Vol. 3, #6. Nov./Dec. 1981. Reprinted *In the Beginning.* Ed. Carl T. Helmers. Rochelle Park, New Jersey: Hayden Book Co., 1983

Morgan, Nelson. *Talking Chips.* New York: McGraw-Hill Book Co., 1984

Scalter, Neil. *Introduction to Electronic Speech Synthesis.* Indianapolis, Indiana: Howard W. Sams & Co., Inc., 1983

Teja, Edward R. and Gonnella, Gary W. *Voice Technology.* Reston, Virginia: Reston Publishing Co., 1983

Witten, Ian H. *Principles of Computer Speech.* London: Academic Press, 1982

SPO256–AL2 Voice Synthesizer. Data sheet number 583–LWC. Fort Worth: Radio Shack. n.d.

Weinrich, David W. "Speech-Synthesis Chip Borrows Human Intonation." *Electronics.* April 10, 1980.

In this chapter you have learned the steps of the research process and the elements of a research paper. In Chapter Ten you will learn to deliver an oral presentation.

CHAPTER ASSIGNMENT

Your instructor should provide you with a research paper assignment. Here is a list of subject areas:

Microchip technology

Portable computers

Trends in company mergers

Popular new products

Advertisements

Employment opportunities

Breakthroughs in technical research

Foreign technology and commerce

Automobile industry

Emerging service industries

TEN

Oral Presentations

PREVIEW

Speakers must explain main ideas simply. Listening is different from reading. Readers can examine a document over and over. Listeners usually have one opportunity to receive information. Speakers should use visuals that depict main points to reinforce comprehension. They should also distribute handouts with main points so that the audience can take some reminders with them. They should organize speeches so that listeners can easily follow. One useful method is to organize by means of a series of questions to which the speaker provides answers.

THE BASICS

Managers often give oral presentations in business and industry. Executive officers must present annual reports to stockholders. First-line managers regularly conduct department meetings. Project teams and boards meet often to listen to presentations on team progress and problem resolution. Field engineers and technicians present instructions on machine operation.

ESTABLISHING THE SPEAKING SITUATION

Some unique characteristics of written communication are depicted in Figure 10-1.

In writing, author and audience never see each other. They communicate through the permanent record of written words. Words can be reread and analyzed over an extended period. In writing, you can detail and examine closely assuming that readers will review difficult material.

Formal and informal oral presentations differ. Figure 10-2 depicts informal oral communciation. Informal oral communication has the following characteristics:

- Limited audience
- Little preparation
- Listeners constantly influence the message

It occurs in the locker room, around the water cooler, in the parking lot outside work, and at business meetings where participants know each other well

Writer ⟶ Text ⟶ Reader

Characteristics:

- *Permanent life*
- *No audience participation in composition*
- *Author imagines the audience*
- *Organization and language are standardized*

Advantages:

- Convenient to read and reread
- Permanent record of the message
- Reproduction in large numbers possible

FIGURE 10-1   Written Forms of Communication

enough to feel informal. Listeners can often ask the speaker for clarification of ideas if they do not understand something.

Formal speaking situations are depicted in Figure 10-3. There is greater distance between audience and speaker. Formal speaking has the following characteristics:

- Wide audience
- Extensive preparation
- Listeners receive the message

Formal speaking situations require speakers to prepare a written speech ahead of time. In preparing it, speakers must make style and content fit the audience. Since listeners cannot ask questions freely, the speakers must be sure to provide a clear sequence of main points.

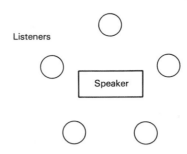

Characteristics:

- Brief, temporary, and remembered life
- Main speaker, composes spontaneously directly to listeners
- Listeners influence speaker's message through questions and body language
- Organization and language are informal

Advantages:

- Extemporaneous performance
- High level of listener-speaker interaction
- Audience indicates immediate impact of message

FIGURE 10-2   Informal Oral Communication

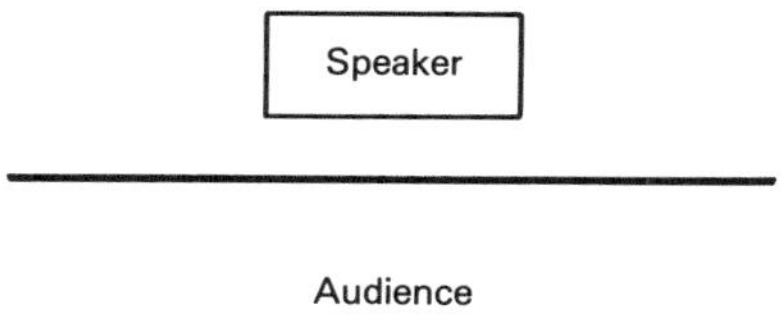

```
┌──────────────┐
│   Speaker    │
└──────────────┘
```

Audience

Characteristics:

- Unless recorded, brief, temporary, and remembered life
- Main speaker prepares message based on estimates of audience interest
- Limited audience participation — speaker controls question asking and observes body language
- Organization and language are formal but fluid — the speaker can ad lib as necessary

Advantages:

- Convenient to listen to
- Uninterrupted oral performance
- Availability of audience feedback

FIGURE 10–3   **Formal Oral Communication**

DECIDING ON A SPEECH TYPE

You should know three speech types: impromptu, extemporaneous, and manuscript.

Impromptu

Impromptu speeches are not prepared. Speakers choose their words during delivery before the audience. Informal speaking situations call for impromptu speeches. Speaker and listeners are usually close associates. Clarification of the message can be requested at any time. The chances are greater of using inappropriate language or making inaccurate statements in impromptu speaking than in other types. Unprepared speakers can easily speak incorrectly.

Extemporaneous

Extemporaneous speeches have a partially prepared delivery—speech content and ideas are outlined before delivery. Exact words of the speech are not prepared. Extemporaneous speakers are usually experienced at giving speeches on their topic. They can shape their thoughts and words as they speak by following a prepared outline and by recalling excerpts from past speaking performances.

Experienced teachers are usually good extemporaneous speakers. As students, we have all recognized the fluid performance of an experienced teacher in contrast to the slower, more hesitant performance of new or substitute teachers. Politicians are also good extemporaneous speakers, especially when they are on the campaign trail giving virtually the same speech at several locations in a brief period.

In business, extemporaneous speaking is used when speakers are in customary roles. Managers at monthly meetings follow an outline and speak extemporaneously. A human resources vice-president visiting company locations explaining new fringe benefits would also speak extemporaneously, at least after the first few presentations. An outline for an extemporaneous speech resembles a topic outline for a research paper.

Manuscript

In manuscript speaking, both words and content are prepared before actual delivery. The speaker reads from a prepared text. Manuscript speaking works best for speakers who either feel unsure of their knowledge or are delivering a speech on a topic that requires precise language. Inexperienced speakers usually adopt a manuscript speech format to allay their fears of forgetting or misrepresenting information. Technical speeches with complex information and business speeches at awards banquets, stockholders' meetings, and conventions are read from manuscripts.

DECIDING ON A SPEECH PURPOSE

Speeches usually have one of three purposes: informing, persuading, or demonstrating.

Informing

Informative speakers deliver facts to the audience. They introduce the main points up front and use transitions (such as first, second, third, etc.) to go from one main point to the next. If you give a speech, be sure that main points are organized in a suitable order, such as most to least important. Highlight the most important facts of the speech in the introduction and reemphasize them in the conclusion. Use attention-getting devices such as questions, illustrations, and visuals to keep the audience interested.

Persuading

Persuasive speeches, similarly, place main points up front, use transitions and organizational sequences, summarize important information in the introduction, and stress it again in the conclusion. They also employ argumentative techniques, such as summarizing opposing views, distinguishing your view from the oppositions, and refuting the opposition point by point. Attention getters, such as questions, examples, and visuals, are used to support your position. Leave neutral information out because it will detract from the strength of your argument. An impassioned delivery certainly complements the effectiveness of a well-organized and honest persuasive presentation. A one-sided treatment of an issue, no matter how impassioned, will not convince anybody.

Demonstrating

Demonstration speeches show how a process is performed. The same speaking principles apply to demonstration speeches as to the other two types. The physical arrangement of the speaking situation must allow the audience to see and understand the process being demonstrated. Tools, equipment, and materials to be used in the demonstration must be available and set up to be used easily by the speaker. Main points in demonstration speeches are organized as process.

DEVELOPING AN APPROPRIATE STYLE

Since the audience sees and hears speakers, speech style is more than the words of the speech. Appearance in clothing, hair style, posture, and facial expressions are all characteristics that determine speech style. Gestures of the hands, face, head, and body are part of the speech style. In addition, voice, including volume, articulation, and tone, must be considered.

Distance between speaker and audience determines in part the formality of a speaking situation. Edward T. Hall has noted the importance of distance in oral communication. At 5.5 feet, speakers in the United States become formal. They use an overloud voice and describe information for the general public to hear. Between 8 to 20 feet, speakers assume a group address mode. Their voices are very loud and their posture and words are more controlled and carefully prepared. Twenty to 24 feet indoors and 100 feet outdoors are the outer limits of a formal-speaking situation. At distances of 5 feet and less, speakers address people informally.

Nonverbal cues, such as voice, gestures, and appearance, are perceived cumulatively by the audience as the speaker's attitude. Hall has identified three cultural patterns that make up attitude: formal, informal, and technical. Formal and informal patterns are natural. They are performed almost subconsciously. In informal speaking situations, these natural patterns of behavior are followed thoughtlessly.

A third pattern of behavior is technical. This consists of a series of very intentional acts performed to create a desired impression. You should follow a technical pattern when giving a formal speech. You should be yourself, but at the same time, you should follow a prescribed pattern of behavior in dress, gestures, facial expressions, and voice. The audience will expect you to follow these conventions.

CUES FOR FORMAL SPEAKING

If the speaker displays an attitude of boredom, by speaking in a monotone, wearing drab clothing, and slouching at the podium, guess how the audience will perceive the speech? You probably guessed correctly: *boring.* If the speaker emanates excitement and desire to communicate by speaking in a voice that alters vocal patterns for emphasis of important points, wears impressive clothing, and stands straight but relaxed at the podium, the audience is likely to perceive the speech as exciting. Speakers should always try to display attitudes of interest and confidence by speaking loudly and enthusiastically, by using gestures appropriately (not too much) to emphasize important points, and by wearing a hairstyle and clothing that are fashionable and appropriate for the situation.

In addition to boredom, avoid attitudes of superiority and fear. Superiority is derived from speaking down to the audience by being pompously self-confident. Perhaps the best way to avoid a superior attitude is to concentrate on communicating information rather than creating a superior effect or impression on the audience. Speakers who are more concerned with how they look and act than how well they are delivering the intended message often come across as being superior. Remember, you should project a favorable impression so that the audience will listen to your message.

Fear is the most natural reaction to have in a public-speaking situation. We often refer to this fear as stage fright or as "having butterflies." It is important, however, to control this fear. Audiences become very embarrassed for a speaker who emanates fear. It makes the audience afraid that something is wrong. If left uncontrolled, the fear may stifle a speaker by causing hesitations, mispronunciation of words, or freezing up.

The best remedy for fear is knowing your subject and purpose. Build up your confidence with the audience by demonstrating your knowledge. Cite important facts. Be totally prepared. Sometimes fear can be eased by breathing deeply several times at points in the speech where pauses are appropriate. Deep breathing relaxes body muscles and reduces physical tension.

Another strategy is to meet audience members individually before giving a speech. Making introductions and shaking hands with members of the audience develops self-confidence and reduces fear. A third method is to view the speaking engagement as a challenge, like playing a sport. Overcoming the fear is part of the game, like getting up to bat or receiving a tennis serve. If you stumble in a speech, remember that the audience has great respect and affection for speakers who stumble and then regain composure to make a strong finish.

MAKING IT FIT: SITUATION, SPEECH, AND STYLE

How do you put together a good speech? First, consider the situation. Three basic distinctions between written and oral discourse are pace, density of ideas, and organization.

Situation

Oral communication is more quickly paced than written communication. Listeners hear the speech, and it is gone—it cannot be heard again unless it is recorded. Ideas are less dense in speeches than they are in written texts. In the same length of time, a listener cannot understand as much as a reader because the eye reinforces information more strongly than the ear.

Finally, speech organization must be simple. To enhance comprehension, a speech should have obvious transitions, such as "The first issue I would like to discuss today is . . . ," followed by "This brings me to my second issue . . . ," and finally, "The third and final issue of discussion I will address is. . . ." In comparison to written communcation, a speech should have less depth, be simpler in content and organization, and have more obvious transitional devices to keep the audience focused on the main points.

Environment

As a speaker you should also consider the physical environment. Examine the room for equipment capabilities, such as the number of electrical outlets (their distance from the equipment, and the need for three-pronged plugs), lighting (determine if it will interfere with any planned visuals), and acoustics (check to be sure that your voice will be understandable).

Notes

What kind of notes should you use during the speech? Impromptu speeches do not require notes. Extemporaneous speeches require at least an outline of main points. Manuscript speeches require a completely written text. But if you feel unsure of your speaking abilities or your topic, consider using the following procedure in preparing your speech:

1. Estimate the number of words that you will need in your speech by multiplying 120 times the number of minutes you are required to speak. For example, if you are giving a 4- to 6-minute speech, you can estimate the number of words needed to be between 480 (4 × 120) and 720 (6 × 120).
2. Write out the entire text of the speech. An easy way to do this is to base your speech on an essay or research paper you have previously written which is appropriate for the audience. You will have to change the style of the written text so that it is appropriate for a listening rather than a reading audience. The oral style should have less depth, meaning fewer elaborate details and more concentration on major points, simplified content and organization, and

more numerous and more obvious transitional devices. Use a friendly second-person style so that you are speaking to the audience as well as discussing your topic.

3. Type or print the final version of the oral text on large (5 × 8) cards lengthwise. Use all uppercase letters and double-space the lines for ease of reading.

4. If you wish, mark the script for pauses using a series of slashes, such as / for a breath, // for the end of a major idea, and /// for a major pause, used to draw attention to a major idea. You can also underline major ideas that need to be emphasized. Place brackets around blocks of the text that are of secondary importance—some or all bracketed material can be included if time permits, or they can be omitted if time is tight.

5. Visual aids should be coordinated into the text. By jotting a note in the margin or between lines of the text, you can cue yourself to when appropriate visual aids, such as overhead transparencies, posterboard illustrations, film strips, or videos, should be activated. Remember that visuals should be prepared and ready to go *before* the speech.

NAME _____ DATE _____

TITLE OF SPEECH _____

INTRODUCTION	Poor	Fair	Good	Excellent	Superior
Contact established	1	2	3	4	5
Objective clear	1	2	3	4	5
Subject well chosen	1	2	3	4	5
BODY					
Central idea clear	1	2	3	4	5
Illustrations	1	2	3	4	5
Did the main points form an easy-to-remember pattern?	1	2	3	4	5
CONCLUSION					
Were the main points summarized?	1	2	3	4	5
Did the closing words give an appropriate, rounded-out effect?	1	2	3	4	5
DELIVERY					
Appearance	1	2	3	4	5
Voice	1	2	3	4	5
Gestures	1	2	3	4	5
Eye contact	1	2	3	4	5

_____ TOTAL

Strong points? _____

What does he need to improve? _____

Critic _____

6. After preparing all this material, you have to practice. First, read over the speech several times to become familiar with the information. Second, practice delivering the speech in an empty room or at home. Third, practice the speech a few times in front of your friends or anyone who is willing to listen and watch. As you practice, try to become less dependent on the manuscript. You are probably prepared to deliver the speech when you can give it while maintaining eye contact with the audience 70 to 80 percent of the time you are speaking.

Use the evaluation sheet provided below to check the quality of your performance. Have friends who are observing you speak fill out the form and discuss their perceptions of your performance with you prior to your actual presentation.

CHAPTER ASSIGNMENT

Revise the research report example "Phoneme Synthesis" from Chapter 9 into a speech manuscript using the suggestions mentioned above.

APPENDIX A

Writing a Resume and Covering Letter

When you are applying for a job, either during school or after graduation, you will be required to write a resume and covering letter and submit them to companies for review before you are invited to interviews. A resume is a summary of your credentials; it includes information about your education, work experience, and special skills that qualify you for particular occupations. Look over the two examples of resumes on pages 202 and 203.

Notice the different styles of the resumes. The basic information in each is about the same, but the ways that this information is presented influences the reader's perceptions of the person represented by the resume. Which style do you like best? Why? Which do you like least? Why? Remember, the company employee who is screening resumes to arrange job interviews really only "knows" the job applicants by reviewing the written versions contained in each resume. So when you are preparing your own resume, remember these points:

1. Make the document impressive: use high-quality paper; leave plenty of white space around all four sides of each sheet; include boldfaced or double-stroked headings and subheadings; avoid crowding information; have the resume typeset, if possible.

2. Try to tailor each resume to each job applied for: you may not be able to accomplish this because of the expense involved, but try composing special resumes on either a good-quality typewriter or word processor for the top 5 to 10 companies on your list.

3. Use action words and describe accomplishments instead of routine duties: instead of writing "Grill Cook: Food preparation and cooking," write "Learned inventory control procedures and perfected culinary skills." Every cloud has a silver lining; if you think hard about your part-time jobs in school, you should discover several important skills you learned that are applicable to the job for which you are applying—but you have to use your imagination.

4. Stress characteristics in your background that will be of primary importance to a future employer. If you have had a good deal of related work experience, stress that; if you have little work experience but a great deal of related educational experience, stress the educational information. Front-load your resume: put your strong-

Qualification Brief

DANIEL G. ROSE

PRESENT ADDRESS:
1938 Summit St.
Columbus, Ohio
(614) 294-2024
MESSAGES: (614) 253-1713

PERMANENT ADDRESS:
3729 Menchhofer Rd.
Coldwater, Ohio
(419) 678-3769

EDUCATION: DeVRY Institute of Technology
Columbus, Ohio

DEGREE EARNED: Bachelor of Science Degree in Electronics Engineering Technology
Graduation: October 1986
GPA - 3.47/4.00

CURRICULUM OUTLINE:

Technical
* Electronic Devices
* Digital Systems
* Micro Hardware and
  Software Systems
* Micro Peripherals
* Communications
  Systems
* Control Systems

Programming
* Basic
* Assembly
* Pascal
Software Used to
Program Microprocessors
Includes: 8085, 8086
8088, MC 68000
Economics

Related Courses
* Differential Equations
  Calculus
* Physics
  Management
  Marketing & Accounting
  Public Speaking
  Technical Writing

* These courses are complemented by over 500 hours of lab experience

HONORS:

Achievements
• Institute of Electrical and
  Electronic Engineers (IEEE)
  Society
• IEEE Executive Committee
• Kiwanis Award: Given for Leadership, Academic, and Athletic Achievement.
• Received Nomination to Air Force Academy.

Projects
• Designed and Built an 8085
  Microprocessor Using HP 64000

EMPLOYMENT EXPERIENCE

12/83 - present: United Parcel Service; Columbus, Ohio
Position: Sorter
Responsibilities: Sort parcels at a rate of 1200 packages per
hour with a 98% accuracy rate.

Skills Obtained: Consistanly worked above quota in both
production and accuracy. **Reliability:** Have
not missed a day of work in past year.

Previous Work Experience: Worked and helped manage family farm for 10 years.

Skills Obtained: Marketed grain and livestock, serviced large
equipment, maintained operating capital.

EXTRACURRICULAR ACTIVITITIES:

President & Student Advisor, Coldwater Future Farmers of America
President & Treasurer, Coldwater 4-H club
Captain; H.S. Football Team, Coldwater

Personal and Professional References Available upon Request

PATRICK W. MENTER

Temporary Address
4280 Vineshire Drive
Columbus, Ohio 43227
Ph. (614) 231-1472

Permanent Address
4301 South Airport Road
Bridgeport, Michigan 48722
Ph. (517) 777-7491

EDUCATION:

Bachelor of Science Degree in Electronic Engineering Technology
Obtained at DeVry Institute of Technology, Columbus, Ohio
Graduate October 1986, **GPA 3.13/4.0**

AREAS OF MAJOR STUDY:

TECHNICAL

Communication Systems
Microprocessor Systems
Control Systems
Electronic Devices
Digital Circuit Design
Circuit Analysis
Calculus/Laplace
Physics

COMMUNICATION

Public Speaking
Literature
Psychology
History
Technical Writing

BUSINESS

Marketing
Management
Economics
Social Issues

PROGRAMMING

Basic
Pascal
Assembler 8085/86,
8088,8748,MC68000

The technical and programming courses are complemented with over 550 hours in lab.

HONORS:

Dean's List, President's List - 5 Trimesters

INDIVIDUAL AND TEAM PROJECTS:

Microprocessor based frequency synthesizer…responsible for hardware, software design and implementation.

8085 Microprocessor system…responsible for hardware, software design and emulation of system.

Microprocessor based heater controller…responsible for all facets of hardware and software design.

EMPLOYMENT EXPERIENCE:

CO-OP UNITED STATES AIR FORCE, Newark Air Force Station
DATES: October 1984 to February 1986
TITLE: Electronic Measurment Equipment Mechanic Helper

RESPONSIBILITIES:

Repairing of cable systems and connector boxes…Assisting senior mechanics in troubleshooting and repair of pumpdown stations and gas leak detection devices.

EXPERIENCE SKILLS:

Acquired skills in troubleshooting and analyzing electromechanical machines…Gained ability to take on more responsibility…Developed better defined interpersonal communications skills.

While employed with the USAF gained security clearance, also, obtained certification in high reliability soldering.

McDONALDS RESTAURANT, Columbus, Ohio
DATES: April 1984 to August 1984
TITLES: Fry Cook, Maintenance

RESPONSIBILITIES:

Opening the grill in morning and setting up for the day…stocking the inventory and preparations to close at the end of day as well as closing…Maintaining the drink system.

EXPERIENCE:

Developed interpersonal communication skills…Improved organizational skills…Developed inventorying skills…Enhanced ability to take on responsibility.

INTERNATIONAL TIRE WAREHOUSE, Columbus, Ohio
DATES: August 1983 to January 1984
TITLE: Tire Changer

RESPONSIBILITIES:

Opening and setting up shop in the morning for the day…Inventory and organizing the stock…Changing tires on all types of vehicles.

EXPERIENCE:

Aquired skills in inventory…Gained exposure to dealing directly with public…Furthered ability to deal with mechnical problems.

RELOCATION: Open

REFERENCES: Available Upon Request

est and most unique job-related attributes first in the resume. A reader will lose interest as he or she reads through your resume; if you bury important information toward the end, it is less likely to be read or recognized as being significant.

5. Remember that although there are standard characteristics that are contained in most resumes (e.g., educational background and work experience), there is no best way to prepare all resumes. When preparing your own, emphasize your own unique characteristics.

6. Finally, omit all personal information, such as gender, age, marital status, and health because it is not necessary to include it. In fact, it is usually illegal for companies to hire people based on such personal information.

A covering letter accompanies the resume; it should contain four specific pieces of information: a statement of application for a particular job or type of job, a reason or several reasons why you have applied to that company, a summary of your credentials and personal goals as they relate to the job for which you are applying, and a definite request for an interview along with information about how, where, and when you can be reached to arrange an interview. A set of guidelines for a covering letter, a model, and an example letter follow.

Securing the Interview

The Covering Letter

The purpose of a covering letter is to establish enough interest in you that the employer will want to contact you and arrange an interview. Every covering letter should include these three elements:

1. It should tell why you are writing. Be specific.
2. It should highlight your qualifications and/or interest in the position for which you are applying.
3. It should refer to the resume which you have enclosed to provide additional information about your background.

Covering Letter Do's and Don'ts

Don't . . .

- Use a standard, printed covering letter.
- Be vague or general. If you make a statement, back it up with a specific reason or example.
- Use indefinite phrases like ''. . . if you have openings'' or ''. . . please contact me when. . . .''

Do . . .

- Type each covering letter individually. Enclose a letter with each resume you send.
- Address your letter to a specific person by name and title, whenever possible.
- Use a good grade of letter-size bond paper.
- Be careful with spelling and punctuation.

- Keep it short. Use simple, direct language. Be brief, clear, and businesslike.
- State exactly what kind of position you are applying for, how you heard about the company, and why you feel you would be an asset to their firm.

Important Hints

- Let your letter reflect your individuality but avoid appearing familiar, cute, or humorous. You are writing to a stranger whose sense of humor you know nothing about. The tone of your letter should be professional in the strictest sense.
- Remember that companies receive many resumes, all with covering letters. Keep it short and concise; sum up what you have to offer as an introduction to your qualifications as outlined in your resume.
- Try to express in your letter why the reader would want to interview you. Tell about one special quality you know that he or she would want to know more about.
- If you have had contact with the company previously, mention it in your letter. Chances are that the person you spoke with will remember your conversation when your résumé crosses his or her desk.

Following is a useful format to use when you construct your covering letter. It should help you organize the information you will want to include.

Like the resume, the covering letter should look impressive. If possible, use high-quality paper that matches the paper used for the resume, and leave plenty of white space for margins, at least an inch all around. Think of the covering letter as a written performance of how you might behave in a job interview. When we discussed oral presentations, we noted that the attitudes of boredom, superiority, and fear were to be avoided because they would turn off the audience. If these attitudes or ones like them creep into your covering letter, especially into the section in which you summarize your credentials and personal goals, then the audience, the potential employer who is reading your letter, will also be turned off. How do you avoid troublesome attitudes? Stick to the facts. Impress the reader with your ability to sumamrize your credentials and goals objectively.

Now try writing your own resume and covering letter.

Your Present Address
City, State, Zip Code
Date of Writing

Mr. John Blank
Title
Company
Street Address
City, State, Zip Code

Dear Mr. Blank:

First Paragraph—Tell why you are writing; name the specific position, field, or type of work about which you are asking. Tell how you heard of the opening or organization.

Second Paragraph—Mention one or two qualifications you think would be of greatest interest to the employer. Tell why you are particularly interested in the company, location, or type of work. If you have had related experience or specialized training, point it out.

Third Paragraph—Refer the reader to the enclosed application form or resumé, as a medium which will give additional information concerning your background and interests.

Fourth Paragraph—Close by making a request for an interview and a confirmation of an appointment at their earliest convenience. Make sure your closing is not vague, but makes a specific action from the reader likely.

Sincerely,

(Your handwritten signature)

Type Your Name

Enclosure (Indicates that you have sent a resume)

1412 Allen Road
Columbus, OH 43201
Date

Ms. Gail Godfrey
XYZ Corporation
123 Main Street
Your Town, USA 12302

Dear Ms. Godfrey:

As you requested in our phone conversation on Thursday, May 5, I am sending you my resume and application for the position of Customer Engineer. As you know, I will be graduating from the DeVry Institute of Technology in June 1983 with a bachelor of science degree in electronics engineering technology.

While attending DeVry Institute of Technology, I have had the opportunity to work with the following equipment: digital volt meters, oscilloscope, 80-85 microprocessor, Apple II computers, and Heathkit digital trainers, just to name a few.

During my employment at White Castle, I have had extensive customer contact. This, coupled with my educational experience has provided me with the job skills necessary to benefit your company.

I have enclosed a copy of my resume for your review. I would like to meet with you at your earliest convenience to review my qualifications. If I do not hear from you within two weeks I will call to inquire about the status of my resume.

I look forward to hearing from you soon.

Sincerely,

Frank Smith

Encl.

APPENDIX B

Research Paper Sources

Following is a list of possible sources of information.

Books

Dewey Decimal System [especially *Pure Science* (500) and *Technology and Applied Science* (600) catagories]

Library of Congress System [especially *General Works* (A), *Science* (Q), and *Technology* (T) categories]

Card catalog entries (author, title, and subject cards) and placement of information on the card
  Call number
  Author line
  Title and publishing information
  Collation (length and size of book)
  Content summary
  Subject headings or "tracings"
  Classification data (Dewey Decimal number and Library of Congress classification.)

Guides to books (choose most appropriate)
  American Book Publishing Record (1960-)
  American Library Directory (1919-)
  Book Review Digest (1905-)
  Books in Print
  Cumulative Book Index
  International Catalogue of Scientific Literature
  Library of Congress Catalogue
  National Referral Center for Science and Technology
  National Union Catalogue
  Publisher's Trade List Annual (1948-)
  Subject Guide to Books in Print (1957-)
  Technical Book Review Index

Periodical Indexes

Note the importance of using professional journal articles.

Bolton's *Catalogue of Scientific and Technical Periodicals*
Ulrich's *International Periodicals Directory* (1932-)
World List of Scientific Periodicals Published in the Years 1900-1960

Also of interest:

> *Applied Science and Technology Index* (1958–)
> *Current Index to Conference Papers in Engineering* (1969–)
> *Current Index to Conference Papers: Science and Tech* (1970–)
> *Current Papers on Computers and Control* (1969–)
> *Engineering Index* (1906–)
> *Reader's Guide to Periodical Literature* (1900–)
> *Science Citation Index* (1961–)
> *Abstracts Indexes* (Note convenience of reading abstracts prior to reading articles)
> *Computer Abstracts* (1957–)
> *Computer and Control Abstracts* (1969–)
> *Dissertation Abstracts International,* Section B (1938–)
> *Electrical and Electronic Abstracts* (1903–)
> *Electro and Lytical Abstracts* (1963–)
> *Electronics and Communication Journal* (1967–)
> *Engineering Abstracts* (1900)
> *Information Science Abstracts* (1966–)
> *Science Abstracts* (1898–) Sections B (computers) and C (electronics)
> *Solid State Abstracts* (1960–)

Bibliographies of Bibliographies
Note the convenience of examining bibliographies to locate texts.

> Besterman's *A World Bibliography of Bibliographies*
> *Bibliographic Index*
> *A Cumulative Bibliography of Bibliographies* (1938–)
> Dalton's *Sources of Engineering Information* (1948–)
> Holmstrom's *Records and Research in Engineering and Industrial Science* (3rd edition, 1956)

Reference Works
Note the usefulness of dictionaries and encyclopedias.

Encyclopedias

> *Collier's Encyclopedia*
> *Columbia Encyclopedia*
> *Encyclopedia Britannica*
> *Engineering Encyclopedia*
> *Harper Encyclopedia of Science*
> *McGraw-Hill Encyclopedia of Science and Technology*
> *Van Nostrand's Scientific Encyclopedia*

Dictionaries

> *The Basic Dictionary of Science*
> *Chambers Dictionary of Science and Technology*
> *Dictionary of Electronics*

Dictionary of Scientific and Technical Terms
Int'l Dictionary of Physics and Electronics

LIBRARY REPORT

Selecting and Limiting a Subject

Characteristics of suitable subjects: interesting; related to major field; familiar; restricted in scope; has sufficient published material. Three general types of suitable subjects:

1. A project you are working on
2. Making a practical decision
3. Discovering new practical knowledge

(Make a list of possible topics and choose the most appropriate.)

Available library sources of information related to a selected topic—consult the card catalog, guides, indexes, references works, and bibliographies to discern how much available information exists.

Reducing the scope of a selected topic:

- Limit the subject to a time period.
- Limit the subject to a particular facet of the subject.
- Limit the subject according to the reader's sophistication.

Making an Initial Plan

1. Make a list of things you as a writer wish to discover.
2. Add to the list things the reader will wish to know.
3. If you don't know enough to make a list, do some general reading.
4. Be prepared to revise the preliminary list.
5. From the list develop a flexible controlling idea.

Reading and Taking Notes

1. From the preliminary list begin to do research reading.
2. For each source read, prepare a coded bibliography card (code, author, title, publication information, page numbers).
3. For each piece of pertinent information, prepare a coded (corresponding to the bibliography card) note card (topic notation, card number, code, page numbers, and note).
4. Try to paraphrase information briefly. Avoid extensive quoting and limit the amount of information on each card.
5. Be sure that you understand the information recorded on cards.

Preparing the Final Outline and Writing the First Draft

1. Use headings from note cards to develop logical outline headings and subheadings.
2. From headings, generate an appropriate method of development and maintain a logical order of mention.

3. According to the logical order of mention, write the first draft using information written on the note cards.

4. As you compose the first draft, write information in your own words, include transitional devices between facts, and discuss the facts in terms of the controlling idea of the paper.

Documenting the Text

(Every unoriginal statement in the report must be documented.)

Place footnotes in the text according to an appropriate system:

- Author-date system
- Number system
- Footnote-bibliography system

(See the MLA or APA style sheet for specifics concerning documentation.)

Revising the Rough Draft and Preparing the Final Copy

Read through the rough draft placing yourself in the role of the reader; judge it critically from that standpoint. Check the rough draft for specific problems and revise it.

- Grammar
- Transitions
- Spelling
- Logical organization
- Coherence
- Completeness
- Documentation

Once the rough draft is completed, prepare illustrations, cover, title page, letter of transmittal, table of contents, list of figures, abstract.

Carefully type or have typed the final copy of the report after a final appraisal of content, clarity of expression for the intended audience, preciseness of language, and revision areas noted above. In general the typed copy should have 1-inch margins all around, be double spaced (except for transmittal letter and abstract), and be subdivided into appropriate subheadings.

See Chapters 8 and 9 for more information on report formats and research procedure.

APPENDIX C

Rules for Using Numbers

- Numbers in the millions are denoted with a combination of numerals and words:

    1.5 millions

- For larger quantities (e.g., billions, trillions, etc.), use either numerals or scientific notation:

    1,000,000,000   or 1×10^8

- Decimals and fractions should be presented as numerals:

    0.15 $2\frac{1}{2}$

- Approximations should be written out in words:

    The length of that parking lot is approximately one hundred feet.

- Information that includes many numbers should be presented in tables, graphs, or charts as numerals.

- Two numerals should never be placed beside each other as modifiers; one of the amounts should be written out.

- Symbols, not abbreviations, should be used to denote units of measure.

- Multiplication is indicated by a raised dot (·); division is indicated by a slash (/).

- Units equal to 1 or less than 1 are singular (e.g., 0.9 inch).

- Equations should be apart from the text centered on a separate line.

- All mathematical symbols should be centered on the same level.

- Equations and symbols should be punctuated as words in the sentence.

APPENDIX D

Word Meanings

Be sure to use words to denote their correct meanings. Study the following list of commonly confused words.

Terms	A	AN
Meanings	(used before a word beginning with a consonant sound)	(used before a word beginning with a vowel sound)

Terms	ABILITY	CAPACITY
Meanings	being able to perform	power to contain

Terms	ABOUT	APPROXIMATELY
Meanings	rough estimate	accurate estimate

Terms	ACCEPT	EXCEPT
Meanings	to receive	exclude

Terms	ADVISE	INFORM
Meanings	to counsel	to provide information

Note: ADVICE is a noun meaning "counsel."

Terms	AFFECT	EFFECT
Meanings	to influence	a result, to result in

Terms	ALL TOGETHER	ALTOGETHER
Meanings	every item or person together	entirely

Terms	ALLUDE	REFER
Meanings	to reference indirectly	to name

Terms	ARE	OR
Meanings	to be (verb)	(conjunction used between two possibilities)

Note: OUR is a first-person possessive pronoun.

Terms	BECAUSE OF	DUE TO
Meanings	by reason of	attributable to

Terms	BESIDE	BESIDES
Meanings	next to	in addition to

Terms	BETWEEN	AMONG
Meanings	involving two	involving three or more

Terms	BIG	LARGE
Meanings	refers to bulk	refers to capacity

Terms	BRAKE	BREAK
Meanings	to stop motion; a device that stops motion	to shatter or split; time off from work

Terms	CAN	MAY
Meanings	implies ability	implies permission

Terms	CENTER	MIDDLE
Meanings	point of reference	central area

Terms	CHOOSE	CHOSE
Meanings	to select (present tense)	selected (past tense)

Terms	CLOTHES	CLOTHS
Meanings	apparel	rag; woven material

Terms	COMPLEMENT	COMPLIMENT
Meanings	unit that completes	praise

Terms	CONTINUAL	CONTINUOUS
Meanings	frequently repeated	without interruption

Terms	COURSE	COARSE
Meanings	direction planned program	rough texture

Terms	CONSCIENCE	CONSCIOUS
Meanings	psychological entity; indicates right and wrong	to be aware

Terms	DATA	DATUM
Meanings	facts, information	single fact

Terms	DESERT	DESSERT
Meanings	to leave; arid, sandy land	sweet food after a meal

Terms	DISINTERESTED	UNINTERESTED
Meanings	impartial	indifferent

Terms	DO	DUE
Meanings	to perform an act or task	required

Terms	EFFECTIVE	EFFICIENT
Meanings	performs correctly	minimizes waste

Terms	*e.g.*	*i.e.*
Meanings	for example	in other words

Terms	ENSURE	INSURE
Meanings	to take precautionary measures	to purchase insurance

Terms	EVERYONE	EVERY ONE
Meanings	all people	each person

Terms	FORTH	FOURTH
Meanings	forward	one more than three

Terms	FARTHER	FURTHER
Meanings	physical distance	nonphysical distance (e.g., concepts, ideas)

Terms	FEWER	LESS
Meanings	countable items	quantity: sugar, flour, wheat

Terms	IMPLY	INFER
Meanings	to suggest in an indirect way	to conclude from evidence given

Terms	INCREDIBLE	INCREDULOUS
Meanings	unbelievable	unable to believe
Terms	ELECTRIC	ELECTRICAL
Meanings	involved with electricity	refers to but does not carry electricity
Terms	LEAD	LED
Meanings	a type of metal	past tense of "to lead"
Terms	MATERIEL	MATERIAL
Meanings	military or organizational equipment and supplies	matter composing a finished product
Terms	MORAL	MORALE
Meanings	ethical	group or individual enthusiasm
Terms	NOTED	NOTORIOUS
Meanings	famous	infamous
Terms	PERSONAL	PERSONNEL
Meanings	individual; intimate	group of workers
Terms	OVER	MORE THAN
Meanings	on top of	larger quantity
Terms	PRACTICABLE	PRACTICAL
Meanings	feasible	sensible
Terms	PRINCIPAL	PRINCIPLE
Meanings	sum of money head of a school	basic truth
Terms	THAT	WHICH
Meanings	introduces a restrictive modifier	introduces a nonrestrictive modifier
Terms	ULTIMATE	PENULTIMATE
Meanings	final	second to last
Terms	WEATHER	WHETHER
Meanings	atmospheric conditions	if

APPENDIX E

Abbreviations and Symbols

Following are standard letter symbols for units of measure. (*Note:* The same form is used for singular and plural senses.)

A, ampere
Å, angstrom
a, are
a, atto (prefix, one-quintillionth)
aA, attoampere
abs, absolute (temperature and gravity)
ac, alternating current
AF, audiofrequency
Ah, ampere-hour
A/m, ampere per meter
AM, amplitude modulation
asb, apostilb
At, ampere-turn
at, atmosphere, technical
atm, atmosphere (infrequently, As)
at wt, atomic weight
au, astronomical units
avdp, avoirdupois
b, barn
B, bel
b, bit
bbl, barrel
bbl/d, barrel per day
Bd, baud
bd. ft., board foot (obsolete); use fbm
Bé, Baumé
Bev (obsolete); see GeV
Bhn, Brinell hardness number
bhp, brake horsepower
bm, board measure
bp, boiling point
Btu, British thermal unit
bu, bushel
c, ¢, ct; cent(s)
c, centi (prefix, one-hundredth)
C, coulomb
c, cycle (radio)
°C, degree Celsius
cal, calorie (also: cal_{IT}, International Table; cal_{th}, thermochemical)
cc, (obsolete), use cm^3
cd, candela (candle obsolete)
cd/in², candela per square inch

cd/m², candela per square meter
c.f.m., (obsolete), use ft^3/min
c.f.s (obsolete), use ft^3/s
cg, centigram
c·h, candela-hour
Ci, curie
cL, centiliter
cm, centimeter
c/m, cycles per minute
cm², square centimeter
cm³, cubic centimeter
cmil, circular mil
cp, candlepower
cP, centipoise
cSt, centistokes
cu ft (obsolete) use ft^3
cu in (obsolete) use in^3
cwt, hundredweight
D, darcy
d, day
d, deci (prefix, one-tenth)
d, pence
da, deka (prefix, 10)
dag, dekagram
daL, dekaliter
dam, dekameter
dam², square dekameter
dam³, cubic dekameter
dB, decibel
dBu, decible unit
dc, direct current
dg, decigram
dl, deciliter
dm, decimeter
dm², square decimeter
dm³, cubic decimeter
dol, dollar
doz, dozen
dr, dram
dwt, deadweight tons
dwt, pennyweight
dyn, dyne
EHF, extremely high frequency

emf, electromotive force
emu, electromagnetic unit
erg, erg
esu, electrostatic unit
eV, electronvolt
°F, degree Fahrenheit
F, farad
f, femto (prefix, one-quadrillionth)
F, fermi (obsolete); use fm, fentometer
fbm, board foot; board foot measure
fc, footcandle
fL, footlambert
fm, femtometer
FM, frequency modulation
ft, foot
ft², square foot
ft³, cubic foot
ftH₂O, conventional foot of water
ft·lb, foot-pound
ft·lbf, foot pound-force
ft/min, foot per minute
ft²/min, square foot per minute
ft³/min, cubic foot per minute
ft-pdl, foot poundal
ft/s, foot per second
ft²/s, square foot per second
ft³/s, cubic foot per second
ft/s², foot per second squared
ft/s³, foot per second cubed
G, gauss
G, giga (prefix, 1 billion)
g, gram; acceleration of gravity
Gal, gal cm/s²
gal, gallon
gal/min, gallons per minute
gal/s, gallons per second
Gb, gilbert
g/cm³, gram per cubic centimeter
GeV, gigaelectronvolt
GHz, gigahertz (gigacycle per second)
gr, grain; gross
h, hecto (prefix, 100)
H, henry
h, hour
ha, hectare
HF, high frequency
hg, hectogram
hL, hectoliter
hm, hectometer
hm², square hectometer
hm³, cubic hectometer
hp, horsepower
hph, horsepower-hour
Hz, hertz (cycles per second)
id, inside diameter
ihp, indicated horsepower
in, inch
in², square inch
in³, cubic inch
in/h, inch per hour
inH₂O, conventional inch of water
inHg, conventional inch of mercury
in-lb, inch-pound
in/s, inch per second
J, joule

J/K, joule per kelvin
K, kayser
K, kelvin (degree symbol improper)
k, kilo (prefix, 1,000)
k, thousand (7k = 7,000)
kc, kilocycle; see also kHz (kilohertz), kilocycles per second
kcal, kilocalory
keV, kiloelectronvolt
kG, kilogauss
kg, kilogram
kgf, kilogram-force
kHz, kilohertz (kilocycles per second)
kL, kiloliter
klbf, kilopound-force
km, kilometer
km², square kilometer
km³, cubic kilometer
km/h, kilometer per hour
kn, knot (speed)
kΩ, kilohm
kt, kiloton; carat
kV, kilovolt
kVA, kilovoltampere
kvar, kilovar
kW, kilowatt
kWh, kilowatthour
L, lambert
L, liter
lb, pound
lb ap, apothecary pound
lb, avdp, avoirdupois pound
lbf, pound-force
lbf/ft, pound-force foot
lbf/ft², pound-force per square foot
lbf/ft³, pound-force per cubic foot
lbf/in², pound-force per square inch
lb/ft, pound per foot
lb/ft² pound per square foot
lb/ft³ pound per cubic foot
lct, long calcined ton
ldt, long dry ton
LF, low frequency
lin ft, linear foot
l/m, lines per minute
lm, lumen
lm/ft², lumen per square foot
lm/m², lumen per square meter
lm-s, lumen second
lm/W, lumen per watt
l/s, lines per second
L/s, liter per second
lx, lux
M, mega (prefix, 1 million)
M, million (3M = 3 million)
m, meter
m, milli (prefix, one-thousandth)
M₁, monetary aggregate
m³, cubic meter
m², square meter
μ, micro (prefix, one-millionth)
μ, micron (name micron obsolete); use μm, micrometer
mA, milliampere
μA, microampere

mbar, millibar

μbar, microbar

Mc, megacycle; see also MHz (megahertz), megacycles per second

mc, millicycle; see also mHz (millihertz), millicycles per second

mcg, microgram (obsolete, use μg)

mD, millidarcy

meq, milliquivalent

MeV, megaelectronvolts

mF, millifarad

μF, microfarad

mG, milligauss

mg, milligram

μg, microgram

Mgal/d, million gallons per day

mH, millihenry

μH, microhenry

mho, mho (obsolete, use S, siemens)

MHz, megahertz

mHz, millihertz

mi, mile (statute)

mi^2, square mile

mi/gal, mile(s) per gallon

mi/h, mile per hour

mil, mil

min, minute (time)

μin, microinch

mL, milliliter

mm, millimeter

mm^2, square millimeter

mm^3, cubic millimeter

mμ (obsolete); see nm, nanometer

μm, micrometer

μm^2, square micrometer

μm^3, cubic micrometer

$\mu\mu$, micromicron (use of compound prefixes obsolete; use pm, picometer)

$\mu\mu$f, micromicrofarad (use of compound prefixes obsolete; use pF)

mmHg, conventional millimeter of mercury

μmho, micromho (obsolete, use μS, microsiemens)

MΩ, megohm

mo, month

mol, mole (unit of substance)

mol wt, molecular weight

mp, melting point

ms, millisecond

μs, microsecond

Mt, megaton

mV, millivolt

μV, microvolt

MW, megawatt

mW, milliwatt

μW, microwatt

MWd/t, megawatt-days per ton

Mx, maxwell

n, nano (prefix, one-billionth)

N, newton

nA, nanoampere

nF, nanofarad

nm, nanometer (millimicron, obsolete)

N·m, newton meter

N/m^2, newton per square meter

nmi, nautical mile

Np, neper

ns, nanosecond

$N·s/m^2$, newton second per square meter

nt, nit

od, outside diameter

Oe, oersted (use of A/m, amperes per meter, preferred)

oz, ounce (avoirdupois)

p, pico (prefix, one-trillionth)

P, poise

Pa, pascal

pA, picoampere

pct, percent

pdl, poundal

pF, picofarad (micromicrofarad, obsolete)

pF, water-holding energy

pH, hydrogen-ion concentration

ph, phot; phase

pk, peck,

p/m, parts per million

ps, picosecond

pt, pint

pW, picowatt

qt, quart

quad, quadrillion (10^{15})

°R, rankine

°R, roentgen

R, degree rankine

R, degree reaumur

rad, radian

rd, rad

rem, roentgen equivalent man

r/min, revolutions per minute

rms, root mean square

r/s, revolutions per second

s, second (time)

s, shilling

S, siemens

sb, stilb

scp, spherical candlepower

s·ft, second-foot

shp, shaft horsepower

slug, slug

sr, steradian

sSf, standard saybolt fural

sSu, standard saybolt universal

$stdft^3$, standard cubic foot (feet)

Sus, saybolt universal second(s)

T, tera (prefix, 1 trillion)

Tft^3, trillion cubic feet

T, tesla

t, tonne (metric ton)

tbsp, tablespoonful

thm, therm

ton, ton

tsp, teaspoonful

Twad, twaddell

u, (unified) atomic mass unit

UHF, ultrahigh frequency

V, volt

VA, voltampere

var, var

VHF, very high frequency

V/m, volt per meter

W, watt

Wb, weber
Wh, watthour
W/(m·K), watt per meter kelvin
W/sr, watt per steradian
W/(sr·m²), watt per steradian square meter

x, unknown quantity
yd, yard
yd², square yard
yd³, cubic yard
yr, year

Following are signs and symbols in common use.

MATHEMATICAL

— vinculum (above letters)
÷ geometrical proportion
—: difference, excess
‖ parallel
‖s parallels
≠ not parallels
| | absolute value
· multiplied by
: is to; ratio
÷ divided by
∴ therefore; hence
∵ because
:: proportion; as
≪ is dominated by
> greater than
⊏ greater than
≧ greater than or equal to
≥ greater than or equal to
≷ greater than or less than
≯ is not greater than
< less than
⊐ less than
≶ less than or greater than
≮ is not less than
⋖ smaller than
≦ less than or equal to
≤ less than or equal to
≥ or ≥ greater than or equal to
≲ equal to or less than
≦ equal to or less than
≨ is not greater than equal to or less than
≳ equal to or greater than
≩ is not less than equal to or greater than
≗ equilateral
⊥ perpendicular to
⊢ assertion sign
≐ approaches
≑ approaches a limit
≙ equal angles
≠ not equal to
≡ identical with
≢ not identical with
卌 score

≈ or ≐ nearly equal to
= equal to
~ difference
≃ perspective to
≅ congruent to approximately equal
≑ difference between
⌾ geometrically equivalent to
⊂ included in
⊃ excluded from
⊆ is contained in
∪ logical sum or union
∩ logical product or intersection
√ radical
√ root
∛ square root
∛ cube root
∜ fourth root
√ fifth root
√ sixth root
π pi
ε base (2.718) of natural system of logarithms; epsilon
ϵ is a member of; dielectric constant; mean error; epsilon
+ plus
✚ bold plus
− minus
▬ bold minus
/ shill(ing); slash; virgule
± plus or minus
∓ minus or plus
× multiplied by
▬ bold equal
number
℔ per
% percent
∫ integral
| single bond
＼ single bond
／ single bond
‖ double bond
⦀ double bond
⫽ double bond
⬡ benzene ring
∂ or δ differential; variation

∂ Italian differential
→ approaches limit of
∼ cycle sine
⌡ horizontal integral
∮ contour integral
∝ variation; varies as
∏ product
Σ summation of; sum; sigma
! or ⌐ factorial product

MEASURE

℔ pound
ℨ dram
ƒℨ fluid dram
℥ ounce
ƒ℥ fluid ounce
O pint

MISCELLANEOUS

§ section
† dagger
‡ double dagger
℀ account of
℅ care of
卌 score
¶ paragraph
þ Anglo-Saxon
₵ center line
♂ conjunction
⊥ perpendicular to
″ or " ditto
∝ variation
℞ recipe
⌋ move right
⌊ move left
○ or ⊙ or ① annual
⊙⊙ or ② biennial
∈ element of
℈ scruple
ƒ function
! exclamation mark
⊞ plus in square
♃ perennial

Index